Treaty

TREATY
Let's get it right!

A collection of essays from ATSIC's treaty thinktank and authors commissioned by AIATSIS on treaty issues

ATSIC

AIATSIS
Australian Institute of Aboriginal and Torres Strait Islander Studies

First published in 2003 by Aboriginal Studies Press for the Australian Institute of Aboriginal and Torres Strait Islander Studies, GPO Box 553, Canberra, ACT, 2601.

Reprinted in 2004

Front cover image: Australia Day Protest, courtesy the Fairfax Photo Library.

Back cover: Treaty watermark. This watermark was designed by Tony Albert and symbolises an eye looking towards the future where coexistence and cooperation exists between both Indigenous and non-Indigenous Australians.

Photographs of the National Treaty Conference 2002 were taken by Sandy Piers Photography.

This publication has retained each individual author's style preferences. Any variability in style is a consequence of these individual preferences. AIATSIS has not applied its standard house style in support of the ATSIS preference for individual author styles.

ISBN 0 85575 433 8

Foreword

The purpose of this book is to publish the outcomes from public discussion about a treaty from Corroboree 2000 until now. The *let's get it right* approach reflects the complexity of the issues needing to be resolved on the road to a treaty and emanates from a reconciliation convention attended by Aboriginal leaders in Melbourne in May 2000. After this convention ATSIC's commitment to a treaty led to the convening of a National Treaty Support Group and think tank to oversee a public information and awareness strategy, a political strategy and a framework for the further development of a treaty. This publication is part of ATSIC's developmental framework strategy. The essays were commissioned by ATSIC and AIATSIS to respond to issues raised by a treaty and to provide theoretical and practical direction within the treaty debate.

Over the past three years treaty promotional material has been widely distributed, workshops have been held around the country and a series of public lectures and forums have been convened so that governments, industry, schools, universities and other interested groups could have an opportunity to engage in debate about the issues that surround a treaty. This campaign is an ongoing process and this publication is an important part of ATSIC's facilitation of discussion, complementing other ATSIC publications on the treaty concept such as *Treaty Issues* and *Treaty Frequently Asked Questions*.

As part of their role in stimulating discussion and debate, think tank members wrote from specialised areas of interest and this collection of essays contains a number of models for securing a treaty on the one hand, and on the other hand, matters that the treaty development process will need to address or incorporate.

Mansell focuses on distinguishing the concept of self-government from a model based on the political concept of equality. A major point made by Mansell is the right of Aboriginal people to choose and lead discussion on the model for a treaty that is preferred and that a model for a treaty based on 'equality'—necessarily assimilatory in character, is not a foregone conclusion.

Behrendt's discussion centres on treaties with first nations peoples in the Canadian jurisdiction including discussion about the *Inherent Right to Self-Government* policy enacted in 1995. While elaborating on the mechanisms for treaty making in Canada, Behrendt identifies the need for a flexible approach in the construction of a framework for treaty negotiating in Australia. In this sense the negotiation framework would need to be able to respond to and resolve such questions as who would have the capacity to negotiate for Indigenous parties; who would be identified as Indigenous and why; the potential third party status within Australia's federation of States in treaty negotiations between Aboriginal peoples and governments; the need to reconcile inherent power imbalances between parties; and the primary need of establishing a framework that would reflect the aspirations of Aboriginal peoples.

Dodson analyses the way in which treaty making can be accommodated within the Australian Constitution. This discussion about the merits of a constitutional framework for the treaty concept contemplates agreement-making at local, regional, State and national levels.

Langton and Palmer discuss the trend toward agreement-making pre and post the enactment of the *Native Title Act* (Cth) 1994 and identify the need for a statutory or constitutional means of protecting the rights of Aboriginal people in agreements that are brokered. In this sense agreement-making is identified as a substitute, but hitherto inferior way, of recognising the rights of Aboriginal peoples to land, water and mineral resources.

Janke and Quiggan examine how a treaty or treaties would be more effective in dealing with a range of intellectual property issues, in particular, recognition of collective ownership. This essay discusses the ineffectiveness of native title and heritage laws and copyright and trademark property laws in protecting Indigenous peoples' rights to cultural resources, arts, songs, stories and knowledge.

Rigney focuses on how a treaty has the capacity to influence current consultative arrangements in the education portfolio. Rigney envisages the treaty concept as providing a framework through which, for example, the use and practice of Aboriginal languages could be preserved, and by association, so too the practice of Aboriginal culture.

Taylor examines the framework for defining a person as Aboriginal, identifies the extent of diversity between Aboriginal peoples and suggests that the integrity of the 'test for Aboriginality' is also a test of the integrity of the framework developed to negotiate a treaty or treaties.

NIYMA—National Indigenous Youth Movement of Australia contribute a perspective from Indigenous youth. This essay invites Aboriginal people to look at and identify themselves outside 'white culture' and to set goals and strategies in response to spiritual / cultural prerogatives. NIYMA identify the symbolic value of a treaty and prior to entering into negotiations with governments, the necessity for Aboriginal peoples to first identify a 'vision for the future' and the role and function of a treaty in that vision.

McGlade's essay analyses sovereignty and native title and demonstrates how a treaty can provide a remedy for the lack of recognition of Indigenous sovereignty.

Davis details the human rights framework from which human rights treaties are negotiated in international law and demonstrates how this framework could be used as the basis for negotiating a treaty in Australia. Davis argues that if this framework were to be used it would be possible to enshrine both individual and collective rights in a treaty through recognition of human rights conventions already established in international law.

Cronin analyses the history of administrative practices in relation to the concepts of governance and self-determination and offers that self-determination can be achieved if administrative / decision-making processes are in the hands of Aboriginal people / Aboriginal governance structures. Cronin identifies the necessity for the treaty concept to reflect Aboriginal governance structures and in this sense envisages the capacity of the treaty concept to build the capacity of Aboriginal organisations to develop and sustain autonomous governance structures.

Nakata traces the way in which funding arrangements differ at local, State and federal levels and analyses how these arrangements are the key to understanding relationships between Indigenous peoples and governments. Nakata emphasises that the treaty concept is a governance issue and that there is a clear need for governance structures to accommodate or contemplate the mix of tradition and colonialism inherent in service delivery issues. The focus in this essay is the relationships between regional autonomy and national, State and local frameworks for administering policies in Aboriginal and Torres Strait Islander Affairs.

A speech given by Senator Aden Ridgeway at the ten year anniversary of the *Mabo* decision in which he reflects on the outcomes in Aboriginal Affairs over a ten year period has also been included. Senator Ridgeway notes that the *Mabo* decision did not remedy the injustices of the past because a social compact (treaty) did not eventuate from the decision. 'The proposal for a treaty or national framework agreement to overcome the destructive cultural, social and economic consequences of dispossession is yet to be pursued by any national government.' Senator Ridgeway argues that a treaty is an obvious means of ensuring that governments are accountable to Indigenous Australians and that 'good public policy can only emerge where there has been an honest and accurate analysis of past error and omission, and a genuine commitment to meeting the needs and aspiration of the people affected by the new policy.'

A speech by ATSIC's Treaty Ambassador, Nova Peris OAM, given at Sorry Day in Melbourne 2003, has also been included to demonstrate the capacity of a treaty to reconcile past injustices. Peris talks about the relationship between a treaty and the idea of a democratic nation and discusses the symbolic place of a treaty in the 'life of the nation'.

I support the idea of a treaty because it is the most obvious means of overcoming the paternalism that has characterised the historical relationship between Aboriginal peoples and governments. Calls for a treaty are not new. Captain James Cook's instructions for annexure of a new colony for England included an instruction to make an agreement with the natives. This instruction was not carried out for many reasons. However, the lack of an initial agreement with Aboriginal people has denied Aboriginal people a political status that would allow us to negotiate laws made on our behalf by the Commonwealth government. Formal governmental discrimination against Aboriginal people is therefore historical and present.

Interpretations of the Constitution by the High Court have to this point only just begun to recognise prior occupation of the land by Aboriginal people. Without a treaty the inferior legislation of the *Native Title Act* (Cth) 1994 makes native title an inferior land title. By association native title can be extinguished under the law.

A treaty is therefore, among other things, very much recognition of the rights of Aboriginal peoples.

In the late twentieth century Judith Wright, Nugget Coombs and other prominent people publicly called on the Commonwealth government to set right the wrongs of the past. This action led to the 'Makarrata' proposal in 1979 which called for recognition of prior possession of the continent, acceptance of Aboriginal people as distinct peoples and compensation on the basis that, as a result of prior possession, Aboriginal people are entitled to compensation when dispossessed of their lands. After this proposal was put forward the government appointed a Senate Standing Committee on Constitutional and Legal Affairs but a resolution aimed at addressing the recommendations of the report put to the Senate by Clyde Holding in 1983 was never voted on.

The Makarrata proposal was followed up by Aboriginal people with the Barunga Statement, handed to Bob Hawke in June 1988. This statement had considerable influence under Paul Keating who delivered a speech that addressed much of the text in the Barunga Statement at Redfern in 1992 after the *Mabo* decision had been handed down.

The *Mabo* decision displaced the doctrine of *terra nullius* and replaced it with a new doctrine, *native title*. After *Mabo*, the Council for Aboriginal Reconciliation (CAR) was established as part of the Keating government's response to the recognition that Aboriginal people had prior possession of the land. The other two government responses to the striking out of the *terra nullius* doctrine in the *Mabo* case were the passing of the Native Title Act in 1994 and the appointment of an Aboriginal Social Justice Commissioner.

The two major reports from this era are CAR's Final Report and the Bringing Them Home Inquiry. These reports together with the recommendations of the 1991 Royal Commission Into Aboriginal Deaths In Custody have taken us further along the road to recognition through a treaty of the prior occupation of the continent by Aboriginal people. Without this recognition Aboriginal people do not have equal negotiating power in the development of laws made by the Commonwealth government.

The *let's get it right* approach reflects the historical governmental barriers to equality under the law in Australia that can be found, for example, in an 1847 petition to Queen Victoria from the Secretary for the State for the Colonies, Earl Grey, John Batman's treaty with Aboriginal people in 1835, the Warrnambool Standard of 1888, or the Barunga or Eva Valley Statements of the late 20th century. All this history demonstrates the striking inequities in political power that exist without a treaty.

In the early twenty-first century Australia is still coming to terms with the magnitude of the effects of dispossession on Aboriginal people. Over the past three years ATSIC has focussed on the treaty issue in a way that has been aimed at providing the Aboriginal people and the broader community with as much information as possible to answer the questions that the prospect of a treaty between Aboriginal peoples and governments raises.

None of the issues surrounding the objective of gaining a treaty are easy ones to reconcile. This body of work tackles the questions that have been ignored or swept under the carpet and takes us further along the road to a treaty.

Treaty discussions and debates have raised the level of interest in rights and unfinished business issues. I continue to progress the debate to prick the conscience of all Australians. A Treaty or Bill of Rights challenges all Australians to accept Indigenous rights to our land.

Geoff Clark

Contents

Preface

'Treaty ... let's get it right' is an important contribution to a national dialogue in Australia, a nation that has been shaped by a history that contains little trace of Treaty or peaceful co-existence amongst its Indigenous and non-Indigenous peoples.

Treaty has been a part of the Indigenous political agenda for many years still deliberations and discussions about Treaty have been few and far between. The recent acknowledgement by the Council for Aboriginal Reconciliation that this country was settled without treaty or consent of the Indigenous peoples put Treaty where it rightfully belongs—an issue that must now be discussed, debated, possibly rejected or perhaps embraced.

In 2000 the Aboriginal and Torres Strait Islander Commission established a National Treaty Think Tank whom it charged with raising awareness of treaty issues. In 2001 the Australian Institute of Aboriginal and Torres Strait Islander Studies (AIATSIS) became a partner to this responsibility and commenced the engagement of treaty research, including a Treaty seminar series and Treaty Visiting Research Fellowship. I was fortunate to be engaged as the AIATSIS Treaty VRF in 2001 wherein I undertook to edit this collection of Treaty essays.

'Treaty ... let's get it right' is primarily concerned with communicating treaty matters to a wide as possible audience, especially the youth. Whether they be Indigenous to this country or descended from the many countries that now make up this multicultural nation, there can be no doubt that they will be the future judges of Treaty. Hopefully this collection of papers will be of some help to them as they learn of Treaty and what it may or may not mean in Australia.

Whether one is a supporter or not of Treaty, there can be no doubt that this book breaks new ground in its consideration of the many possibilities and aspects of an Australian treaty process, an important first step in any domestic treaty process.

The contributors to this book give no certain answers, nor do they address all the issues that could possibly be associated with a national treaty dialogue. However, they give an important voice to Treaty and the many subject matters that have been left largely unheard.

The essay papers engage in a broad range of topics including Aboriginal and Torres Strait Islander sovereignty, constitutional change, governance, histories of treaty, settlement and agreement making within and outside of the native title sphere, issues for the Torres Strait, intellectual and cultural property, international human rights law, perspectives of youth, international experiences with treaties, education and language, concepts of citizenry, matters of identity.

All contributors, from the National Treaty Think Tank and the individuals approached by AIATSIS to write papers for this book, are Indigenous people from many parts of Australia. And they raise a great diversity of subject matters and personal opinions in 'Treaty ... let's get it right'. Like many Indigenous peoples, past and present, they have a passion for Treaty that resonates through this book.

Hannah McGlade

Acknowledgements

Acknowledgement of and special thanks to the following people are necessary for without them this book would not have been possible:

Aboriginal people and Torres Strait Islanders who attended community consultations because without this investment of time or energy the framework for this book could not have been developed

Hannah McGlade for her contribution as book editor

ATSIC's Treaty Ambassador, Nova Peris for advocacy and promotion of the treaty concept to Indigenous and non-Indigenous people

ATSIC, in particular the elected arm; Treaty Secretariat staff in National Office who convened the Think Tank, Treaty Support Group and National Treaty Conference with Australians for Native Title and Reconciliation (ANTaR) and the Australian Institute of Aboriginal and Torres Strait Islander Studies (AIATSIS); and Treaty Co-ordinators in State Policy Centres, Network Offices and Regional Offices who co-ordinated community consultations

Members of ATSIC's National Treaty Think Tank:
- Professor Marcia Langton
- Professor Larissa Behrendt
- Professor Michael Dodson
- Dr Martin Nakata
- Lester-Irabinna Rigney
- Glenn Shaw
- Michael Mansell
- National Indigenous Youth Movement of Australia (NIYMA)

Members of ATSIC's Treaty Support Group:
- Patrick Dodson
- Bob Weatherall
- Commissioner Anderson
- Former Commissioner Dickie Bedford
- Former Commissioner Patricia Thompson
- Former Commissioner Brian Butler
- Commissioner Dillon
- Commissioner Doolah
- Commissioner Gordon
- Mandawuy Yunupingu
- Rhonda Jacobsen
- Rod Towney
- Peter Yu

AIATSIS commissioned authors:
- Megan Davis
- Louise Taylor
- Darryl Cronin
- Terri Janke
- Robyn Quiggan

AIATSIS for co-ordinating a treaty seminar series, supporting the work of the Treaty Visiting Research Fellow (Hannah McGlade) and commissioning some of the contributions to this book

Melbourne University, the University of Technology Sydney and AIATSIS, partners in the Agreement, Treaties and Negotiated Settlements linkage agreement through the Australian Research Council; Melbourne University in particular for the on-line data base and co-ordination of a seminar series and University of Technology Sydney and the University of New South Wales for supporting the research focus of this book

ANTaR for supporting the treaty concept and accepting the challenge of promoting the treaty to the broader community through education and awareness raising workshops

The Independent Education Union, in particular Lynne Rowley and Diat Collope, for promoting the treaty concept to their members

National Indigenous Radio who supported the treaty concept through broadcasts to remote communities

The Indigenous Law Bulletin for focussing an edition on the treaty concept

James Cook University and Murdoch University for hosting conferences about the treaty concept

Special thanks also to conference speakers and participants, and to Regional Councils who supported community consultations in their regions.

Citizenship, Assimilation and a Treaty
Michael Mansell

Granting Australian citizenship to indigenous peoples should not be conditional on them surrendering their historic rights. But that is the offer on the table.

Glossary of Terms

Aboriginal Australians: the original people who lost their country and consented to be citizens of Australia. Their lost rights are replaced with those of other Australians.

Australian Aboriginals: the original people whose lands were invaded and are now occupied. All past rights are not lost, although they are unable to be exercised. Can still enjoy all rights of Australian citizens without losing their inherent rights.

Australians: the people who created the nation of Australia and who show allegiance to that nation.

Assimilation: making indigenous people the same in all respects as Australians.

Indigenous Australians: same as Aboriginal Australians.

Integration: making indigenous people the same as Australians while retaining their culture and identity.

Citizenship: a. (politically) indigenous people becoming legitimate members of the Australian nation in exchange for giving up previous rights. b. (legally) indigenous people deemed to be citizens by fate of Australian law. Distinguished from political citizenship acquired by consent.

Legitimate: the establishment of the right to govern by a principle or a rule. Australian governments legitimately govern their citizens because they were elected to do so— by virtue of the rule or principle of consent. Distinguish from moral legitimacy.

Moral legitimacy: the right or wrong, or good and evil of government claims to legitimacy. Australian governments may legitimately rule their own citizens because of the principle of consent; but there is no moral legitimacy to govern indigenous peoples without their consent. The foundation for Australia's claim to sovereignty is by rule of force. There is no moral foundation because the invasion and subsequent domination were wrong.

Sovereignty: the right of authority in a people to control their territory, and those in it. Sovereignty can still exist even if a people are prevented from exercising it. Can also be exercised by force and domination without a moral right.

Introduction

The idea of a treaty is good. It could settle all outstanding disputes between indigenous peoples and the government. Prime Minister Howard has already rejected the idea of a treaty. He argues that as Aborigines are also Australians, people cannot make a treaty with themselves.

The immediate focus of a treaty is hardly about the attitude of present political leaders. That would be too shallow a beginning. The core issues revolve around the status of the indigenous peoples. Are Aboriginal and Torres Straits Islanders distinct peoples, able to make binding political agreements with governments? Or are they only Australian citizens, whose claim against their government is purely moral?

Central to the whole treaty debate is the indigenous vision. Where do Aboriginal and Torres Straits Islanders see themselves as being in the next 20-odd years? How can a treaty help get them there?

These complex issues are for the indigenous peoples to resolve. A treaty could advance the indigenous cause, but only if the goal is known.

1. The two competing outcomes of a treaty

(a) All crown lands returned to Aborigines. The Torres Strait islands to the Islanders. Aborigines able to govern themselves on their own land; the TSI are on theirs, if that was their choice. Economic and cultural sea and fresh water zones for the indigenous peoples. Aborigines decide the values and content of education for Aboriginal children. Having authority to plan their futures. From that base making the improvements to give indigenous peoples a high standard of living, and choices of how they lived. This is one version of a treaty.

(b) A different aim is for equality. This version takes white society and all it offers as something to duplicate. The goal is for access to participate in the political system, share in the economic benefits, be part of the culture that makes up the Australian nation and not be discriminated against. The goal under this model is for forms of indigenous autonomy and return of some lands within the limits of Australian fairness. This is the base to provide indigenous peoples with a high standard of living, and choices of how they lived.

Both models involve indigenous peoples living and working beside white Australians. That is a social reality for either model. Where the models differ is in their political philosophy. The first is centred on indigenous independence—politically speaking. The second accepts dependence on Australia—again politically.

The most controversial part of the first option is that of Aboriginal government. The Torres Strait Islanders could easily govern themselves, and less controversially, due to their geographic location. The islands form their territory. Their isolation from the population centres of Australia means less controversy. Yet the same question arises for the TSI people as it does for Aborigines: is political independence their aim in a treaty? Or is it to be part of Australia?

2. Current policies

The choices for Aborigines are for assimilation at one end of the spectrum, to self rule at the other. The current policies that apply to the indigenous peoples of Australia can be characterised as assimilationist in nature. The white race overwhelmed the indigenous peoples. Dispossession of all the lands was complete, as has been the domination of the two indigenous peoples by the whites. Only fairly recently have measures been taken to return lands to indigenous peoples. The 1976 Northern Territory Land Rights legislation was a forerunner to State legislation up until 1995. Native title and purchase of lands through the Commonwealth ILC body are current forms of recognising or acquiring lands for indigenous peoples.

Generally, Aboriginal children are taught the same curriculum as white children. That curriculum is based on white values. The economy and political systems are European. The law is that of the whites. The nation of Australia is, in all respects, very much a white one into which Aborigines and Torres Strait Islanders must fit.

There are many reports by government instrumentalities that claim Aborigines and Torres Strait Islanders must be part of, and subject to, Australian authority.

The argument for a treaty presupposes change. Existing policy and practice would therefore need to be reviewed.

(a) The meaning of citizenship

There is a widely held view that the best interests of Aborigines and Torres Strait Islanders are served by being citizens of Australia.

There are two aspects to citizenship: the first is that Aborigines and Torres Strait Islanders are deemed to be citizens of Australia, that is, citizens in the legal sense. By virtue of the Australian Citizenship Act 1948, being born to an existing permanent resident or citizen of Australia automatically confers citizenship. But that is only "legal" citizenship.

The second aspect deals more with an individuals "moral" stance- involving an allegiance. Often referred to as 'full' citizenship, this is gained when full equality with "other Australians" is reached. The Aboriginal "passage to full citizenship remains incomplete while the indigenous people remain the most disadvantaged group" (Australian Citizenship Council 2000, p30). Indigenous people were citizens without rights, according to this argument, until the right to vote, anti-discrimination laws, the formation of ATSIC and native title changed the scene (Australian Citizenship Council 2000).

Accordingly, once equality in the areas of health, education, employment, imprisonment rate, alcohol and drug dependency, depression and suicide is achieved indigenous peoples will have achieved full citizenship (Australian Citizenship Council 2000), and should be happy.

Yet we have to recognise that citizenship cannot provide Aboriginal entitlements, it can only curtail them. In the Native Title Report, Social Justice Commissioner Dr Bill Jonas (2002, p 9) points out:

> The real problem with citizenship rights...is that they are not capable of transforming the poverty and destitution that marks so many Aboriginal peoples' lives. They were not intended for this purpose

There is another down side to citizenship. It is not offered without strings attached—it comes at a heavy price. The price to be paid for is the abandonment of indigenous sovereignty, and with it the loss of self-determination. Any rights would be limited to those granted by the parliaments or recognised by white law. There would be no inherent rights. The rights and entitlements of the two indigenous peoples would largely depend on popular opinion and government policy, like they do now. Once the indigenous peoples throw their hat in the ring with the rest, their rights are likewise curtailed.

> Australian democracy guarantees us our civic freedoms and our fundamental rights and equality...all Australians are obliged to support the basic structures and principles of Australian society—our Constitution, democratic institutions and values—which guarantee us our freedom and equality and enable diversity in our society to flourish. (Australian Citizenship Council 2000, p 18)

Apparently, this is not supposed to be assimilation. The report of the Citizenship Council (2000, p 19) states that social cohesion does not mean, *"you must all become like us"*. The report failed to explain how this could be avoided.

The Reconciliation Council's Final Report spelt out the most recent position on the future for Aborigines and Torres Strait Islanders. In its declaration (2000, p 109), the Council's political stance was for *"a united Australia"*, self-determination had to be exercised *"within the life of the nation"* and the lands no longer belonged to Aboriginal people because the land was *"ours"*. Morally, the statements seek to legitimise the dispossession and dominance, while encouraging a form of equal access.

In his speech to an ATSIC national policy conference in March 2002 Minister Ruddock said:

> "The question of rights is prominent in the conference agenda... I am all for individuals being able to determine their own destiny... there needed to be a new emphasis on supporting individuals to make decisions for themselves. We must aim for a future in which Indigenous people can share equitably in the social and economic opportunities of the nation."(Ruddock 2002)

The point the Minister makes is that the government will only stand by an indigenous decision that is in line with that of the government. For the government, political assimilation is essential, and after that indigenous people can make individual choices about their futures.

The reaction from Aboriginal leaders to the Minister's statement indicates the indigenous sensitivity to anything that smells like assimilation. Former Council of Reconciliation Chairman, Pat Dodson (Saunders 2002) insisted the Government hold talks with Aborigines because he feared the motives of the Ruddock statement were division and assimilation. Dodson warned *"We have to stop being co-opted into the system because the more we do that the more we participate in our own demise"* (Saunders 2002).

Human rights watchdog, Dr Bill Jonas, supports Patrick Dodson. Dr Jonas (2002, p 9) comments *"We need to adopt a rights approach that does have the capacity to transform social, economic and political relations in Australia."*

There is indeed a fine line between gaining equality through citizenship, and succumbing to assimilation forces. If this danger was real, and known to indigenous peoples, would the type of equality being offered still be taken up? In other words, is the government being honest about the meaning of its plans for indigenous peoples?

(b) The policy of assimilation

From Federation until the 1960s, official policy for Aborigines was protection and assimilation. In September 1951 the Native Welfare Council, comprising Commonwealth and State ministers, met in Canberra and stated the policy to be:

> all Aborigines and part-Aborigines are expected eventually to attain the same manner of living as other Australians and to live as members of a single Australian community, enjoying the same rights and privileges, accepting the same responsibilities, observing the same customs and influenced by the same beliefs, hopes and loyalties as other Australians. (Our Future Our Selves, 1990, pp 1–2)

In those days indigenous peoples had little input into government policy.

(c) Political mainstreaming

The political system—parliaments and voting was designed by whites for whites. Representative democracy has its place where all other things are equal. But Aborigines are in a minority and will be increasingly so as migration figures show. Reliable estimates place the indigenous population at around 350,000. Over 3 million people have become citizens under migration since 1949 (Australian Citizenship Council 2000, p26).

Indigenous participation in Australian politics will be minor. Participation would be more window dressing, than effective. Australia gets indigenous peoples to surrender their right to political independence in exchange for being a powerless minority within the white system. Yet there is little doubt about the pressure, from many quarters, for indigenous peoples to succumb.

Integration, like citizenship, is meant to bring all people under the one umbrella while allowing for individual differences. In this case, the "one umbrella" refers to the political, economic, legal and social systems established by whites. It is now called Australia. Integration accommodates individual social and cultural differences, but not collective political differences.

The carrot is that you can stand for election but realistically cannot be elected to office by your own people. The exceptions might be in the Northern Territory or in some seats in WA (Buxton 1998).

Indigenous participation in Australia's political system is political assimilation. Will political absorption make Aborigines and Torres Strait Islanders socially the same as "other" Australians? Being the same is not meant that indigenous people have to actually end up physically looking the same as whites. It means white values, behaviour and attitudes so overwhelm individual indigenous people that eventually, these values are adopted in preference to indigenous ones. In other words, indigenous people would remain in name only.

One commentator puts the dilemma this way:

> The strain of Aboriginal policy, torn between the separatist and integrationist tendencies, must be relieved by an honest acknowledgment that the real policy is actually self-determination— within-boundaries... [Aborigines] will become part of the modern world in their own time and in their own way... if not this generation then the next. The only surviving elements of an Aboriginal identity may be race and history. (Johns 2001, p 18)

The "modern world" means white Australia. Even the element of hope about identity in this otherwise pessimistic assessment may be unfounded. Co-founder of Link-Up, Dr Peter Read makes the following comment on what he has observed:

> [Young Aborigines] are beginning to challenge the idea that you are Aboriginal, full stop. They are now saying, 'Why can't I say I'm Italian or Irish as well?' (Scott, 2002, p18).

This may reflect urban pressures for young Aborigines. It is hardly representative of rural areas.

Without a distinct political base, indigenous people will become dependent on the political system into which they are merged. Additional pressure to conform will come from the economic system of capitalist Australia. John Altman, from the Centre for Aboriginal Economic Policy Research, stated the obvious:

> ...nowhere are the differences between Indigenous institutions and those of the colonisers more marked than in the economic system... there seems no doubt that most indigenous people, whether urbanised or in remote locations, wish to maintain their distinct identity and cultural autonomy. How can this be reconciled in modern Australia with economic equality? (Johns 2001, pp 14–15)

Privatising delivery of services (currently called consultancies or "outsourcing") and of the local community store; getting education for the sole purpose of getting a job or running a private business; moving away from collective ownership of land to private, are some examples of how the values of the Australian economy would change the collective economic behaviour of indigenous people.

The warnings need to be heeded, not ignored. JRR Tolkien, author of *The Lord of the Rings*, lamented the English loss of myths and legends connecting the English to their past. Aborigines and Torres Strait Islanders are being pushed to embrace a system that will guarantee their demise as distinct peoples.

3. Who has the right to decide the indigenous future?

The National Report of the Royal Commission into Aboriginal Deaths in Custody (p 199) stated:

> ... running through all the proposals that are made for the elimination of [Aboriginal] disadvantage is the proposition that Aboriginal people have for two hundred years been dominated to an extraordinary degree by the non-Aboriginal

society and that the disadvantage is the product of that domination. The thrust of this report is that the elimination of disadvantage requires an end of domination and an empowerment of Aboriginal people; that control of their lives, of their communities must be returned to Aboriginal hands.

The Queensland Government's 1991 Aboriginal and Islander Review Committee discussion paper entitled "Towards Self-Government" stated:

> Aboriginal and Torres Strait Islander communities consulted by the Committee had no doubt about the survival of their rights. The Committee was often asked why the Queensland and Commonwealth Parliaments, and the Australian High Court, must be the ultimate adjudicators of Aboriginal and Torres Strait Islanders' rights. The question is important because it highlights a fundamental issue relevant to Aboriginal and Torres Strait Islander self-government. Whatever the legal situation, Aboriginal and Torres Strait Island people do not regard any powers to govern which they exercise as being 'derivative' or originating from any mainstream government. (Gardener-Garden 1992, p 18.)

These two bodies point out that taking decision making away from indigenous peoples is a major part of the problem. The logic is that it is a treaty must look at political self-rule. If there are to be limits of self-rule, those limits should be negotiated, not imposed.

4. Indigenous statements and positions

In 1938 Jack Patten and Bill Ferguson wrote the manifesto *Aborigines claim citizen rights* (Johns 2001, p 9). The manifesto called for racial assimilation. The manifesto was written in an era when the white Australia policy was overpowering. Fighting against the trend of everything being white must have felt a lost cause.

The push for citizenship rights in the 1967 referendum was a push for equality of access. As many Aborigines led the 1967 civil rights movement the outcome could be said to be part of the Aboriginal agenda. The 1970s saw a movement away from access rights of individuals to a collective rights agenda. Land rights, Aboriginalisation of organisations and even Aboriginal administration of government programs, coupled with fiery demands, amounted to a rejection of assimilation. The mood was for collective self-determination.

Even the 70s and 80s push for more Aboriginal people to be given jobs in the public service was not a reverting to individualism: it was more a call for people to be able to either run their own affairs or have a greater say. The government's replacement of the Department of Aboriginal Affairs with ATSIC was its response to the self-determination push by indigenous people.

ATSIC's propaganda materials and annual reports describe indigenous people as "indigenous Australians" or as "Aboriginal Australians" (ATSIC 2002); as do many indigenous leaders, including both indigenous Chairs of the Reconciliation Council. Behind that phrase ATSIC continues to argue the case for equality, integration and citizenship.

It is difficult to find a definitive contemporary statement by Aborigines about Aboriginal aspirations. ATSIC, government reporting bodies comprising at least some Aborigines, and even the indigenous bureaucracy are seen, at least publicly, as influential.

The more radical views usually come from local organisation leadership, or the community itself. Freethinking is heard more often from the so-called uneducated Aboriginal community. There are no signs of radical political thought coming from Aboriginal graduates. Does this mean that education is teaching Aboriginal students to accept the merit of white political, economic and social doctrines?

Edna Collard, from West Australia, wrote (2002) about Aborigines being on the electoral roll. She said "This would seem to me to... be selling out to the political system of the invader. [D]oesn't this mean [giving] up sovereignty?"

If it does, ATSIC is unconcerned. ATSIC maintains that for indigenous people to vote in ATSIC elections they must also enrol to participate in general elections. ATSIC acknowledged its position conflicted with implied loss of sovereignty, and that forcing Aborigines on to the general roll could lead to penalties for not voting (ATSIC 2002).

Professor Marcia Langton (2001) agrees with ATSIC "...the right of Aboriginal people is inferior to that of other Australians. For Aboriginal people in Western Australia it is not compulsory to vote, while for other Australians it is."

The inference from the ATSIC/Langton argument is that all laws and policy governing individual behaviour should be the same for indigenous people as it is for others. Is this not a form of assimilation?

Why a treaty is needed to deal with access rights is not at all clear. Access already exists. A treaty to guarantee access would be no more effective than existing anti-discrimination laws. A "treaty" between the state and one section of the community would have the effect of domestic legislation, not of international law. This is because indigenous peoples, once having accepted the legitimate right of governments to govern them, are bound by the decisions.

Placing the "treaty" in the Constitution would have no greater effect. Constitutional entrenchment of the right of access sounds very grand. In practice it would change little. Aborigines denied access can currently sue under anti-discrimination laws. If these rights were placed in the Constitution they can still sue. What would be different?

A standard that makes all equal might come back to haunt those who seek it. Non-discrimination laws aimed at achieving a level playing field could be used against Aborigines having any different rights. One law for all means customary law is subject to the white law. The Brandy case showed how anti-discrimination laws can work against Aborigines. Those same laws can be used against Aborigines stopping white access to their lands. One system means maintaining the right of politicians to decide indigenous policy, and allocate resources. One law is now used to stop indigenous people from fishing without a permit, unless they have native title. Isn't this what Aborigines are complaining about?

5. Some other implications for the equality policy

(a) Land rights

The cost for Aborigines and Torres Strait Islanders gaining equality is the loss of any claims to their country. If the land belongs to "all" citizens, no one section could logically claim the land as theirs. The right to decide their own collective destiny is lost too, as the indigenous destiny becomes meshed in the collective destiny of all Australians. Self-determination would apply to Australia, not to any group within it. The trade off? To gain access to the benefits of Australian society.

(b) Declarations on indigenous rights

Often, government or the High Court "declares" that certain Aboriginal rights do not exist. Decisions by governments, or the High Court, are binding on all Australian citizens. Citizens give up their right to govern, or to decide the law, and defer to those institutions.

However, the decisions of these bodies, while binding on Australian citizens, are binding only on those citizens. Decisions by the High Court rejecting the existence of Aboriginal sovereignty (Coe v C/W 1979; Coe v C/W 1993), for example, declare the law for Australian citizens. The declaration has no binding effect at all on Aborigines as a sovereign, independent people. The High Court's declaration merely means that Australian law does not recognise Aboriginal sovereignty.

A legal ruling by the High Court against Aboriginal sovereignty does not mean that Aboriginal sovereignty does not exist. It simply means white law does not recognise it. The question of the existence of sovereignty is entirely in the hands of the people who assert its existence, in this case Aborigines. The Court cannot be the absolute ruler on the point because neither the Court nor the Australian nation, has obtained the consent of indigenous peoples to decide.

Action was taken by Aboriginal leaders Paul and Isobel Coe (Coe v C/W 1979; Coe v C/W 1993), to test the High Court's position on Aboriginal sovereignty. This was not implied consent for the institutions of the Australian state to sit in judgement on Aboriginal rights. Those cases, like the Mabo case, simply tested the internal position of Australian law.

It would be entirely different if it were shown that indigenous peoples had consented to abandon a distinct right to exist as a people, and become citizens of another nation, in this case Australia. That process implies the loss of other rights, a point that governments seize.

(c) Treaty with whom?

Another difficulty is defining the parties. If indigenous peoples are already Australians, with whom are they to make a treaty? It is silly to say citizens can make a treaty with their own government. It would put a strain on language to call that a treaty. Perhaps the answer is in the Humpty Dumpty approach.

Alice said to Humpty, *'glory' doesn't mean a 'nice knock down argument.'*
"When I use a word", Humpty Dumpty said in rather a scornful tone, "it means just what I choose it to mean—neither more nor less." (Carroll 1871, Ch VI)

(d) Moral basis for equality

The foundation for equality appears to be based on a fresh start. Indigenous peoples forget what they had, and whites what they took. Historian Henry Reynolds often describes the call for Aborigines to stop digging up the past as hypocritical, for Australia reveres the fallen warrior on ANZAC day, and celebrates the date of white invasion, centenaries and bi-centenaries, federation etc.

The equality argument means indigenous prior ownership is irrelevant because the land now belongs to "everyone". Well, not quite everyone. Those whites having a legal interest in land, keep it. So too do indigenous groups who have native title or some form of land rights. How many would this be, and how do their holdings compare with white ownership?

With a fresh start how then could native title and other Aboriginal rights be logically maintained? The answer seems to be that if whites can bring their gains into the mix then why can't Aborigines. But the mix would be so unequal. This approach would entrench the existing inequality against which so many have campaigned.

It could be argued that as a treaty is a negotiated settlement, the outcome could be more pragmatic than logical. If there were no land, sea areas and other rights included there would be no treaty. Indigenous peoples would walk away. But where would they walk to?

If negotiations began on the basis that indigenous people were citizens of Australia, that is the position they must revert to. If so, where is the incentive for Australia to genuinely enter into negotiations in good faith? The government gets what it wants, with or without a treaty.

If indigenous people were not just citizens but were sovereign peoples, a break down in talks would lead to a very different result. The indigenous peoples could resort to their right of self-determination as sovereign peoples, and threaten to pursue full independence by other means. The incentive is for Australia to negotiate to dissuade indigenous peoples from pursuing this path.

To seek to enter into negotiations with a nation state on behalf of a people without a philosophical, moral and political foundation discredits the cause and belittles the people. Such a huge undertaking of finalising a people's future demands a more dignified approach. Compare the Aboriginal Provisional Government vision—for Aboriginal people to take our place among the nations and peoples of the world, not beneath them.

(e) Australia's moral dilemma

Truth and frankness can be provocative, especially where assumptions are challenged. Some moral pain will have to be felt by Australia because of what has, and is happening, to indigenous peoples. There is a need for Australia to *"recognise the injustice of the past and confront lingering assumptions of ethnic superiority... [and that there must be] a public repudiation of past assumptions... [because] in so far as they are statements of collective guilt, they imply that guilt can be successfully expiated... They are more of a means for the non-Aboriginal people of laying the unjust past to rest and building a new foundation for guilt-free legitimacy."* (Mulgan 1998, p 189).

6. A political settlement as a better alternative

A final settlement that compromises claimed rights of all parties (including the Australian government) so they can co-exist, is a political, not a social settlement. Australia wants to maintain its territorial integrity and its ability to govern all inside that territory. Indigenous peoples might want self rule. Territory, rights over the territory and ability to carve out indigenous futures are all issues the government must address.

Common ground needs to be found. Indigenous peoples do not contest Australia's international boundaries but do contest its claims over indigenous areas within that greater territory. Indigenous peoples do not dispute Australia's international economic or security zones.

There is not likely to be a dispute about Australia's exclusive right to govern urban areas within Australia.

There is, however, dispute about Australia's claim to legitimate right to govern all people, everywhere in Australia. Such a claim is inconsistent with any moral base. It stands against Aboriginal self-rule. Forms of joint or exclusive government of certain indigenous areas might well be the subjects of a settlement. Australian governments still impose their will on indigenous peoples without consent.

7. The basis for a political settlement

A political settlement recognises that indigenous peoples are not coming to the negotiating table as defeated people but as sovereigns: emphasising equality of scale with government, not with other individuals. All manner of things affecting the futures of the respective peoples—Aborigines, Torres Strait Islanders, and Australians—are, according to this theory, up for grabs. This includes political rights and relationships. Social benefits in housing, health, jobs and quality of life generally would flow from political arrangements, instead of as a substitute for a political settlement.

Aboriginal sovereignty does exist. Before whites invaded Australia, Aborigines were the sole and undisputed sovereign authority. The invasion prevented the continuing **exercise** of sovereign authority by Aborigines. The invasion and subsequent occupation has not destroyed the **existence** of Aboriginal sovereignty.

Australia has exercised its authority over Australia and Aborigines by force, not through any legitimacy. The distinction between the existence of a right and the exercise of it is relevant to the competing sovereign claims made by Australia and

Aborigines. The one has exercised sovereign powers without a legitimate right to do so, the other, while having the legitimate right to exercise sovereign powers, has been prevented from doing so. Preventing a people exercising their sovereign rights does not mean that a people lose the right.

If you lose your car to a thief, you lose the ability to exercise control over the car. You do not lose the right to the car.

Australia hotly disputes the proposition I embrace. Likewise indigenous people hotly dispute Australia's absolute right to rule. Somewhere within this standoff is room for negotiation. Australia is not about to concede any jurisdiction arguments in favour of indigenous peoples and the latter are not likely to give up the right to push for self-determination. The whole point of a political settlement is to find ways to resolve such impasses.

Support for a treaty

The history of white/black conflict in Australia should drive government to negotiate a treaty with both Aborigines and Torres Strait Islanders. The negotiations should be in good faith. The government could act on behalf of its immigrant population to deal with history truthfully, and its consequences honourably.

Ill treatment alone may not be a reason justifying a treaty. It is different when that ill treatment involves invasion of someone else's country, murder, racial segregation, a prejudiced legal system, theft of children and all based on the belief of racial superiority. Today's Australians occupy and use the indigenous lands for themselves. If Australians take advantage of past wrongs they also take the responsibilities that attach to those benefits. One such responsibility is restitution for the original owners.

The need for a settlement does not require argument. The nature and character of the settlement does. Is a treaty with Aborigines and Torres Strait Islanders meant to be a political settlement or a social contract?

Conclusion

The discussion about a political settlement is briefer than that dealing with the equality model. This is not because the political settlement arguments are undeveloped. It is purely because I fear the equality and citizenship approach will tend to dominate the debate. There needed to be an analysis of that approach.

The idea of a treaty gave rise to expectations of a political settlement between the Australian government, representing the immigrant population, and Aborigines and Torres Strait Islanders. A final settlement could clarify the political relationship between the groups, and dealt with the social and economic arrangements that flowed from that relationship.

It would be disappointing if the treaty debate degenerated into an excuse to hurry up and cement the assimilation of the indigenous peoples into Australia's political, economic and social systems.

The approach to a treaty by the two indigenous peoples should be conducted as if it were an exercise of their right to self-determination. The choice about the long-term futures of the two peoples is for them, and them alone, to decide. Having arrived at a vision, the two peoples would be better equipped to negotiate with the nation state of Australia.

The choice which indigenous peoples make is not the real issue: the right to make that choice is. If the choice is for assimilation, integration or citizenship, then so be it. It is the same if the choice is for social integration but political independence. The Australian government would need to clarify that it agrees with indigenous people having the right to choose. That choice must be an informed expression of the free will of the people, not one imposed by government.

Australian Governments have always acted in the interests of white people. That has been the dominant government policy. A new start requires a declaration that this selfish approach to race issues is in the past. That simple statement would create the potential for more dignified relations.

Should the government insist that indigenous peoples come to the table as individual citizens and not as peoples, it is clear nothing will have changed. Indigenous negotiators engaging government as citizens would undermine their peoples' position.

Whether the indigenous peoples will agree, after being properly informed, to assimilate, or be politically independent, I cannot say. Nor, truthfully, can anyone else. The whole treaty debate gives indigenous peoples a rare opportunity to talk about their futures. The treaty requires a focus on the future. It does not mean the day to day issues will disappear overnight. They will remain all the longer if a future for indigenous peoples is not carved out by indigenous peoples.

Michael Mansell is Secretary of the Aboriginal Provisional Government which campaigns for the right of Aborigines to choose their own destiny, and a lawyer.

Practical Steps Towards a Treaty: Structures, Challenges and the Need for Flexibility

Larissa Behrendt

With the re-emergence of a treaty between Indigenous and non-Indigenous Australians as a focus for the Indigenous rights debate, there is much expectation about what such an agreement may achieve. The utility of a treaty is something that has been discussed by the Aboriginal leadership for over two decades.

Patrick Dodson sees it as an opportunity to set down broad principles that will facilitate and guide further discussions about unfinished business,

> We have got to have an agreement between the government and Aboriginal people. This would probably need a referendum. That agreement would need to recognise our prior ownership and occupation of this land. Part of the Labor Party platform was to recognise a treaty with us but the government has taken no action. A treaty would contain broad principles—the points of departure—for discussions about other rights, such as those to land, language and culture (Dodson, 2002).

In calling for a referendum, he also believes that there needs to be a change in the way that non-Indigenous Australians see Indigenous people and the way that they conceptualise the relationship that Indigenous people currently have with the dominant culture.

Gallarrwuy Yunupingu identifies the cultural distinctiveness of Indigenous people and that the lack of a treaty or agreement could be a basis for recognising Indigenous sovereignty:

> Instead of forcing Aboriginal people to celebrate the bicentennial, the government should be passing a constitutional amendment which recognises us as the first owners of the country. There has never been any agreement signed between the Aboriginal and non-Aboriginal people as there has been with other indigenous peoples ... So we need to begin to talk about sovereignty. We are a people, even if we are classified by languages. Our culture and belief in the land made us a distinct people. Even the urbanised Aboriginal people—who are a creation of non-Aboriginal society—have a sense of belongingness (Yunupingu, 2002).

Yunupingu implies that cultural distinctiveness gives rise to a right to a distinct political unit and also indicates that a treaty can become a catalyst for the recognition of Aboriginal rights.

The Senate Standing Committee on Constitutional and Legal Affairs in its report,

Two Hundred Years Later, also recognised the need for a resolution to the issues left outstanding by the lack of an agreement making process:

> ..., the Committee is of the view that if it is recognised that sovereignty did inhere in the Aboriginal people in a way not comprehended by those who

applied the terra nullius doctrine at the time of occupation and settlement, then
certain consequences flow which are proper to be dealt with in a compact
between the descendants of those Aboriginal peoples and other Australians
(House of Representatives Standing Committee, 1983).

A treaty could provide, among other things, a symbolic recognition of sovereignty
and prior occupation, a redefinition and restructuring of the relationship that
Indigenous peoples have with Australia, the granting of better rights protection and
the basis for regional self-government.

With this promise, it is not surprising that a treaty remains a clear focus for the
recognition and protection of Indigenous rights. It is currently a key ATSIC initiative
and has been supported in the Final Report by the Council for Aboriginal
Reconciliation as part of the way forward.

For the idea of a treaty to move forward, two conversations have to take place.
Firstly, a discussion about the content of a treaty or treaties needs to occur in order to
define the rights and interests to be articulated and protected. Secondly, the issue of
the framework and process of a treaty or treaties needs to be considered. These two
questions are interrelated. A broad understanding of what a treaty is supposed to
achieve and contain will assist in determining the appropriate type of process for
negotiations and the most suitable legal form for the resulting agreement.

Subject matter

Although there are notable cultural, social and economic differences in Indigenous
communities throughout Australia, there is much common ground in responses to the
question of what Indigenous people will want in a treaty. It is possible to assert this
by looking at expressions of Indigenous self-determination such as the Barunga
statement, the Eva Valley statement and Patrick Dodson's 4th Vincent Lingiari
Memorial Lecture, 'Until the Chains are Broken'. These articulations can assist with
mapping the spectrum of rights we could predict would be identified for inclusion in
a treaty. These rights include everything from the right not to be discriminated
against, the right to enjoy language, culture and heritage, our right to land, seas,
waters and natural resources, the right to be educated and to work, the right to be
economically self sufficient, the right to be involved in decision-making processes that
impact upon our lives and the right to govern and manage our own affairs and our
own communities. A treaty could also be used to provide a symbolic recognition of
sovereignty and prior occupation, redefine and restructure of relationship between
Indigenous peoples and Australia and provide the basis for regional self-government.

From this range of claims it can be seen that the issues identified as subject matter
for a treaty include matters that the legal system has attempted, albeit often
unsuccessfully, to protect (such as freedom from racial discrimination, native title and
heritage protection). The agenda also includes several rights for which there has not
been strong or any legal protection (self-government).

One issue that arises from the scope of these claims is that there may be some matters that do not need to be dealt with by a treaty. Another issue is that there must be flexibility in the way in which content is articulated. This requirement of ensuring that Indigenous communities across Australia get the best outcome for their particular circumstances highlights the attractiveness of treaty-making at a local or regional level to best accommodate the specific needs and aspirations of different Indigenous groups. Therefore, a national treaty should be a standard-setting document for local or regional treaties containing fundamental, bottom-line principles and, at the same time, it should provide mechanisms for local and regional decision-making processes.

A Treaty process

There are two models that can provide a guide to treaty making processes that have an overarching structure but allow for agreement making at the local or regional level: Indigenous Land Use Agreements under the *Native Title Act 1993* and the agreement making processes in Canada.

A. Indigenous Land Use Agreements: A Legislative Model

Provision for agreement making between Indigenous and non-Indigenous parties is made under the *Native Title Act 1993*. Indigenous Land Use Agreements are of interest in this context because they can facilitate agreements about native title without the need for native title determinations. As a result of the 1998 amendments there are now three types of Indigenous Land Use Agreements provided for under the act:

- *body corporate agreements*: these agreements are relevant where native title determinations have been made over an entire area and there are registered native title bodies corporate in relation to the area. All registered native title bodies corporate must be parties to the agreement. These agreements can cover any matter relating to native title. The resulting agreement can be registered (*Native Title Act 1993*, ss. 24 BD-BI and ss. 24 BC).

- *area agreements*: these agreements apply to areas where there have been no native title determinations or determinations have not been made over the whole area. They cannot be made if there are registered native title bodies corporate in relation to the whole area. All registered native title claimants and bodies corporate must be parties to the agreement. In the absence of native title bodies corporate, native title claimants or their representative bodies for the area must be the parties. An area agreement can cover any matter relating to native title. Because these agreements occur in the absence of a native title determination, the process for their registration is more complex than for body corporate agreements (*Native Title Act 1993*, ss. 24CA-CL).

- *alternative procedure agreements*: like area agreements, these agreements are made over areas where there have been no native title determinations or determinations have not been made over the whole area. They cannot provide for the extinguishment of native title since potential native title claimants may not be parties to the agreement. It can provide for other matters related to native title. Like area agreements, there is a complex registration process for these types of agreements (*Native Title Act 1993*, ss. 24CA-CL).

Indigenous land use agreements, being able to provide for "matters related to native title", can cover a range of issues, including:

- the doing of future acts
- future acts that have already been done
- withdrawing, amending or any other matter in relation to an application for the determination of native title or compensation for native title:
- the relationship between native title rights and interests and other rights and interests in the areas,
- compensation for any past act, and
- any other matter concerning native title (except extinguishment in the case of alternative procedure agreements) (Native Title Act 1993, ss. 24CA-CL).

When ILUAs are registered, they have the effect of a contract. That is, the agreement will take effect as a contract at common law and will bind the parties to the terms and conditions of the agreement. In this way, registration creates legal certainty for the parties over the matters covered by the agreement. Native title holders who are not parties to the agreement are bound by it though the *Native Title Act 1993* which sets out notice and objection procedures.

Although it had been proposed that registered agreements have the force of legislation, this was not included as part of the legislative scheme. However, the *Native Title Act 1993* expressly states that there is no prohibition on governments legislating to the effect of its obligation. Nor is there anything in the Act or otherwise to prevent the government from legislating to give force to the obligations of other parties under the agreement or third parties who may be affected by the agreement, such as sub-contractors.

ILUAs are attractive not just because of the certainty they can provide parties but because they are less expensive than litigation with more ownership of the outcome by the parties. However, it should also be remembered that, despite these benefits, just because there is not litigation, the process of negotiation still requires resources, including time. There is also an argument that the voluntary nature of ILUAs is tenuous since, once it is registered, its contractual force binds all native title holders and contracting parties. This gives rise to questions about the power imbalance between the parties who are negotiating and the effectiveness of the mechanisms within the *Native Title Act* to ensure that all native title holders are consulted (Kee, 2001).

ILUAs cover all matters related to native title (except for extinguishment in certain circumstances). For such an agreement to be considered as capable of meeting the expectations of a treaty there would need to be an extension of the subject matter that could be included in such agreements, requiring an expansion from matters related to native title to matters that related to self-government.

B. Canadian Land Claims Processes and the Inherent Right to Self-Government: A Policy Model

Treaty making has re-emerged as a way in which to define the relationship between First Nations and the Crown in right of Canada.

In 1973, the Comprehensive Claims Process and the Specific Claims Process were introduced as part of a federal government response to the decision in *Calder v Attorney-General of British Columbia* in which the Supreme Court of Canada indicated that an Aboriginal title may be recognisable at common law ([1973] SCR 313). The Comprehensive Claims Process was implemented where claims to Aboriginal title had not been addressed through treaty or agreement with the Aboriginal community. Sometimes these land claims were accompanied by claims for varying forms of self-government. The Specific Claims Process was implemented where First Nations felt that there was non-fulfilment of Indian treaties and lawful obligations or improper administration of lands and other assets.

These processes were viewed as positive because they provided for, 'consideration of a wide range of issues, participation by the Aboriginal groups most closely involved, ratification by elected officials, and constitutional entrenchment of guarantees.' (Elliott, 1997). However, the disadvantages of these processes have also been identified with criticism focused on the slow pace of settlement (Elliott, 1997). The delay in the settlement of claims has been attributed to a variety of factors including disunity among claimant groups and between government parties, a succession of different parties such as a change in federal or chief negotiators, the impact of claims on third parties and the need to resolve overlapping Indigenous claims (Elliott, 1997). To assist with the resolution of claims, some large claim areas have been split and negotiated in segments. Other factors that seem to affect the process of negotiations include the format of negotiations, the personalities of the negotiators, geographical distances between negotiating parties and support or opposition from outside groups.

On the other hand, negotiations have often been assisted by interest in economic development. The discovery of oil reserves helped to accelerate the conclusion of the *Alaska Native Claims Settlement Act* and the James Bay Hydro development assisted with the conclusion of the *James Bay and Northern Quebec Agreement* and the *Northeastern Quebec Agreement*.

The process for the resolution of claims began with the Aboriginal group establishing the validity of their claim. For a comprehensive claim, they have to establish traditional and continuing occupancy of land not dealt with by treaty or eliminated by legal means. For a specific claim, a breach of a provision or obligation under the treaty has to be shown.

If the claim was accepted, the process was as follows: (1) a framework agreement to set out the parameters of the discussion, (2) agreements-in-principle on particular matters, and then (3) a final agreement that was then signed, ratified and implemented. These Final Agreements enjoy the protection of the Canadian Constitution (*Constitution Act 1982*, s35 (1)).

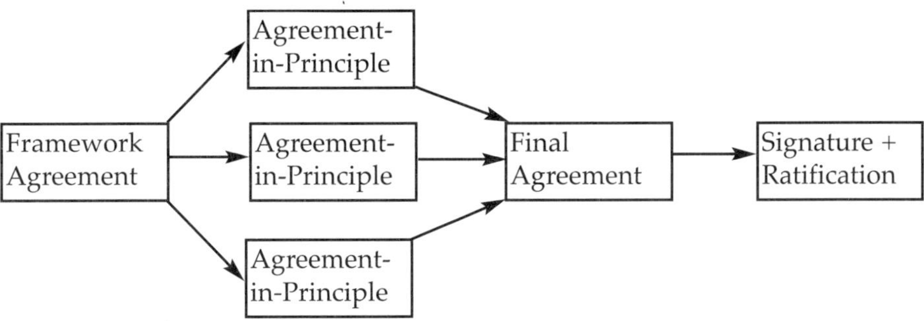

Canada implemented an *Inherent Right to Self-Government* policy in 1995 which allows for processes to reaffirm and renegotiate treaties that are already in existence and to negotiate treaties where they were not entered (Department of Indian and Northern Affairs, 1995). The policy recognises that self-government is an inherent right held by Aboriginal people that predates the 1982 Constitutional amendment and therefore attracts constitutional protection (Department of Indian and Northern Affairs, 1995). The Canadian Government has defined the right of self-government as follows:

Recognition of the inherent right is based on the view that the Aboriginal peoples of Canada have the right to govern themselves in relation to matters that are internal to their communities, integral to their unique cultures, identities, traditions, languages and institutions, and with respect to their special relationship to their land and their resources (Department of Indian and Northern Affairs, 1995).

In the policy, the Federal Government emphasises its preference for negotiating the content and implications of the inherent right to self-government with Indigenous peoples at a community-based level, viewing litigation as a last resort. The Supreme Court of Canada has emphasised that the legislature, rather than the judiciary, is the appropriate arbiter of this matter. (This was the approach emphasised by the Court when remitting the case back to trial in Delgamuukw v. British Columbia (1997) 3 SCR. 1010).

The *Inherent Right to Self-Government* policy identifies the matters that the Federal Government will negotiate on and this is an interesting guide for future discussions about the content of a treaty in Australia. The policy lists:

- *subject matters that constitute the inherent right to self-government.* These matters are defined as being matters 'internal to the group, integral to its distinct aboriginal culture, and essential to its operation as a government or institution'. Included are marriage, education, health, adoption and child welfare, Aboriginal language, tradition and religion, social services, administration of Aboriginal laws, including the establishment of Aboriginal courts or tribunals and the creation of offences of the type normally created by local or regional governments for contravention of laws, policing, land management, natural resource management, agriculture, hunting, fishing, trapping, management of public works, housing, local transportation, and the licensing, regulation and operation of businesses located on Aboriginal lands.

- *subject matters considered by the Federal Government to be beyond the internal matters of the First Nations but which it has conceded are negotiable.* These include matters such as divorce, labour/training, penitentiaries and parole, environmental protection, fisheries co-management, gaming, and emergency preparedness.

- *subject matters considered to be outside of the inherent right to self-government.* These include matters such as powers related to Canadian sovereignty, defence and external relations, management and regulation of the national economy, maintenance of national law and order and substantive criminal law, navigation and shipping, and postal services.

This model has facilitated the renegotiation of existing treaties in light of the extended understanding of self-government. The Canadian policy provides a guide as to the subject matter that can be taken into account as part of the negotiations and allows for specific agreement making at a regional level.

Challenges

The experience with both the registration of Indigenous Land Use Agreements and the modern Canadian agreement making processes can be used to highlight and predict the challenges for a treaty process in Australia.

A: Mandates: As the focus of the treaty debate turns to processes and frameworks, the issue of who is going to have the authority to represent, negotiate on behalf of and sign for Indigenous parties is going to become increasingly important. Deciding the issue of representation is going to be a difficult one. The use of existing representative structures would be one option. ATSIC has a regional and national structure but it is far from clear whether this is one that Indigenous people will feel best represents their community and its role in negotiations is going to be controversial. Similarly, land councils, although an established regional structure, are often plagued by the same community politics that place ATSIC in an awkward position.

State and national conventions that elect representatives may be another way to proceed. This model would allow for greater (and grass roots) participation in the selection process and can also allow issues to be aired and discussed in large forums. It is a model that can provide for input from Indigenous men and women, elders and youth.

Consideration of mandate issues within the Indigenous community must be coupled with Federal Government commitment to create a clear mandate to negotiate the framework and substance of the treaty.

B: Indigenous Identity: The Canadian experience shows that when there are benefits that flow from a treaty, the issue of band membership becomes a contentious one and the difference between "status" and "non-status" Indians a matter of great tension in Indigenous communities. A treaty or a series of treaties will bring the issues of identity and qualification for inclusion to the forefront and we will need to be prepared to deal with this.

As we have already seen from the native title debates, there is fracturing within the Indigenous community over who appropriate beneficiaries are for identified Indigenous rights. The recognition of rights to land has seen traditional owners pitted against Indigenous people whose families have moved in to or were forced to move in to the claim area three to four generations ago.

It is a reflection of how little Indigenous rights have historically been protected in our country that Australia has a much more flexible approach to proof of aboriginality. Heritage, self-identification and acceptance by the Indigenous community are the defining elements in official requirements of proof. When there are treaty benefits, the issues of who can claim can become more contentious, contested and political. The impact of these issues of identity on the stolen generations will be disproportionate as they are the ones less likely to be integrated into Indigenous communities or be able to show attachment and connection to traditional lands. This distinction between Indigenous people included in the pool of treaty beneficiaries and those who are not will create divisions within our communities and create notions of "real" and "not real" Indigenous people. This may also create different classes of Indigenous people with different rights.

C. States as Parties: Treaties, as agreements between nations, have been traditionally between the Indigenous people and the Federal Government of their colonising nation-states. However, in the Canadian context, this two party approach has been changed to a tripartite negotiation. The *Inherent Right to Self-Government Policy* states that treaty negotiations now take place between the provinces, federal government and First Nations people. [1] The inclusion of provinces as third parties to the negotiations was claimed to be as a matter of practicality based on the transfer of natural resources from Federal to Provincial hands through various agreements and a 1930 constitutional amendment.[2]

However, the result of this inclusion of another party at the table is a power shift. It leaves the Federal Government often in the middle ground, rather than the opposition, since the provinces are often more conservative and less willing to compromise. Inclusion of the provinces at the negotiation table has meant that the First Nations' bargaining position is eroded.

This is a clear move away from the Canadian Government's exclusive jurisdiction over Aboriginal matters under s. 91(24) of the *Constitution Act 1867*. This tri-party negotiation also reflects the change from Indian treaties being seen as agreements between two sovereigns to the treatment of such agreements as a matter internal to the Canadian state.

Although we have a different constitutional structure in Australia, it is important that we ensure that any attempt to increase the number of parties at the table is not successful. Like Canada, our federal government has power (at least under the races power or the external affairs power) to make agreements with Indigenous people. Inclusion of the states and territories at the negotiating table may seem more attractive where they are less conservative and more willing to negotiate than their federal counterparts. The issue of appropriate negotiating partners is further complicated when the issues affect local government and conceivably three levels of Australian government could be at the negotiating table.

Inclusion of parties other than Indigenous peoples and the federal government should be avoided as it creates a disadvantage for Indigenous peoples who then have to negotiate with several parties.

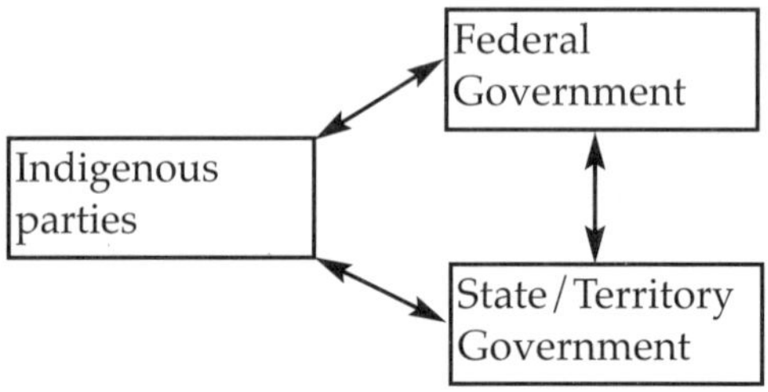

As the Canadian experience shows, this can lead to a situation where the less conservative level of government acts as a mediator between the Indigenous party and the more rigid government. This "good cop/bad cop" routine can obscure the real alliances between the parties and the fact that both levels of government are part of the State.

The preferred model of negotiation is to have the Federal Government as the negotiating party on behalf of the State and have them responsible for bringing state, territory and local governments on side.

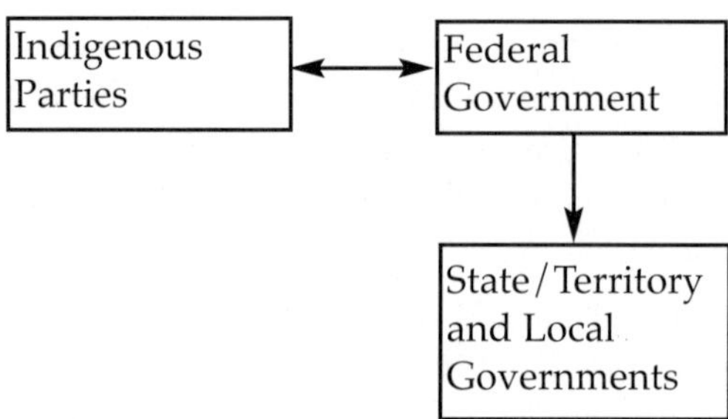

D. Inherent Power Imbalance between the Parties: There is an inherent power imbalance in any negotiation where one party is both the arbiter and a party to the negotiations. Where the treaty negotiation is between Indigenous peoples and the Australian state and directed by the Australian legal system, there is an inherent bias in favour of the government. A more pronounced power imbalance occurs where one of the parties to the negotiations is also the one to interpret the agreement. In the context of treaties, a power imbalance occurs where one arm of government (the judiciary) interprets a treaty entered into by another arm of government (the legislature). Although the doctrine of the separation of powers would treat them as different entities with different functions, both represent the Crown in right of Australia.

The power imbalance can be alleviated by the creation of an independent body to interpret and enforce a treaty. Suggestion of an appropriate independent model in the Australian context has already been made. On 12 May, 2000, Patrick Dodson presented his Wentworth Lecture, "Beyond the Mourning Gate—Dealing With Unfinished Business", in which he proposed that an independent 'Treaty Commission' be established to draft a Treaty between the Australian Government and Aboriginal peoples. He suggested that the content of the treaty be based upon matters raised by the Reconciliation Council and any other matters relayed before it. His Treaty Commission would comprise a membership of forty people, twenty proposed by the government and twenty proposed by ATSIC. This Commission would be established independent of government. To complete the treaty, Dodson suggested that the two parties then choose their representatives to negotiate the treaty, which would then be placed before the Aboriginal people for consideration by referendum.

E. Fidelity to Indigenous Aspirations: A challenge for Indigenous negotiators will be for the end result to be faithful to Indigenous claims to sovereignty and other aspirations. A treaty process will be one that requires negotiation and compromise. It will involve, through the negotiation process, a move from the aspirational to the pragmatic and those who feel that the end result is less than they can live with will feel betrayed by the final agreement. This will be particularly so for those who are left out of the group of beneficiaries. We can see this occurring with native title with those whose claims for native title were not eligible under the legislative scheme of the *Native Title Act 1993*.

This will be a special challenge for the issue of sovereignty, the notion that we are a separate and distinct nation. It has already become apparent in community consultations about a treaty that the issue of sovereignty is one that is important to Indigenous people and held on to as a fundamental belief.

The key for negotiators will be to ensure that they have a clear understanding as to what the core issues being sought for inclusion in a treaty and how far they are mandated to compromise. They will then need to be careful that the core issues are not compromised.

Responsiveness to communities through flexible processes will allow greatest fidelity to self-determination. For this reason, regional and local agreement making will increase feelings of ownership and assist in ensuring that final agreements capture the aspirations of the community. The federal framework that facilitates those regional and local agreements will need to ensure that it can provide enough scope for regional and local agreements to achieve the things that Indigenous people (men and women) and their communities want. It will also need to ensure that it can protect the rights recognised in those local and regional treaties in order to make them meaningful.

F. Resources: It is essential that the framework for any treaty-making process get balance right between Indigenous and non-Indigenous parties to ensure that there is an equal playing field between the parties. To this end, adequate resources, an appropriate timeframe, respectful procedures and a culturally appropriate process must be developed and maintained throughout the negotiation process.

A fluid, on-going process

Treaty making has seen a long term negotiation process that, if successful, takes decades to conclude. This becomes a trap, as Indigenous peoples have to wait a long time for the benefits of negotiations.

There are two ways in which this long term model of treaty-making could be altered to pass on the benefits of a treaty to Indigenous people and their communities more quickly.

The first is to ensure that agreement making that is already occurring at a local and regional level—whether under native title legislation or through other mechanisms—is allowed and encouraged to continue while federal negotiations about process and framework take place. This means that agreement making that can achieve practical outcomes for Indigenous people will not be put on hold while a national process is established, something that may take decades. It also means that those communities who already have the agency and the capacity to negotiate and exercise self-determination can go ahead and do that.

The national framework, when concluded, should have standards against which other agreements can be tested. This could mean that, where appropriate, regional and local agreements concluded before the federal agreement could be negotiated to the extent that standards within those documents are less than the standards set out by the federal framework. This would not be dissimilar to the process being undertaken in Canada where old treaties, whose content is often narrow, are being reinterpreted and renegotiated in light of the more expansive *Inherent Right to Self Government* policy.

Another way to ensure a fluid, on-going process is to provide for progressive treaty making. Rather than waiting until the whole content of the treaty is negotiated, it could be that each issue, as it is agreed upon and ratified, becomes part of the treaty but is implemented from that date. This would mean that the easier issues, as they were resolved, would come into effect and allow Indigenous people to enjoy the benefits of those clauses without having to wait for the more difficult issues to be resolved. This approach would also mean that treaty-making could be an on-going process. As new issues may arise—biotechnology, genetic engineering, intellectual property, water rights—which earlier negotiators did not anticipate, they could be negotiated and incorporated into the treaty. This more flexible approach to treaty making will also better reflect the on-going relationship between Indigenous and non-Indigenous Australians since, like any relationship, it is fluid, flexible and changeable.

Where to from here

While there appears to be increasing interest in a treaty, it is important to also focus debates not just on what the content of such an agreement or agreements may be but also on some of the challenges in developing a process to negotiate a treaty. It is important to anticipate these challenges and find workable solutions to them to ensure that they do not become divisive and derail the process.

Expressions of self-determination can give an indication of the content of a treaty and this information can also be used to anticipate the most suitable form a treaty can take. Greatest flexibility will be achieved through a model with national principles that allow for regional and local decision making on key issues.

We can also predict some of the problems with process —states at the table and the inherent power imbalance—and foreshadow the divisive issues —mandates, inclusion and Indigenous identity. Dealing with these issues effectively will ensure that the treaty process, whatever it ends up looking like, will deliver the best long-term benefits to the parties.

The effectiveness of a treaty process can be further enhanced by finding fluid and on-going ways to structure and enforce treaty making, particularly where that flexibility will allow the benefits of any agreement to reach Indigenous peoples and their communities quickly.

Professor Larissa Behrendt is Professor of Law and Indigenous Studies and Director of the Jumbunna Indigenous House of Learning at the University of Technology Sydney and Director of Ngiya, the National Institute of Indigenous Law, Policy and Practice. She graduated from the University of New South Wales in 1992 and has since graduated from Harvard Law School with her Masters of Laws and Doctorate.

Unfinished Business: A Shadow Across Our Relationships

Mick Dodson

In this paper I seek to examine the concept that there is 'unfinished business' and how this business is central to the process of negotiating a treaty or treaties.

I remember greeting with some enthusiasm the introduction to the Parliament and the passing of the *Council for Aboriginal Reconciliation Act* in 1991. To me the passing of this Act represented great hope, a new opportunity and a chance to bring on reform and deliver social justice to Aboriginal and Torres Strait Islander peoples. There was unanimous cross party support for the Act so there was good reason to be optimistic. We also had the report of the Royal Commission into Aboriginal deaths in custody around the same time. Then in 1992 the Council of Australian Governments endorsed the *National Commitment to Improved Outcomes in Aboriginal and Torres Strait Islander Affairs* (AGPS 1992). Overcoming Indigenous disadvantage was definitely on the government agenda. The assault on disadvantage was meant to run side by side with reconciliation. The objective of Reconciliation was described as the 'achievement of a united Australia, which respects this land of ours; values the Aboriginal and Torres Strait Islander heritage; and provides justice and equity for all.' (AGPS 2000).

As we all know the Council for Aboriginal Reconciliation has delivered its final report, is now defunct and reconciliation is still perhaps but a dream. The federal government is yet to fully respond to the Council's final report.

Unfinished business

Defining what unfinished business is is as good a place as any to start this examination. Although the notion may mean different things to different Indigenous people, and attract different descriptions and definitions, its fundamental importance is not disputed. For example, an Indigenous person who is a member of the stolen generations may view the key outstanding issues in a treaty process in quite a different way to someone who has had a relative die in custody, or someone who has had their native title rights extinguished by historical act or transaction. Further, there are many Indigenous Australians who regard the question of Aboriginal and Torres Strait Islander sovereignty as the most pressing and important piece of unfinished business for the nation to address. It is important therefore that in the process of dealing with unfinished business in the treaty making process, we include all points of Indigenous view on the subject, including those views that reject or diminish the importance of the issue. This paper does not explore every single view on the issues but it does look at the way that the government or government-funded reports have responded to or couched the concept.

The Council for Aboriginal Reconciliation in their final report did not use the term 'unfinished business' when dealing with this issue, rather it chose to use perhaps a more politically friendly term—'unresolved business'. In Appendix 3 of their report the Council defined unresolved issues to mean:

> Any issue, whether already identified or identified through the processes of this Act, that is an impediment to achieving reconciliation until it is addressed; including but not limited to: the recognition of the right to equality; the protection of Aboriginal and Torres Strait Islander cultures, heritage and intellectual property; the recognition of Aboriginal and Torres Strait Islander customary law; a comprehensive agreements process for the settlement of native title and other land claims; regional autonomy and constitutional recognition (AGPS 2000).

The Council's guidance as to the meaning of unresolved business is useful, but in my view, what we are really talking about when we use the term 'unfinished business' is the yet to be met legitimate grievances of Aboriginal and Torres Strait Islanders, including the sovereignty question that arises directly from the consequences of the colonisation of this country by the British.

Everything mentioned in the Council's report including the right to equality, culture, heritage and intellectual property rights, recognition of customary law and other issues too many to mention, have been addressed in some report somewhere in the last three decades, so coverage of these issues is not new, it is unfinished. Unfinished business is about confronting the legacy of the past and re-aligning the relationship between Aboriginal and Torres Strait Islander peoples and government and the peoples of Australia (see Patrick Dodson's Wentworth Lecture—*Beyond the Mourning Gate—Dealing with Unfinished Business*, AIATSIS, 2000). It is also deeply rooted in questions of identity and how Indigenous Australians perceive themselves and accept these perceptions. These outstanding matters directly affect the relationship between Indigenous and non-Indigenous Australians and the future of that relationship. Unfinished business is very much about the 'unresolved relationships between Indigenous peoples and the wider community' (Huggins 2002).

If we are talking about treaty making in a new Australia these matters must be central to that process. The resolution of these matters by agreement is essential to a lasting reconciliation. So important are they that there must in my opinion be an up front agreement to negotiate about them before any treaty process is entered into.

Getting the parties, the commonwealth government in particular, to the table of treaty making, is the single biggest task facing Aboriginal and Torres Strait Islander peoples. In the present political climate we should not be deluded—this is indeed a Herculean undertaking, but it cannot be an impossible task. We have achieved great things in the past and we need a great deal of patience and perseverance to achieve present goals.

Setting the agenda is not so hard; however negotiating the adoption of the agenda by all stakeholders will require a great deal of skill. To begin with, identifying what we are talking about so far as unfinished business is concerned is not going to be too difficult because most of the work has already been done. Itemising or particularising the unfinished business is not in my view very hard. Generating national collective political will to implement the agenda is the real difficulty.

Establishing the means by which we might reach a national collective political will to get on with a treaty process is not within the scope of this paper. However, it must be appreciated by Indigenous and other Australians who are supportive of a treaty and a treaty making process, that enormous efforts must be put into education, awareness raising and confidence building across the nation. Without such parallel strategies the process will fail. The Aboriginal and Torres Strait Islander Commission (ATSIC) has already embarked on a number of programmes and projects in this regard. Co-ordination of the various strategies is the key to success.

Professor George Williams has provided excellent advice on the framework for a strategy including:

- focus on the long not the short term;
- making sure the process is not just about politicians;
- looking at incremental not immediate change and rejecting minimalist approaches;
- getting the community involved and owning the process; (and I would suggest the outcomes);
- educating the community and having models they can understand;
- Australia-wide bipartisan support;
- the reform process should also become part of the reforms (Williams, AIATSIS, 2001).

The factors above should underpin and inform the overall strategic treaty framework. Perhaps what Williams is saying is that Aboriginal and Torres Strait Islander peoples and our supporters must win all the moral ground and argument, as well as win the battle over ideas, by convincing all Australians there is nothing to lose but much to win. It is therefore important in my view that as a first step in a treaty process we need to establish the framework within which we are to proceed and the way in which we might address unfinished business. Therefore the principles that might underlie a treaty in broad national terms include:

- Recognition of Aboriginal and Torres Strait Islander peoples as the first peoples of Australia and of the distinct rights which flow from this;
- Agreement to the necessary reforms for a more just society;
- The setting of national standards to inform local or regional treaties and agreements.

In my opinion a single national treaty is impossible to achieve in Australia mainly because I believe Indigenous Australians would not agree to this. My preferred approach is for a national treaty framework model, which allows for treaty making on a national, state-wide regional or local basis.

In supporting a national framework model I do not deal directly with the key issue of Indigenous sovereignty. It is clear to me that this question must be addressed at some stage in the treaty process. The model I support remains silent on this issue. Michael Mansell has written that the question of sovereignty 'is the single hardest issue to get people to move their position on' (Mansell, 2002). He raises some very pertinent questions about Indigenous sovereignty such as, how did the British invasion become legitimised and how in the process did Indigenous peoples legitimately lose their sovereignty? There are at present no answers to these questions and perhaps they might be best left unanswered in the interest of a successful treaty process. As Mansell concedes, it is 'not necessary for either side to concede sovereignty ... the treaty could simply be silent or acknowledge both' (Mansell, 2002).

A national framework could allow for treaties that could be comprehensive, deal with multiple or single issues, or merely address some specific local issue. There could even be a national single-issue treaty dealing with sovereignty. But why should we do it this way? There are many remaining to be convinced that this is the right way and that we need a treaty.

Why do we need a treaty or treaties?

There are a number of things about the British invasion, which although they are now not seriously contested, remain important. In the first place our rights have never been formally recognised by the invaders, their descendants or past government. Second, our rights have been affected by a lopsided relationship with the newcomers who saw us as 'primitives' with no rights and with no concept of 'civilised' customs. A treaty or treaties could have recognised and protected Indigenous rights and led to a just constitutional basis for the Australian federation.

We were completely overlooked as relevant parties in the formation of the Australian federation. If a treaty had been in place and constituted by the principles noted above, the structure of federation would no doubt have incorporated Aboriginal rights in the federal system.

The need for a treaty today is based on the reasonable basis that Aboriginal and Torres Strait Islander societies have been injured and harmed throughout the colonisation process and just recompense is owed. I do not maintain that this is the only basis for a treaty, which is to say that the process cannot and should not just be about compensation.

It is important to realise that a national framework treaty or agreement would allow Indigenous communities and other local, regional, state and territory stakeholders to sign treaties with each other at those levels. Finally, and perhaps above all, a treaty process will deliver the ultimate certainty to the relationship between Aboriginal and Torres Strait Islanders and the rest of the country's population.

The framework

I am suggesting four ways in which we might construct a legal foundation so a treaty could be negotiated in Australia between Indigenous peoples and the commonwealth government. These are,

- An agreement under international law in the form of a treaty;
- An agreement that is supported by the constitution;
- An agreement that is supported by legislation;
- A simple agreement.

This is not to say that there are not other approaches available.

I favour an agreement that is supported by the constitution and this paper deals with that approach. However some brief discussion of the other three forms a treaty might take is included.

An agreement under international law in the form of a treaty

The immediate issue implicit in this approach is the continued existence of Aboriginal and Torres Strait Islander sovereignty. This option is a proposition that would have two sovereign parties, the commonwealth of Australia and the Aboriginal and Torres Strait Islander people who would enter into an agreement enforceable under international law. The key question that arises is, can Indigenous Australia legitimately negotiate a treaty with non-Indigenous Australia?

This approach poses some difficulties in the Australian political context because not only do sovereign parties have to have the capacity to conclude treaties under international law, but they must also be sovereign entities possessing international personality. The Commonwealth of Australia is obviously regarded internationally as a sovereign entity and possesses international personality. This is a much more difficult thing for Aboriginals and Torres Strait Islanders to establish. But the question of the legal international status of Indigenous Australians is seen by many Aboriginals and Torres Strait Islanders as part of the unfinished business requiring attention.

An agreement that is supported by legislation

Any legislation passed by the Commonwealth parliament must fall within the scope of power given to the parliament by the Australian constitution. There are two potential heads of power within such scope: section 51 (xxvii)—the races power; and section 51 (xxix)—the external affairs power.

Through the so-called races power the commonwealth parliament has passed legislation like the ATSIC Act, the Northern Territory Land Right Acts and the Native Title Act, however it is possible for this power to be used in a discriminatory fashion, for example, the Hindmarsh Island and Native Title Amendments Act legislation discriminate against Indigenous people.

There appears to be no doubt that the commonwealth parliament has the power under these sections of the constitution to make *special laws*, (without predetermining the content of what they might contain), to give effect to a treaty or treaties but there is an obvious political limitation to the use of this power. This has been most recently exemplified by the amendment by the present government to the Native Title Act.

The vulnerability arises from the capacity of later parliaments (depending on which political party or parties have a temporary majority) to substantially repeal or amend such legislation. This potential political exposure represents a substantial impediment to implementing a treaty or treaties under this head of power.

The Commonwealth Parliament also has power under the constitution to make laws with respect to external affairs under section 51 (xxix). This section gives the Parliament the power to enact legislation governing and regulating all Australia's relations with other countries. This is a very broad power and generally the conduct of external affairs does not require legislative action as these matters are usually accomplished by Executive action. It is arguable that this power enables the Commonwealth Parliament to make laws on an indefinite array of subjects provided each meets the description of an external affair. A treaty or treaties with the Indigenous peoples of Australia would fall into such a description. For example, the poor socio-economic circumstances of Aboriginal and Torres Strait Islanders are of concern to many countries with strong links to Australia. If the reason (in part) is to allay these concerns and improve international relations with these countries then the use of the power in this context could arguably be described as an external affair. Recent criticisms by United Nations human rights bodies are a case in point.

The Commonwealth Parliament can also enact laws by reference to matters referred to it by State Parliaments. The most recent example concerning Indigenous issues was the *Framlingham and Lake Tyers Bill* of the Victorian parliament.

A simple agreement

A treaty or treaties could be negotiated in the form of an agreement within the realm of the statutory and common law of contract. The contract or agreement could create legally enforceable rights and obligations. This is essentially the way in which the United States of America dealt with Native American tribes within 1788 and 1842. 242 treaties were made during this time. The power to make treaties in the United States comes from Article I section 8 of the American constitution.

An agreement that is supported by the Constitution

The idea of inserting a new section 105B in the Constitution was covered in a paper by Gil Shaw and tabled at the hearings of the Senate Constitutional and Legal Affairs Committee on the feasibility of a compact in 1982. This option, of legally securing a treaty, involves including the entire text of the document in the Australian Constitution. Such a proposal could set the basis of relationships between the Commonwealth and Aboriginal and Torres Strait Islander peoples and how they would be conducted in the future.

Such an approach has its advantages, for example in providing certainty, but could prove to be inflexible, and it would be difficult to change or to remove problems that may be encountered in the operation of the treaty. Obtaining approval for such a proposal would also be very difficult and as I indicated earlier, I think Aboriginal and Torres Strait Islander people are unlikely to agree to this approach.

A bare statement of principles however, perhaps providing a framework for the future relationship, might gain approval from the electors. However, any detailed text, even in the unlikely event that all Australians agreed on it, would be next to impossible to get into the Constitution, especially given the history of the failure of referenda in Australia.

Agreeing on working and content appears to be the most difficult task. These matters would first have to receive support from Indigenous peoples. A bill for law is then required from the federal parliament followed by agreement to the bill by a majority of people in a majority of states. Given this difficulty, it might be easier to argue around an existing precedent set in constitutional law.

Inserting a special section into the Constitution would give a broad enabling power to the Commonwealth Parliament in terms of negotiating a treaty or treaties with representatives of Aboriginal and Torres Strait Islander peoples. This section could be modelled on the present section 105A.

Section 105A

If the proposal outlined above received support from the electors at a referendum it would give the Commonwealth Parliament plenary powers to enter into treaties. This potentially gives great security to Aboriginal and Torres Strait Islander peoples and would not require the support (although desirable) of the States. It would also avoid the need for the Commonwealth to have to rely on some other (uncertain) enabling power presently existing in the constitution, like s 51 (xxvi). In a 1932 judgement, Rich and Dixon J.J. found, in respect of sub-section 5 of s105A, that:

> The effect of this provision is to make any agreement of the required description obligatory upon the Commonwealth and the States, to place its operation and efficacy beyond the control of any law of any of the seven Parliaments, and to prevent any constitutional principle or provision operating to defeat or diminish or condition the obligatory force of the Agreement.

As suggested to a Senate Legal and Constitutional Affairs Committee investigating the feasibility of a treaty in 1981, a new section 105B could perhaps be inserted to enable the Commonwealth to have the power to make the treaties as presently spelt out in the first paragraph of 105A. This paragraph would then be followed in very broad terms by a non-inclusive list of things that might form the content and substance of treaties. The terms of the treaties could set other requirements, for example forms of dispute resolution and the power to vary the treaty provision by the parties. The new 105B would also require an automatic validation of the treaty or treaties entered into before the new section took effect. This would allow existing agreements, if so desired, to be brought under this new section. There could also be a power for the parliaments to pass laws enabling them to carry into effect the terms of the treaty or treaties. This would mean the Commonwealth could authorise the States, in certain agreed circumstances, to exercise this Commonwealth power.

A possible 105B, along the lines of the version that follows, has been presented to the 1981 Senate Constitutional and Legal Affairs Committee:

(1) The Commonwealth may make a treaty or treaties with persons or bodies recognised as representatives of Aboriginal and Torres Strait Islander peoples of Australia with respect to the status and rights of those people within Australia including but not limited by the following:

(a) estoration of Aboriginal and Torres Strait Islander peoples or to some of them of their lands which were owned and occupied by them prior to 1770;

(b) compensation for the loss of any land incapable of being restored to the Aboriginal and Torres Strait Islander people or some of them;

(c) matters of health, educational employment and welfare;

(d) matters of political status, representation and organisation, including self-government;

(e) matters of inherent sovereignty and the sharing of sovereignty;

(f) matters of language, culture, heritage and intellectual and cultural property;

(g) the law, including Aboriginal and Torres Strait Islander law and custom, relating to the exercise of judicial power by the Commonwealth of Australia or any State or any Territory within Australia;

(h) any other matter identified by Aboriginal and Torres Strait Islander peoples in relation to their status as first peoples and nations.

(2) The Parliament shall have the power to make laws for the validating of any such treaty or treaties made before the commencement of this section. Such laws shall not be altered, amended, rescinded or repealed by the Parliament without the free and informed consent of the Aboriginal and Torres Strait Islanders party to the treaty or treaties as well as a two-thirds majority vote of the members of both houses of the Parliament entitled to vote.

(3) Any treaty or treaties made may be varied or rescinded by the parties thereto and as such shall supersede any prior treaty or treaties for the purposes of this section.

(4) Subject to sub-section (2), the Parliament shall have the power to make laws for the implementation by the parties of such treaty or treaties.

(5) Any laws passed under clauses 2 and 4 shall be binding upon the Commonwealth, the States and Territories within Australia, notwithstanding anything contained in this constitution or the constitutions of the several states or the self governing laws of any territory or any law of the Commonwealth, or any State or Territory.

(6) Any variation or alteration or rescinding of this section shall occur in the following manner

(a) notwithstanding section 128, a bill for a law for a referendum shall not be introduced into the Parliaments without the Parliament having obtained two thirds majority support of the Aboriginal and Torres Strait Islander peoples, and;

(b) the terms of the treaty or treaties permits such alteration, amendment or rescinding, and if so, are complied with.

Sub-section (5) would give full force of the Constitution to laws passed to affect the treaty or treaties. This approach removes the complexity of trying to incorporate the text of a treaty into the Constitution.

Scope of content

Questions of the scope and content of a treaty bring us back to where we started. The scope of the content is limitless and only bounded by the imagination and willingness of the negotiators. Unfinished business at the national, regional and local levels will require identification and settlement.

Matters mentioned above dealing with a broad constitutional enabling power might form the basis for the content of treaties. What the content of these treaties is is largely an issue for the negotiating parties, what Australians, black and white, can agree on and what their imaginations will allow. Some of the content might include,

- The prohibition of racial discrimination;
- Recognition of the rights of equality;
- Recognition of the principle of non-discrimination.

In my opinion the ideal situation would be to have these three principles embedded in the Australian Constitution by an Australian Bill of Rights.

Other matter for inclusion might include,

- Access to education and training;
- Employment;
- The recognition of distinct Indigenous identities;
- The protection of laws, cultures and languages;
- The effective implementation of relevant recommendations from a variety of reports;
- Law and justice issues;
- Resolution for the stolen generations;
- Control, ownership and management of land, waters and resources;
- Benefits from resource development;
- Economic and social development;
- Reparation and compensation;
- Self-determination;
- Self-government;
- Constitutional recognition.

This is by no way intended to be an exhaustive list. The negotiation process must have the flexibility to allow for new or more specific issues to be identified for negotiation in the future. However, the identification of the content of treaties might be achieved through agreed processes under a constitutional mandate as mentioned above, which would allow the parties to reach agreement on principles that would underpin the negotiations.

The lessons of history

I have already outlined some of the work we have already done on the issue of unfinished business. We should not forget where we have been and what we have done as a nation, not only in the interests of not repeating the mistakes and injustices of the past, but also to make something of the hard work we have done over these years. We need to revisit the myriad reports that have been produced over the past three decades. They themselves in most cases represent unfinished business. Findings have not been acted upon, recommendations remain unimplemented and many just gather dust on some shelf somewhere.

There have been major efforts in the last twenty years or so to address the myriad issues confronting Indigenous peoples and governments and the rest of Australian society. Much of the unfinished business is detailed in these reports. Major national reports have been

- The Recognition of Aboriginal Customary Law
- Aboriginal Deaths in Custody
- Bringing Them Hone (the Stolen Generations Report)
- The Social Justice Package.

There have also been a plethora of other relevant reports at the national level dealing with just about every conceivable topic. For example, in the health portfolio alone there have been reports on mortality and morbidity, alcoholism, mental health, dental health, traditional healing and hospitalisation, health care programs and Aboriginal involvement and self-determination in health care. There have also been reports on our recreation needs, native title, land rights and social justice. We have even had distinguished scholars from the United Nations report on our human rights situation. Not to be forgotten are the results of the lengthy and sometimes acrimonious negotiations with the former Prime Minister, Paul Keating, over the High Court's decision in the *Mabo Case*. These negotiations led to the eventual enactment of the Native Title Act, the establishment of the Indigenous Land Fund and the development of a social justice package, the three main responses by the government to the decision.

The Keating government honoured the first two planks; however the social justice package is yet to be implemented even though there were three reports on this issue prepared for the Keating government. These were a report by the Social Justice Commissioner (I was the incumbent at the time) and reports by the Council for Aboriginal Reconciliation (*Going Forward*) and ATSIC (*Recognition, Rights and Reform*).

There was also a submission put in by the Northern Land Council. These reports were to inform the development of the social justice package and together pretty much covered the field of unfinished business. My report, for example, dealt with constitutional reform, regional agreements, funding of citizenship entitlements and rights—such as higher standards of health care, educational opportunities and municipal services, to name a few. Like so many others these submissions are languishing somewhere.

At the national level we have also had countless studies, fact-findings, commissioned research, parliamentary inquiries and the like. We have had papers and manuscripts, books and journals, articles and treatises and a tower of other writings that would easily fill many libraries. These things have been repeated at the state and territory level. The most recent example is perhaps The Gordon Report (640 pages, 197 findings and recommendations). The inquiry found that:

> There was an urgent need for greater co-ordination between government agencies, more training for staff, including cross-cultural training, and more services and better resourced services, especially in remote areas (Koori Mail, August 2002).

Sounds familiar!

These reports have to be dug up, dusted off and revisited to 'find' the unfinished business—we do not have to reinvent the wheel.

Professor Michael Dodson is Chair of the ANU's Institute for Indigenous Australia and a prominent advocate on land rights and other issues affecting Aboriginal and Torres Strait Islander peoples. He is a member and current Chair of AIATSIS.

Negotiating Settlements: Indigenous Peoples, Settler States and the Significance of Treaties and Agreements

Marcia Langton and Lisa Palmer

1. Introduction

This paper is a contribution to the national debate about agreement making and the potential for a treaty between Indigenous people and settler Australia. The paper will draw out the significance of agreement-making for present-day Australian circumstances in order to inform the debate on the negotiated settlement of disputes over resource use, service delivery and other citizenship entitlements in the Australian context.

Agreement making with Indigenous people has been a feature of the Australian policy landscape for over twenty years. There has been a proliferation of agreements between Australian Indigenous people and resource extraction companies, railway, pipeline and other major infrastructure project proponents, local governments, state governments, farming and grazing representative bodies, universities, publishers, arts organisations and many other institutions and agencies. Some are registered under the terms of the Native Title Act. Others are simple contractual agreements that set out the framework for future developments. Strelein (see Williams, 2001:14) noted that the accelerating process of agreement making in Australia necessitates "a national framework and protection for those agreements". Scholz (2001) observes that in native title and agreement making negotiations the government is increasingly pushed by fiscal concerns to negotiate, but once government representatives embark on the process of negotiation this creates its own momentum and communities of interest which become invested in the process of negotiation.

The outcomes of the reconciliation process pursued in the last ten years necessitate an audit of agreement making with Aboriginal people in recent times. There has been some work in the native title field (Edmunds 1998) and in the governance field (Meyers *et al* 2002; Ivison *et al* 2000). However, there is a notable absence of a well-developed body of literature in Australia on treaty and agreement making with Indigenous peoples, either in academic or popular forms, covering broader issues and thus a lack of information on models, processes of negotiation, and forms of entrenchment through statutory or constitutional means. Neither is there an adequate international survey that draws relevance for Australian circumstances, although there has been some work in this field (Meyers *et al* 2002; Stephenson 1997; Ivanitz 1997; Dorsett and Godden 1998).

An audit of agreement making with Aboriginal people in recent times is an important component of a current Australian Research Council Linkage project,

'Agreements, Treaties and Negotiated Settlements with Indigenous Peoples in Settler States: their role and relevance for Indigenous and other Australians', a project in which we are involved. This project also involves ATSIC and researchers from both The University of Melbourne and The University of Technology Sydney and commenced in March 2001. The project aims to examine treaty and agreement making with Indigenous Australians and the nature of the cultural, social and legal rights encompassed by past, present and potential agreements and treaties. It will include an examination of the legal history and foundations of agreements and treaties, an audit of current agreements, including an agreements database, their purposes, status and outcomes, and will include international comparative research on treaty and agreement-making. While many of the agreements we examine will be related to land, our research will also examine non-land based agreements such as those agreements made in the areas of health, education and research.

In this paper we want to give some attention to this idea of agreement making as the principal form of engagement between Indigenous peoples and the state as to resource use, including land, seas and waters, and the resources of the natural world.

2. The Significance of Agreement Making

In 1992 the High Court of Australia overturned traditional views on Aboriginal rights in land in its famous decision in *Mabo (No. 2)* and recognised native title as a form of customary title arising from traditions and customs. The common law recognition of native title by the High Court established that customary rights to land had pre-existed and, under certain conditions, survived British sovereignty. Native title survives in a range of circumstances where it was not extinguished by valid acts by the Crown, not only extinguishing acts such as valid grants of title but also extinguishment acts such as the *Native Title Amendment Act 1998* (Cth) that limit the recognition of native title. The codification of native title in the *Native Title Act 1993* (Cth) ('*NTA*') aimed, among other things, to resolve the retrospective effects of an underlying title which had the potential to invalidate land titles, including pastoral leases issued since annexation.

The National Native Title Tribunal and procedures of the NTA have the purposes of enabling determination or negotiation of native title and non-claimant applications with respect to dealings in land that might be subject to native title. The Act establishes a 'right to negotiate' procedures, which following amendments to the NTA, are conceded only to registered native title bodies corporate and registered native title claimants in relation to certain kinds of future acts (Australian Government Solicitor 1998: 37). Especially important in this context are the sections of the NTA which provide for agreement making, such as consent determinations and Indigenous Land Use Agreements.

Corporations, such as Comalco, signatory to the Western Cape York Communities Co-existence Agreement, are readily prepared to treat with Aboriginal nations, noting in their agreements their ancient identities, the Wik, the Thaayorre, the Alngith, and many others. Corporations acknowledge that pre-existing Aboriginal polities exist as a profound reality in our political and economic landscape. Such agreements are evidence of a willingness among some present day private corporations to do what the colonial governments were by and large unable to countenance, that is, to acknowledge that another group of people were the owners and custodians of the lands and waters of Australia and their descendents have a right to possess, use and enjoy those lands and waters and, within the limits of Australian law, to govern their use and access by others, and to reap any benefits arising from that use and access by others as would any other group of people in rightful possession of a place.

Agreement making emerges in our historical analysis as an instrument of governance within and between the nation state and indigenous nations, or as we refer to them, aboriginal polities. Agreement making has developed as a surrogate instrument of engagement and governance in a context of legal pluralism that has denied rights of self-government. That is, in a settler nation state that coincides with a number of aboriginal polities having their own customary law regimes, agreement-making has evolved among these diverse entities as a means of engaging rationally in dealings in land access and use and resource distribution and governance. However, the Australian Constitution provides no recognition of the existence of aboriginal polities, and it is only in legislation, such as the Native Title Act and to some extent land rights statutes, such as the Pitjantjatjara Act, that lower level of recognition of these polities occurs in order to provide statutory regimes for dealings between resource extractors and the Aboriginal landowning corporations or entities.

The evolving nature of these agreements has raised a number of highly contentious legal, political and constitutional issues. The right to negotiate, a limited and prescribed statutory right under the Native Title Act, serves as the trigger for a series of governance procedures that, in sum, are an inferior substitute for rights of self-government that are found in the Canadian and United States jurisdictions with respect to first nations.

Legal and constitutional pluralism: recognition of indigenous polities and customary law regimes and their relevance to treaties and agreement-making

The Australian Law Reform Commission, in its 1986 Reports on the *Recognition of Aboriginal Customary Law*, discussed the wide variation in a number of overseas jurisdictions of the incorporation of customary law into the legal regimes of nation states. It described, on the one hand, the apartheid era situation in South Africa as a 'coercive form of legal pluralism' with not only separate laws but a separate court structure for the Blacks. Of South Africa's diverse legal history, the Report observed that its legal system had its origins in Roman Dutch law (from the Netherlands) but with a strong infusion of English common and statute law. At the same time, South African law provided for the recognition of the customary law of the Bantu (or Blacks). The recognition of indigenous customary law was 'a vehicle for avoiding the recognition of the equality of all South Africans'. It was 'accompanied by rules maintaining the superiority of the 'white' legal system and its rules' (Australian Law Reform Commission 1986: Section 795).

In contrast, the Report noted that 'many other African countries have, since independence, opted for integrated legal systems, partly in response to the demands of 'nation-building', partly as a reaction against pluralism as a form of 'separate development': 'Some of the states in Nigeria have for example abolished customary courts, preferring instead that customary law be applied in the ordinary courts. Tanzania, Uganda, Zimbabwe and Kenya have also opted for integrated court systems. The Northern States of Nigeria, on the other hand, have retained customary courts and worked on improving them. Other African countries have excluded customary law completely or modified its recognition to meet their new situation. (Australian Law Reform Commission 1986: Section 795)

Assessing the shortcomings and difficulties confronting courts and other bodies in overseas jurisdictions, the Commission found a number of trends that also have become apparent in our study of agreement making in native title contexts in Australia;

- the diversity of experience in different countries, each dependent to a very large degree on its own experience and history;

- the difficulty of classifying many of the 'justice mechanisms' as 'traditional' or indigenous, given that many operate as an extension of the criminal justice system;

- the difficulty, in particular, of limiting 'justice mechanisms' to problems which can be regarded as 'traditional';

- the frequent difficulties encountered (especially in the United States) with jurisdictional and due process requirements;

- the tendency of tribal courts to become more legalistic over time, often as a response to the way the general legal system operates;

- the relatively trivial or limited range of matters dealt with, especially in the criminal law field; and

- the continual encroachments and pressures on the laws, customs, practices and traditions of indigenous people, even in countries where they are in the majority. (Australian Law Reform Commission 1986: Section 802).

The Reports emphasis that, with respect to these various examples of legal pluralism, the level of acceptance by the indigenous people subject to them is a crucial consideration in assessing their validity and success.

The long tradition of legal pluralism in common law jurisdictions is an important foundation for considering the questions of both legal and constitutional pluralism that have arisen in recent Australian literature on the question of a settlement or treaty with Indigenous Australians and the native title agreement making environment that has emerged since the High Court decision in *Mabo No. 2*.

Recent literature on federalism draws attention to how diversity is accommodated in constitutional and political arrangements in various state formations. Thomas Fleiner (2001) of the Institute of Federalism at Frieberg University has proposed in a paper, "Constitutions & Diverse Communities in the 21st Century", that, in Europe at least, a number of different solutions have evolved in European nation-building, particularly expressed in European Constitutions with regard to their diversities. While the German constitution constructs the volk, or one-people, as the equivalent of the nation (conceived as a unity of people, territory, language and polity), Belgium, made up of three Communities, the French Community, the Flemish Community, and the German-speaking Community, recognises this diversity in its Constitution. In the Serbian Constitution, it is stated that "Persons belonging to a national minority shall have special rights which they exercise individually or in community with others." The Bosnian Constitution asserts that it is the will of its various communities in the following: "Bosniacs, Croats, and Serbs, as constituent peoples (along with Others), and citizens of Bosnia and Herzegovina hereby determine that the Constitution of Bosnia and Herzegovina is as follows". This rich diversity of communities of people caught up in several modern nation state formations in Europe contrasts with the settler state situation in Australia where unitary principles of nation-building have been, and remain, dominant in constitutional affairs.

Aboriginal people have continued to argue for the survival not only of customary property rights in land but also ancient jurisdictions, on the grounds that, just as British sovereignty did not wipe away Aboriginal title, neither did it wipe away Aboriginal jurisdiction. Aboriginal governance under the full body of Aboriginal customary laws must, by the same logic as the discovery of native title at common law, survive annexation of Australia by the Crown, even if in some qualified way.

Because of the Native Title Act administrative regime, governments are being forced to treat with Aboriginal people in a variety of ways. We thus find that by default Aboriginal people are, through the cumulative effect of native title determinations both by the Tribunal and by the Federal Court, being treated as peoples. The aboriginal polity has emerged from the factors at work in the environment of dealing with native title holders in relation to economic and land use issues and resource distribution.

The international literature of relevance to this project shows that in the United States of America, Canada and New Zealand, and perhaps elsewhere, negotiated agreements have replaced treaties as the modern arrangement for engagement with Indigenous peoples with respect to resource use (Bartlett 2001, Dorsett & Godden. 1998, Ivanitz 1997, Langton 2001, Meyer *et al* 2002).

Webber (2001) Dean of Law at the University of Sydney, speaking in the AIATSIS Seminar Series "The Limits and Possibilities of a Treaty Process in Australia', observed that, in Canada at least, treaties and agreements function to handle the interface between Indigenous and non-Indigenous governments long into the future. They manage the just apportionment of resources and create institutions which govern territory, rather than ruling on specific proprietary interests.

In the same series, Patton (2001: 16), of the Department of Philosophy at the University of Sydney, pointed out the 'inconsistency in recognising native title on the one hand, and refusing to recognise any form of sovereignty on the other'. In responding to this paradox of the proliferation of agreements with indigenous people governing resource use and the illegitimacy of Aboriginal customary governance of resources, Patton argued that 'Resolving that inconsistency, that paradox, is what needs to be done in order to restore legitimacy' (2001:16). His substantive argument relied on overseas examples of sharing sovereignty and the earlier considerations by a Senate Standing Committee of the Makarrata proposal for a treaty or compact with indigenous Australians. He asks 'whether the present constitutional arrangements do not amount to an illusory and indefensible form of unity, achieved without the consent of and without consultation with the Indigenous people of this country—this is how the present Constitution was achieved' (2001:8). He raises 'the possibility that the Constitution might be altered in ways that could accommodate some form of ongoing residual Indigenous sovereignty,' (2001:8) such as has been raised in Canada where the Canadian Royal Commission into Aboriginal Peoples has proposed the idea of shared sovereignty: Aboriginal inhabitants of Canada could be regarded 'as partners in the sovereignty of the nation on a par with the federal and provincial governments—that they should be considered a third tier of sovereign government' (2001:8).

He also reminds us of the deliberations of the 1983 Senate Standing Committee on Constitutional and Legal Affairs which argued in its Report that little was to be gained by relying too heavily on the precedent of treaty-making in North America and elsewhere for at least two reasons: 'the term 'treaty' did not have, in the 18th and 19th centuries, the precise meaning that it has today in international law. . .' and 'those treaties signed in earlier periods generally have no status as instruments of international law today' (2001:8).

The committee recommended that the government give consideration to the implementation of a compact by amending the Constitutional to provide a broad enabling power to the Commonwealth to enter into an agreement with representatives of the Aboriginal people.

In particular, the committee recommended a constitutional amendment along the lines of s.105A, which was inserted into the Constitution in 1929 in order to give the Commonwealth power to enter into financial agreements with the states. This section provides, in particularly strong form, for the protection of all such agreements against other laws, both state and federal, and all other sections of the Constitution. A provision of this kind, giving the Commonwealth power to make agreements with Indigenous peoples, would provide similarly strong protection for the rights laid down in any future agreements. (Patton 2001: 9)

Michael Dodson (2001) has outlined the laws pertaining to Aboriginal and Torres Strait Islander people in Australia and the way in which the Australian Constitution might be changed to accommodate a greater recognition of Indigenous rights. He supports the 1983 proposal of the Senate Standing Committee on Constitutional and

Legal Affairs to amend s.105 of the Constitution. Such an amendment, particularly if it were supplemented by explicit mention of Indigenous rights and interests in a modified constitutional preamble, would provide an enabling power for the Commonwealth to make agreements or treaties with groups representative of Aboriginal and Torres Strait Islander people. The amendment could then be used to 'entrench' a series of local and regional agreements and to give them constitutional force. The Canadian Constitutional entrenchment of treaties and agreements provides a model which might be used by Aboriginal people in our circumstances, especially in relation to this proposition to amend s.105. There is no evidence that there has been any detriment caused either to Canadian sovereignty or to the Canadian polity by these arrangements. That many recent agreements have been affirmed by the Canadian Constitution is evidence that there are alternatives to the limited framework of the legal cannon in Australia.

In 2001, Rowse argued that a Treaty or national framework agreement would be an effective check on states, more so than the political will of the Commonwealth government in relation to standards of social justice, land tenures and service delivery.

These approaches to questions of self-determination, sovereignty and indigenous self-government were also raised by George Williams (2001:15) in the AIATSIS seminar series. Williams observed that '. . . what we need. . .is to develop a more sophisticated sense of what we understand by sovereignty. . . because of Mabo it is possible to have a legal system that has sovereign laws emerging from different social and historical contexts.'

As Patton (2001) has pointed out what we need in Australia is a revision of Eurocentric judgements about political organisation in Indigenous societies that enable the Constitutional recognition of Indigenous civil polities and customary law.

Trends in Agreement-Making

While many of these same shortcomings and difficulties confront courts, Indigenous groups and others negotiating the recognition of Indigenous rights in the Australian jurisdictions, of itself the emerging culture of agreement-making in Australia is progressing a process of orderly negotiation based on recognition of civil polity, in particular the setting out of principles and rules for managing the relationship between native title, public laws and private rights. As the National Native Title Tribunal Member, Fred Chaney (2001) suggests, by achieving native title agreements you carry things forward; native title act procedures may in fact come to recognise and flesh out the substance of native title rights.

In September 1998 an audit conducted by the National Native Title Tribunal found that there were at the time 1349 agreements struck by native title parties nationwide (See Figure 1). According to the Tribunal this outcome was indicative of a developing culture of mediation and negotiation (NNTT 1999: 15). Of these agreements, 257 related to native title determination applications while a further 1092 were future act related agreements (See Figure 2). These native title determination applications ranged from consent determinations of native title to intra-indigenous agreements over boundaries of native title applications (See Figure 3). The audit data establishes that the number of agreements reached rose significantly each year and according to the Tribunal this is a result of the parties developing an understanding of the native title and agreement making process, building relationships of trust and appreciating the importance of progressing in mediation as opposed to litigating an outcome (NNTT 1999: 17). We make no claims about the content and outcomes of those agreements other than to observe their increase in popularity, and the growth in the use of the *NTA* procedures by native title parties.

The President of the National Native Title Tribunal, Graham Neate (2001), refers to a growing confidence in the process of agreement-making with Indigenous people. One type of agreement increasing in prevalence are Indigenous Land Use Agreements (ILUAs) which can be made both under the terms of the NTA and outside of its terms. The ILUA provisions replace the agreement-making process in Section 21 of the 1993 NTA (which lacked proper protection for agreements once they were made) and provide for legally binding negotiated agreements made voluntarily between people who hold, or claim to hold native title in an area and other people who have, or wish to gain an interest in that area (Wade 2001). Once successfully negotiated, and after procedural hurdles stipulated under the Act have been satisfied, an ILUA is registered as a statutory agreement under the NTA and is enforceable as a contract. Also of significance is that Native Title holders, irrespective of being party to the agreement, are contractually bound and can be sued for any breach.

ILUAs are particularly important and useful when

- There is adequate time to negotiate

- There will be a long term relationship between parties

- Where compensation is likely to be an issue (Wade 2001:3).

In 2001 the NNTT was in the process of assisting 110 separate ILUA negotiations. Many native title claims, especially in Queensland, are proceeding through mediation to consent determination coupled with the use of ILUAs, which in these instances form part of the package of documents which formalise the resolution of native title determination applications. Alternatively ILUAs may be 'stand alone' agreements which deal with native title issues independently of the native title determination process (Neate 2001). In South Australia, the Aboriginal Land Rights Movement (ALRM) and the State Government are involved in negotiations to progress a state-wide ILUA. There are currently 3 pilot projects in SA which are being used to work out and discuss the state-wide ILUA process. Parry Agius (2001) of the ALRM refers to these pilot projects as the 'Substantive Issues Development Phase'.

Another important area of agreement making under the provisions of the NTA is the increasing number of Native Title Consent Determinations. At the end of 2001 the NNTT recorded some twenty-two Native Title Consent Determinations (See Figure 4). These date from the first decision on the 7th of April 1997 to the most recent case in October of 2001. These determinations are resolved through the principle of good faith negotiations.

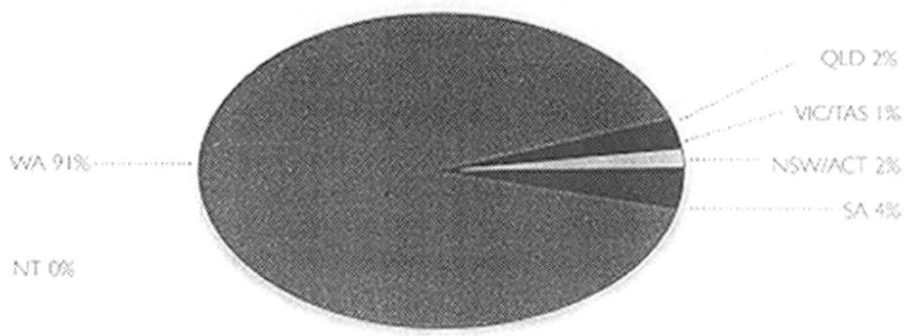

Source: National Native Title Tribunal 1999:15.

Figure 1: Agreements by State and Territory, 1994–1998 (future act agreements included).

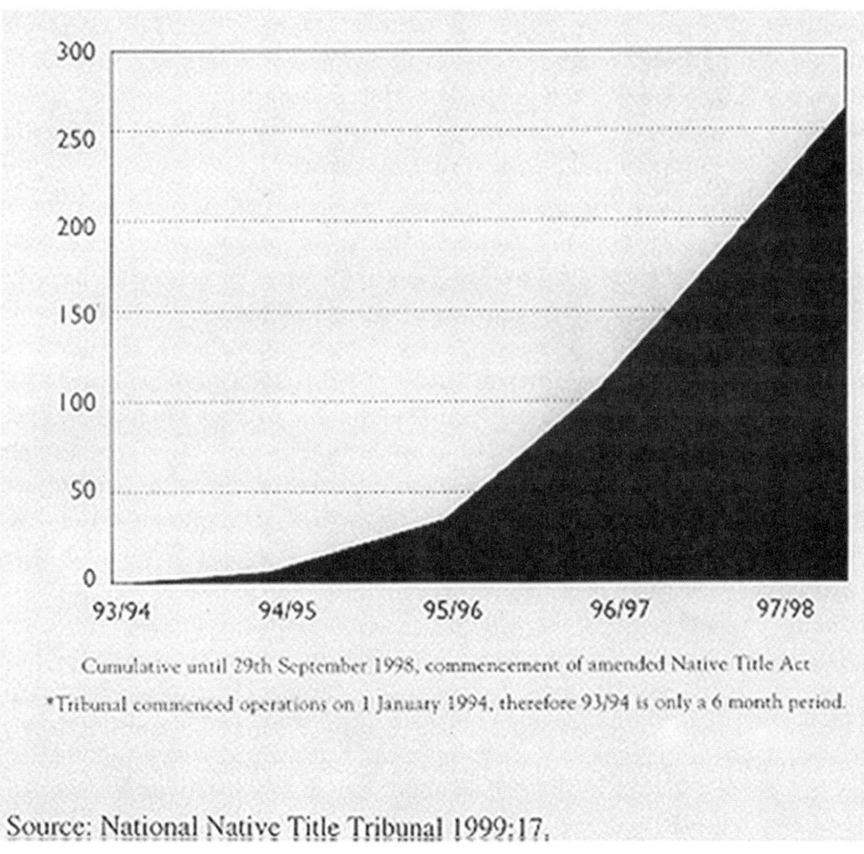

Source: National Native Title Tribunal 1999:17.

Figure 2: Cumulative number of Native Title related agreements by year (excluding future act) 1994–1998.

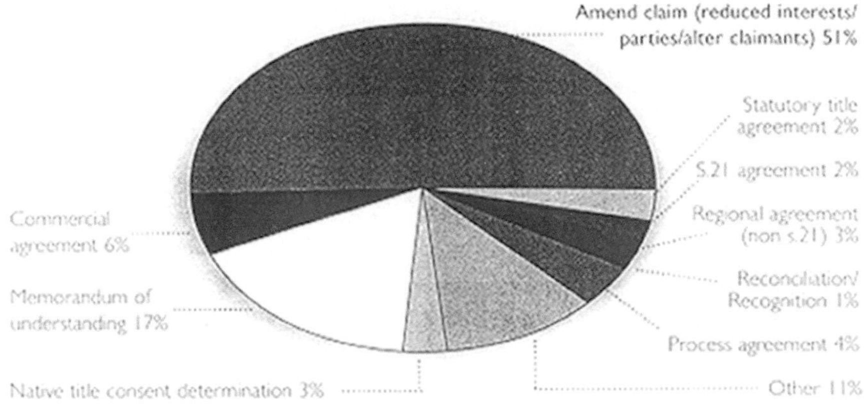

Figure 3: Major components of native title agreements (non future act) 1994–1998.

Another emerging area of significance in the agreement making arena is Environment Australia's Indigenous Protected Area Program. Through this program, Indigenous landowners are supported by Natural Heritage Trust Funding to manage their lands either as independent bodies or through co-management agreements. As of November 2001 there were 15 officially declared Indigenous Protected Areas, 11 co-management projects, and 3–4 projects with interim or seed funding to investigate the possibility of declaring an Indigenous Protected Area.

In response to the Convention on Biological Diversity1992, ratified by Australia in 1993, the Australian Government produced the *National Strategy for the Conservation of Australia's Biological Diversity* (1996). This *National Strategy* recommends a framework in which governments, industry, community groups and individual land owners can work co-operatively to 'bridge the gap between current efforts and the effective identification, conservation and management of Australia's biological diversity' (1996:3). The Strategy also advocates the development and use of collaborative agreements that would recognise existing intellectual property rights and establish a royalty payments system in line with relevant international standards relating to traditional resource rights. This is an emerging form of agreement making that requires further development and research, and will be an important area of focus in our ARC research project.

Conclusion

New legal and political relationships between indigenous peoples and the Australian polity and its constituent parts is a dynamic and rapidly growing phenomenon. Research is needed to inform the debate about the possibility for alternative arrangements in post-frontier Australia.

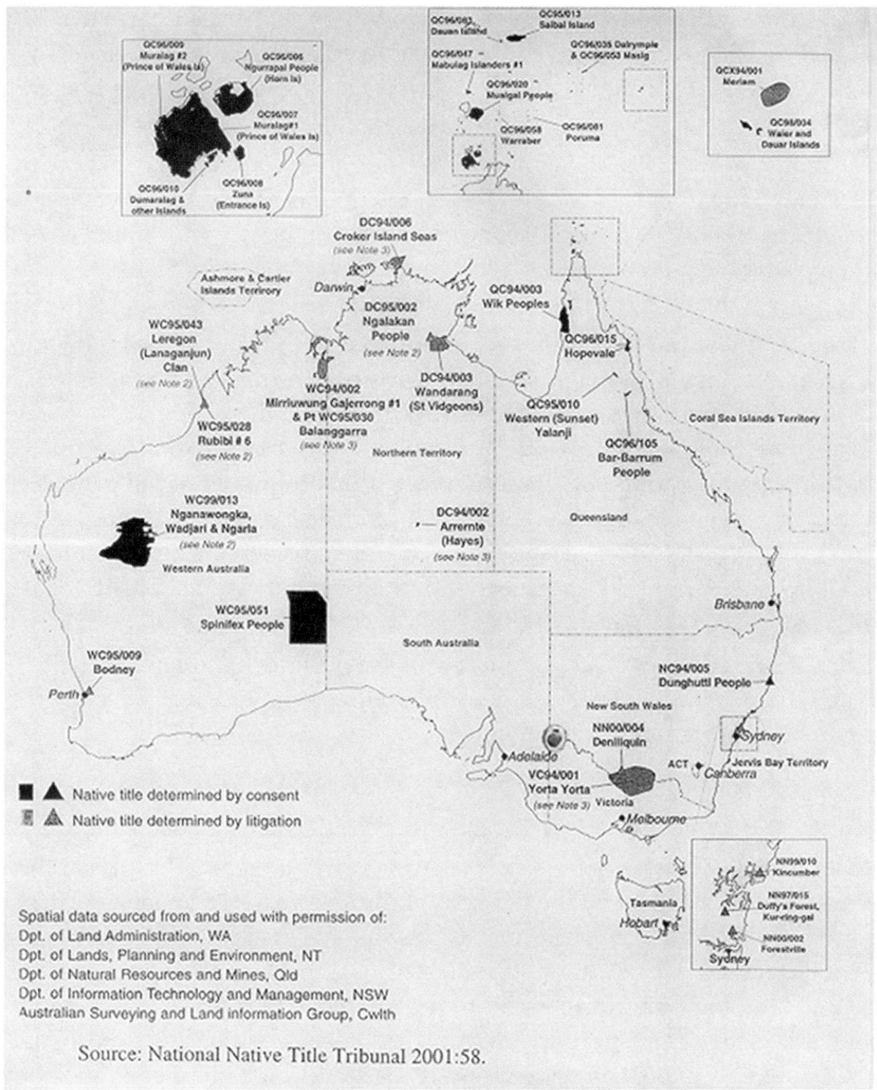

Figure 4: Map showing external boundaries for areas over which native title has been determined as at 30 June 2001.

There is concern about not simply the mechanism but rather the kinds of agreements that any Constitutional change would take into account and might confirm, and the range of issues that need to be looked at in pursuing that path.

There has been a number of propositions put on how to deal with this problem of legal and political pluralism and settler and customary land tenure systems. For instance national Native Title Tribunal Member Fred Chaney (2001) proposes as a resolution to these problems in the context of agreement making that in addition to the acknowledgement of native title there also needs to be a permanent state title which overlies and does not extinguish native title itself. He also states that Aboriginal people need to be given the power to create tenures on their title for Aboriginal and non-Aboriginal people which do not extinguish native title and which would be commercial tenures.

A peculiarly Western Australian view has been proposed by Glen Shaw of the ATSIC Treaty Think Tank. He argues that in relation to Native Title there is a need to shift the focus from the Commonwealth and to negotiate with the States as well. Legislation involving land tenures lies with the States, therefore States by virtue of such legislation define the terms of extinguishments or impairment of Native Title.

In case law, it was the Delgamuukw finding that introduced to the developing body of native title law the idea of native identities as both ancient and adapting, based in traditional practices but with the flexibility to deal with the realities of late modernity. De Costa in his analysis of the British Columbia Treaty Commission process asks, Is the call for 'certainty' in the BC Treaty Process 'the recognition of Indigenous rights, or an indemnity against their assertion?' (2001:9) He also notes that modern agreements in British Columbia should be considered as 'living agreements' with the potential to evolve, rather than achieving final closure in negotiations (De Costa 2001).

What is needed are new ways of looking at the traditional notion of treaties between settler states and indigenous peoples along with research which will untangle these difficult historical problems.

Professor Marcia Langton is the Chair of Australian Indigenous Studies at the University of Melbourne, and the Director of the Centre for Indigenous Natural and Cultural Resource Management. She was previously Director of the Centre for Indigenous, Natural and Cultural Resource Management and Ranger Professor of Aboriginal Studies at the Northern Territory University. An Aboriginal woman with 13 years experience as an anthropologist and 28 years experience in Aboriginal Affairs, Langton is published widely, and is the author of a number of books including *Burning Questions: emerging Environment Issues for Indigenous Peoples in Northern Australia*.

Dr Lisa Palmer is an ARC Postdoctoral Fellow working on the ARC Linkage project, 'Treaties, Agreements and Negotiated Settlements: their role and relevance for Indigenous and other Australians'. Lisa completed her PhD at the Northern Territory University in 2001 on the subject of the relationship between Aboriginal traditional owners, the tourism industry and non-Aboriginal Park Managers in Kakadu National Park.

How Do We Treat Our Treasures? Indigenous Heritage Rights in a Treaty

Robynne Quiggan & Terri Janke

Introduction

Indigenous Australians continue to affirm their rights to ownership of their land, resources, cultural expressions, knowledge and legal systems. Although colonisation and the assertion of British sovereignty placed enormous pressure on the active practice of the customs and traditions, Indigenous Australians continue to declare rights to all aspects of cultural heritage and cultural life on the basis of their status as original owners of land, law and culture. Indigenous cultural and heritage rights include rights to cultural resources, arts, songs, stories and knowledge.

In this current age of globalisation where information is a leading currency, Indigenous heritage has a new value inside and outside Indigenous communities. In the past ten years there has been increased interest in Indigenous heritage by government and industry. Government bodies seek cultural information for environmental management and planning. There are increasing approaches by biotechnology and pharmaceutical companies for use of Indigenous knowledge and resources for new medicines. Indigenous cultural expressions such as art and dance are projected to an international audience. This increased interest has provided opportunities for Indigenous Australians; however it has also opened up the path for exploitation of Indigenous heritage. Examples include instances where Indigenous knowledge has been used without proper consent. This is especially damaging where the knowledge consists of sacred images. Other instances include the rip-off copying of art and the production of fakes. Unchecked plundering of Indigenous people's heritage will result in the same dispossession and disenfranchisement experienced in relation to land.

This paper considers how the recognition of Indigenous rights to heritage which lie at the heart of the life of Indigenous peoples, might be strengthened under the non-Indigenous legal system by a treaty or treaties. These rights are described as "Indigenous Heritage Rights" or "Indigenous Cultural and Intellectual Property (ICIP) Rights" in international standard setting documents (Daes in Janke 1999). This paper will use the term "Indigenous Heritage Rights".

What is Heritage?

An international study on heritage protection undertaken by the United Nations Special Rapporteur Mrs Erica Irene Daes developed a definition of heritage which was used as a basis for Australian consultations for the protection of Indigenous Cultural and Intellectual Property (Daes 1995). This definition was expanded on by

Indigenous Australians and recorded in the report *Our Culture Our Future* (Janke 1999):

> Indigenous Heritage consists of the tangible and intangible aspects of the body of cultural practices, resources and knowledge systems that have been developed nurtured and refined (and continue to be developed, nurtured and refined) by Indigenous people and passed on by Indigenous people as part of expressing their cultural identity including:
>
> - Literary, performing and artistic works (including music, dance, song ceremonies, symbols and designs, narratives and poetry
> - Languages
> - Scientific, agricultural, technical and ecological knowledge (including cultigens, medicines and sustainable use of flora and fauna)
> - Spiritual knowledge
> - All items of moveable cultural property, as defined by the UNESCO Cultural Property Convention 1970, including burial artefacts
> - Indigenous ancestral remains
> - Indigenous human genetic material (including DNA tissues)
> - Cultural environment resources (including minerals and species)
> - Immovable cultural property (including Indigenous sites of significance, sacred sites and burials)
> - Documentation of Indigenous people's heritage in all forms of media (including scientific, ethnographic research reports, papers and books, films, sound recordings).

Indigenous heritage is a living one and includes items based on that heritage which may be created in the future (Janke 1999, p. 12).

The Existing Legal Framework

The Australian legal system includes laws which provide some protection for tangible (physical) and intangible (non-physical such as knowledge, art and stories) Indigenous Heritage. However, the current legal framework offers only limited recognition and protection.

Tangible heritage is protected through a system of Commonwealth and State heritage laws including the *Aboriginal and Torres Strait Islander Heritage Protection Act 1984 (Cth)* (See Janke 1999, pp. 283–298). These laws are primarily aimed at protecting sites and objects of significance to Indigenous people from destruction. In most jurisdictions, (except Victoria which has legislation pertaining to 'folklore') the intangible aspects of a site or object including knowledge, art and stories for instance, are not protected under these laws.

The consistent criticism of these laws has been that they are inadequate mechanisms for heritage protection. For example, in 2000 the Human Rights Committee (HRC) of the United Nations considered Australia's compliance with the International Covenant on Civil and Political Rights. In relation to Article 27 which concerns the rights of minorities in a state to culture, language and religion the Human Rights Committee expressed the following concern with the way in which the Australian Government determined land use. The HRC stated: "securing continuation and sustainability of traditional forms of economy of indigenous minorities (hunting, fishing and gathering), and protection of sites of religious or cultural significance for such minorities, which must be protected under article 27, are not always a major factor in determining land use." (Human Rights Committee 2000, paras 498-528.)

Intangible heritage such as knowledge is protected under intellectual property laws including copyright, patents, trade marks, designs, passing off and breach of confidence laws. This body of legislation focuses on rights to make and protect commercial use of knowledge, inventions, art and other forms of intellectual property. For instance, an artist might use copyright to grant to one company the exclusive rights to reproduce her work. Similarly a company might seek a patent on an invention so it can have the exclusive right to produce that particular formula or machine or method of production.

Australian intellectual property laws and Australian laws regulating the treatment of Indigenous heritage have provided some protection for Indigenous Heritage rights where Indigenous people can meet the criteria for protection, but they fall far short of recognising rights as original or sovereign owners of resources, language and other forms of cultural knowledge.

What Rights Flow to First peoples as Owners and Custodians of their Indigenous Heritage?

The inherent rights that flow to Indigenous peoples from their position as first peoples stem from two sources. The primary source of Indigenous people's rights is the laws, customs and traditions of Indigenous peoples.

Indigenous people ground their rights in their long-standing and enduring connection to land, which predates colonisation. This relationship includes occupation of the land, cultivation and care of the land, and spiritual and cultural practices based in a relationship to land. Rights that flow from that connection to land apply to all aspects of community life and are:

1. Derived from past practice, customary laws and cultural beliefs;

2. Ongoing and necessary for the present and future;

3. Expressed in many ways including rights to Indigenous cultural heritage.

The second source of rights is the set of declarations and international human rights instruments, which record the rights belonging to sovereign peoples and nation states. Indigenous peoples have endorsed many international human rights standards such as equality, self-determination and non-discrimination, and seek to have these applied and respected by colonising governments.

In Australia, Indigenous peoples' rights to Heritage have been expressed in a number of ways. In 1993 a delegation of Indigenous Australian people met and developed the "Declaration Affirming the Self-determination and Intellectual Property Rights of the Indigenous Nations and Peoples of the Wet Tropics Rainforest Area" (Jingara Delegation 1993). The preamble to the Declaration states:

Recognising that the Indigenous nations and Peoples of the Wet Tropics rainforest Area have exercised their inherent right to self-determination in regard to the care, protection, use and control of the forest since time immemorial; and

Acknowledging that in the exercise of that right of self-determination the Indigenous Nations and People continue to foster and develop a unique relationship with their total environment; and

Affirming that the values, processes, Law and Lore which the Indigenous Nations and Peoples have developed throughout that relationship are expressed in their intellectual property rights.

Indigenous Australians have been active in the development of expressions of these rights in international forums where Indigenous rights to heritage are drafted into international instruments.

Recognition of Indigenous Heritage in International Instruments

Indigenous Heritage rights are embodied in the rights recognised in a number of international instruments, such as Article 27 of the International Covenant on Civil and Political Rights which addresses rights to culture, language and religion of minorities. Article 16 of the International Covenant on Economic, Cultural and Social Rights recognises the rights of individuals to participate in cultural life, to benefit from scientific progress and to benefit from their intellectual property.

The Declaration on the Rights of Indigenous People

The most explicit statement of Indigenous rights is found in the Draft Declaration on the Rights of Indigenous People, developed from the work of the United Nations Working Group on Indigenous Populations. Articles 12, 13, 14, 24 and 29 of the Draft Declaration include protection for Indigenous Heritage rights. Article 12 states: "Indigenous peoples have the right to practise and revitalise their cultural traditions and customs..." This includes all manifestations of culture, such as archaeological sites, artefacts, designs, ceremonies, art forms. It also includes the right of return of tangible and intangible cultural property taken without their consent.

During ongoing discussions about the Declaration, the Australian government Representatives "expressed concern with respect to the rights of third parties to ownership within the framework of article 12. The Representative of Australia also expressed concern as to the practicality and feasibility of restitution for past acts; and referred to the need to clarify the term "intellectual property" in articles 12 and 29" (Pritchard 2001, p. 126).

These comments indicate the kinds of objections Indigenous Australians encounter when negotiating Indigenous Heritage rights within Australia. The unwillingness to make restitution is a familiar objection for Indigenous people dealing with matters such as the Stolen Generation and native title. In the case of Indigenous heritage, the use of tea tee oil is an example of an unrecognised commercial use of Indigenous knowledge. The collection, distillation, production and application of tea tree oil is arguably derived from Indigenous knowledge concerning the healing properties of the tea tree. Many companies commercially offer tea tree oil products. How could proper restitution for use of this knowledge be made to Indigenous people? These kinds of issue will need to be thought through by Indigenous communities and negotiators.

Article 13 protects Indigenous peoples rights to their spiritual and religious traditions, customs and ceremonies, sites, ceremonial objects, the right to the repatriation of human remains and to preservation and protection of sacred places including burial sites. These rights currently find some representation in Australian law and policy. The return of human remains is a significant issue for Indigenous Australians. In 2000, the UK and Australian Prime Ministers issued a joint statement pledging their commitment to repatriation of Indigenous remains held in British museums (Fforde & Ormond-Parker 2001, p. 6). In 2002, the Royal English College of Surgeons decided to return its collection of Aboriginal human remains to Australia (Hooper 2002).

Article 14 protects the rights to Indigenous history, language, oral traditions, philosophies, place and community names and the right to an interpreter in political, legal and administrative proceedings.

This Article combines the right of Indigenous people to ongoing language, linguistic identity and to procedural fairness where language differences may be a barrier. Indigenous Australians also include linguistic identity in definitions of Indigenous Heritage includes linguistic identity, but there is little governmental commitment to language rights.

In December 1998 the Northern Territory commenced phasing out bilingual education programs in government schools in Aboriginal communities, and replacing them with 'English as a Second Language' programs based on a policy position that bilingual education was contributing to the low standards of English literacy among Aboriginal students (Aboriginal and Torres Strait Islander Social Justice Commissioner 1999, p. 72). Interpreter services in the Northern Territory have received some government support recently, but improvement is needed to meet standards. Services for Indigenous people engaged in judicial and administrative processes also remain inadequate. The Federation of Aboriginal and Torres Strait Islander Languages (FATSIL) provides policy, research and advocacy initiatives in this area.

Article 24 protects rights to traditional medicines and health practices, including the right to the protection of vital medicinal plants, animals and minerals. It combines these cultural rights with rights of access to health services of all kinds.

Article 29 focuses on the right to protection and control of intellectual property and to develop sciences, technologies and cultural manifestations, including human and other genetic resources, seeds, medicines, knowledge of the properties of fauna and flora, oral traditions, literatures, designs and visual and performing arts. This Article is probably the most comprehensive representation of Indigenous Heritage as defined by Indigenous Australian representatives, but cannot be viewed in isolation from the other articles.

During negotiations of the Declaration it has been suggested that Article 12, 24 and 29 be brought together into a single Article, but Indigenous representatives have resisted amendment of the original Draft of the Declaration. Rights to Indigenous Heritage are also enunciated in international instruments concerned with the interaction of the development and maintenance of biodiversity and economic sustainability.

The Convention on Biological Diversity

The *Convention on Biological Diversity* (1992) is another important international instrument for Indigenous Heritage rights. Australia ratified the Convention in 1993. The most relevant Articles for Indigenous people are Article 8(j) and Article 10. It is important to note that the wording of the Articles water down each country's obligations by use of terms such as "as far as possible and as appropriate" and "subject to its national legislation".

Article 8 of the Convention on Biodiversity:

"Each Contracting Party shall, as far as possible and as appropriate:

> 8 (j) Subject to its national legislation, respect, preserve and maintain knowledge, innovations and practices of indigenous and local communities embodying traditional lifestyles relevant for the conservation and sustainable use of biological diversity and promote their wider application with the approval and involvement of the holders of such knowledge, innovations and practices and encourage the equitable sharing of the benefits arising from the utilisation of such knowledge, innovations and practices."

Article 10 of the Convention on Biodiversity:

"Each Contracting Party shall, as far as possible and as appropriate:

> (a) Integrate consideration of the conservation and sustainable use of biological resources into national decision-making;

> (b) Adopt measures relating to the use of biological resources to avoid or minimise adverse impacts on biological diversity;

> (c) Protect and encourage customary use of biological resources in accordance with traditional cultural practices that are compatible with conservation or sustainable use requirements;

(d) Support local populations to develop and implement remedial action in degraded areas where biological diversity has been reduced; and

(e) Encourage cooperation between its governmental authorities and its private sector in developing methods for sustainable use of biological resources."

Policy and Legislative Conservation and Biodiversity Initiatives

The Australian Government has implemented a number of conservation and biodiversity programs and policies. The "National Strategy for the Conservation of Australia's Biological Diversity" includes Principles intended as a guide for implementation of the Strategy. Two of the Principles relate to Indigenous concerns:

Principle 2: Although all levels of government have a clear responsibility, the co-operation of conservation groups, resource users, indigenous people, and the community in general is critical to the conservation of biological diversity.

Principle 9: The close, traditional association of Australia's Indigenous peoples with components of biological diversity should be recognised, as should the desirability of sharing equitably benefits arising from the innovative use of biological diversity.

The Australian government has implemented a number of land management strategies from monies made available from the sale of the government owned communications company, Telstra. For example, a network of thirteen Indigenous Land Management Facilitators have been appointed, and their primary role is to promote the participation of Indigenous people in sustainable land management and nature conservation. The Indigenous Protected Areas Program was established to provide funding to Indigenous organisations and communities to establish and manage protected areas on Indigenous owned estates and to establish cooperative or joint management arrangements on publicly owned protected areas between Indigenous groups and the relevant government nature conservation agencies. (http://www.ea.gov.au/indigenous/programs.html) Funding can be provided for projects that record and make use of traditional knowledge of native plants, if the project also has a component of planting native vegetation or protecting remnant native vegetation. http://www.ea.gov.au/indigenous/programs.html)

While there are positive aspects to these programs, they fall far short of implementing rights of Indigenous peoples as first peoples to protect Australia's biodiversity. These rights include, rights to be consulted, adoption of the standard of prior informed consent by Indigenous people, assurance of benefit sharing in projects and protection for intellectual property used and generated by projects.

The *Convention on Biological Diversity* provides for prior informed consent to projects affecting resources. Although this right is often assumed to belong to the state party, it is now understood by Indigenous advocates as an inalienable expression of self-determination. On the rights of Indigenous communities Fourmile states that national laws should "empower such communities to set their own conditions with regard to the giving of prior informed consent. Consistent with the right of self-determination, such condition should also include the right to refuse access to territories, biological resources, knowledges and technologies" (Fourmile 2000, pp. 171-172).

In 1999 the Federal government passed the *Environment Protection and Biodiversity Conservation Act 1999 (Cth)*(hereafter EPBC Act). This Act establishes an Indigenous Advisory Committee which "advises the Minister for the Environment and Heritage on the operation of the EPBC Act, taking into account the significance of Indigenous people's knowledge of the management of land and the conservation and sustainable use of biodiversity." (http://www.ea.gov.au/epbc/publications/factsheets/advisory.html)

The *Environmental Protection and Biodiversity Conversation Regulations 2000* provide procedures for checking research and certain activities on Commonwealth territories. This has allowed Indigenous issues to be considered as an important part of management in the territories. One example is the clearance procedure operated by National Parks for use of images from Uluru Kata Tjuta National Park. The Regulations have enabled the Board of Management of the Park, which is run jointly by Mutitjulu community members and Environment Australia representatives to implement a permit system for use of images. Anyone wishing to conduct commercial filming, videoing, photography or art in the Park must obtain a permit from the Director of the National Park.

Recognition of Indigenous Heritage in Indigenous Law

Maatatua Declaration 1993

In 1993 the Nine Tribes of Maatatua in the Bay of Plenty Region of Aotearoa, New Zealand convened the First ICIP (Indigenous Cultural and Intellectual Property) Rights Conference. The Maatatua Declaration was drafted and adopted by the delegates and includes the right to self-determination. The exercise of the right of self determination includes recognition of Indigenous people as exclusive owners and capable of managers of ICIP and intellectual property. In the Declaration Indigenous people express a willingness to offer their ICIP to "all humanity provided their fundamental rights to define and control this knowledge are protected by the international community."

This declaration is another important standard setting instrument, and has been used as a lobbying mechanism by Maori to influence protection of Indigenous heritage rights in New Zealand.

Julayinbul Statement

In 1993, a meeting of Indigenous delegates in Australia developed and endorsed the Julayinbul Statement, which identifies the rights of Indigenous people to continue to live within and protect, care for, and control the environment and Indigenous Heritage. The Statement includes recognition of the right of Indigenous people to define themselves and their Indigenous Heritage. The Statement echoes the Maatauta commitment to share Indigenous Heritage provided fundamental rights are respected. The statement locates Indigenous Heritage within the framework of Aboriginal customary laws.

"Aboriginal intellectual property, within Aboriginal Common Law, is an inherent inalienable right which cannot be terminated extinguished or taken.

Any use of the intellectual property of Aboriginal Nations and Peoples may only be done in accordance with Aboriginal Common Law, and any unauthorised use is strictly prohibited.

Just as Aboriginal Common Law has never sought to unilaterally extinguish English/Australian Common Law, so we expect English/Australian Common Law to reciprocate."

The Statement then calls upon Indigenous people to develop means to implement these principles, and upon governments to review legislation and policy with regard to ICIP, and to implement international standards which protect ICIP rights.

The Julayinbul Statement provides important guidance on standard setting for the development of legal protections for Indigenous Heritage.

Incorporation of Rights into Domestic Law of the Nation State

Having established the scope of Indigenous Heritage, and the nature of the rights to be incorporated, this paper now discusses ways these rights are and might be protected by Australian legislation.

Australian Domestic Law

Review of Existing Legislative and Common Law Protections of Indigenous Heritage

The exploration of legal ways to protect Indigenous Heritage has largely been undertaken by Indigenous people in:-

(i)   native title and heritage law

(ii)   intellectual property laws such as copyright and trade mark law.

The *Mabo v Queensland (No 2)* 1992 175 CLR 1 decision in 1992, recognised Indigenous native title rights to land. The majority held: "Native title has its origin in and is given its content by the traditional laws acknowledged by and the traditional customs observed by the indigenous inhabitants of a territory. The nature and incidents of native title must be ascertained as a matter of fact by reference to those laws and customs." *Mabo v Queensland (No 2)* 1992 175 CLR 1 at para 64. Native title cases since *Mabo* have raised the issues of ownership of land, resources and cultural knowledge. In *Western Australia v Ward, Attorney General (NT) v Ward, Ningarmara v Northern Territory* [2002] HCA 28 (8 August 2002) the High Court clarified its position on the relationship between cultural knowledge and native title. The court held that the rights and interests protected under the *Native Title Act* are rights in relation to land and water only. "In so far as claims to protection of cultural knowledge go beyond denial or control of access to land or waters, they are not rights protected by the *Native Title Act*." (High Court of Australia, *Western Australia v Ward*—Statement (8 August 2002))

Indigenous people have sought protection for sites of importance under the Commonwealth heritage legislation. This legislation has not met the needs of Indigenous people. For example, in NSW, Toomelah–Boggabilla Local Aboriginal Land Council fought for years to stop water-skiing on Boobera Lagoon as it is culturally and spiritually offensive. But even when they achieved a declaration under the Commonwealth Act to stop the power boats, they had to struggle to get it enforced (Quiggin 2001, p. 4). In 2000, the UN Human Rights Committee received submissions from Indigenous people on existing heritage legislation and the delay in reform of the Act. The Human Rights Committee urged the Australian government to finalise its long standing review of Commonwealth heritage legislation and give sufficient weight to "securing continuation and sustainability of traditional forms of economy of indigenous minorities (hunting, fishing and gathering), and protection of sites of religious or cultural significance." (Human Rights Committee 2000, paras 498–528).

Under the *Copyright Act 1968 (Cth),* copyright protects literary, dramatic, artistic and musical works from unauthorised use and dissemination of the work. The copyright owner of an artistic work has a number of rights, including the right to control the reproduction of the work in material form. Copyright vests in the works of individual Indigenous artists and even after a work is sold, the artist retains copyright. The artist can licence rights to third parties to use and receive a fee. An artist can take action against unauthorised use. Indigenous artists such as Johnny Bulun Bulun, Banduk Marika and Bronwyn Bancroft have used copyright law to protect their artwork in the courts. (Johnson 1996, details these cases). Effective management of copyright can act as a means of protecting the cultural integrity of copyright works especially since the enactment of legislation pertaining to moral rights in 2000. Moral rights are rights belonging to creators and include the right to be attributed or credited for a work, the right not to be falsely attributed for a work and the right of integrity. The right of integrity is the right not to have a work treated in a derogatory manner. Derogatory treatment includes altering or mutilating a work, in such a way that the creator's reputation is damaged. Creators can bring an action if these rights are infringed.

Arts organisations support artists and assist them with access to legal services so proper legal arrangements are made for the use of their work. Arts organisations such as Desart are using licence agreements and trademarks to protect Indigenous arts production. Arts organisations such as Desart use trade marks to promote the work of their artists. The National Indigenous Arts Advocacy developed the Label of Authenticity, a certification mark which is licensed by Indigenous artists and attached to their work. These trade mark schemes provide some protection for artists by promoting authentically produced Indigenous products. The success of such schemes however is dependent on the good will of purchasers and users of the art. A need remains for greater marketing and awareness raising of the issues.

Copyright provides limited protection for creators of works. The terms of protection for works is limited to the life of the author plus fifty years. Copyright only vests in original works in a material form. Copyright gives rights to individual creators but there is no recognition of communal ownership, where works are handed down through the generations, and where each generation develops and contributes labour and effort.

There are many types of Indigenous cultural works that do not fit within the legislative scheme of the *Copyright Act 1968* (Cth). For instance, works that were produced a long time ago, and where the author cannot be identified accurately are not easily protected under the *Copyright Act 1968* (Cth). These works are considered to be in the "public domain" where they are free for people to copy without the permission of the creator.

Oral stories, which are not in material form are not able to be protected under the *Copyright Act 1968* (Cth). If the oral story was recorded by the traditional owner, the owner can assert copyright in the recording because a recording is a material form. Problems arise for Indigenous people when someone other than their traditional owner or a member of that clan group creates a literary work based on an oral story. In these cases the writer is recognised under copyright law as the copyright owner. Similar issues arise for Indigenous dance, songs and music.

Intellectual property rights do not recognise collective rights. Indigenous heritage rights are collective rights. Traditional knowledge and songs, stories, knowledge and resources are held for the benefit of the group as a whole. While copyright can provide recognition of individual rights, any measures for protection and recognition should explore the interaction between individual and collective rights, before being relied upon.

Rights to culture are inalienable and cannot be transferred. This raises an interesting question however of whether rights in aspects of culture can be owned by individuals. The issue arises in relation to new works that are created, as obviously these are the subject of copyright and ownership would vest in the creator of the new work. The development of legal protection for Indigenous Heritage should recognise the development of Indigenous culture. It should include new works that follow traditional themes and works that are in the spirit of identity but in response to new mediums. In Australia some example of new Indigenous heritage are the panel boards created originally at Papunya Tula Art Centre. Panel boards are works by Indigenous artists which portray Indigenous themes painted in acrylic on canvas boards. The Aboriginal flag is another example of an Indigenous symbol which is of cultural significance to Indigenous people. Currently copyright in the flag belongs to the recognised creator, Harold Thomas. (See *Harold Thomas v David George Brown and James Morrison Vallely Morrison* [1997] 215 FCA 9 April 1997).

Recent copyright case law has commented on the role of Indigenous customary laws and communal ownership. In *Bulun Bulun v R & T Textiles*, 41 IPR 513 at 524, the applicant claimed that the rights to paint and permit the reproduction of the artistic work is a native title right. The court found that such rights were not native title rights, firstly on the grounds that certain statutory procedures regarding determinations of native title rights were not followed, and secondly, because of a larger conceptual barrier. Justice von Doussa stated:

> The principle that ownership of land and ownership of artistic works are
> separate statutory and common law institutions is a fundamental principle of the
> Australian legal system which may well be well characterised as "skeletal" and
> stand in the road of acceptance of the foreshadowed argument.

The court did recognise however, that the artist owed a fiduciary obligation to the group as a whole to deal with the copyright in a manner consistent with customary obligations. This might allow the clan representative to take action where the author is unknown or unwilling to take action against a third party infringer (*Bulun Bulun v R & T Textiles*, 41 IPR 513 at 524).

Indigenous peoples are exploring ways to recognise communal rights via other structures. The notion of the trust as an appropriate structure to hold cultural assets has been considered. A trust is a legal structure which holds assets for the benefit of an individual or a group. A trust could hold the intellectual property generated in a project. The proceeds from such ventures are put back towards the enhancing of culture. The Yothu Yindi Foundation for instance, is a trust structure that collects a portion of royalties from the commercial exploitation of communally owned material and redistributes it towards community projects such as the recording of cultural songs.

Indigenous people seek the right to control disclosure, disseminate, reproduce and record Indigenous knowledge, ideas and innovation concerning medicinal plants, biodiversity and environmental management. Indigenous people are concerned about increasing bioprospecting and patenting of their scientific knowledge and innovations.

Henrietta Fourmile (1996) has reported on the patenting by a US company of an element found in Smokebush, a plant that has been traditionally used by the Indigenous people of Western Australia for its healing properties. In the 1960s, the WA government granted the US national Cancer Institute (NCI) a license to collect plants for screening for the presence of cancer-fighting properties.

"The specimens were found to be ineffective, but they were held in storage until the late 1980s when they were tested again in the quest to find a cure for AIDS. Out of 7,000 plants screened from around the world, the Smokebush was one of four plants found to contain the active property Conocurovone, which laboratory tests showed could destroy the HIV virus in low concentrations. This "discovery" was subsequently patented. The US National Cancer Institute has since awarded Amrad, a Victorian pharmaceutical company, an exclusive world wide license to develop the patent."(Janke 1999, pp. 24–25)

Amendments to the Western Australian *Conservation and Land Management Act* and the *National Parks and Wildlife Act* also provide the WA Minister for the Environment with the power to grant exclusive rights to Western Australian flora and forest species for research purposes. Following the amendments, the WA government awarded Amrad the rights to develop an anti-AIDS drug. According the Blakeney, (1997, p. 196) Amrad is reported to have paid $1.5million to the WA government and if

Conocurovone is successfully commercialised, the WA government will be paid royalties of $100 million by 2002 (Janke 1999, p. 25).

While Indigenous people generally support development of important medical treatments, they should not be disadvantaged by such work. As a result of the WA legislation and patent law, Indigenous people now face the possibility of being prevented from using any plants which are the subject of an exclusive agreement.

The collection and publication of traditional knowledge by researchers, without the permission, contribution or acknowledgement of Indigenous people is problematic. Indigenous people face difficulties accessing the patent system for protection of traditional knowledge because of the commercial focus of patent law. The law of patents does not protect knowledge where it has been published (for example, by researchers) or where it exists as a natural phenomenon without some "new" innovation.

The recognition of prior rights of Indigenous peoples is not yet recognised by patent law. Some practitioners working in these areas have come together and developed a Code of Ethics to govern their work. The first principle of the Code of Ethics of the International Society of Ethnobotanists addresses the issue of prior rights and states:

> This principle recognises that indigenous peoples, traditional societies, and local communities have prior, proprietary rights and interests over all air, land, and waterways, and the natural resources within them that these peoples have traditionally inhabited or used, together with all knowledge and intellectual property and traditional resource rights associated with such resources and their use.

Drafting New Legislation

There has been wide support for the development of sui generis, or separate, special legislation for protection of Indigenous Heritage.

ATSIC's position (ATSIC, Issues: Intellectual Property http://www.atsic.gov.au/) strongly supports the path of sui generis legislation to remedy the shortfalls in existing legislation identified as follows:

- Emphasis on economic rights over cultural rights;

- Lack of coverage of the range of issues that Indigenous peoples consider as their cultural and intellectual property rights and Traditional Knowledge (eg Oral knowledge passed down through the generations, oral stories, dance etc which are not in written form)

- Protection provided for defined periods of time, instead of permanent protection.

- ATSIC is committed to pursuing additional initiatives including the consideration and development of sui generis legislation to cover all aspects of Indigenous cultural and intellectual property rights and Traditional Knowledge. (ATSIC, Issues: Intellectual Property http://www.atsic.gov.au/)

The proposal to draft sui generis legislation raises many issues. Many questions about the purpose, the scope, enforcement provisions, exemptions and other matters must be resolved before effective legislation can be drafted.

Domestic Law in Other Countries

The experience of other colonised countries can provide useful information on the success of different methods of incorporating Indigenous heritage into national legal regimes. In some instances, countries have developed these laws in order to regulate and ensure national benefits from the research and development activities of multinational companies in regard to biological resources. The rights of Indigenous people have taken a higher profile where traditional knowledge and resources on traditional country hold the keys to this commercial benefit for the nation state.

This paper will focus on the cases of Canada and New Zealand.

Case Study: Canada

The protection of Indigenous heritage in Canada is influenced by a number of issues and watershed events in the legal political life of the nation state including,

(i)   Treaties made with the settlers and the Indigenous peoples at the time of occupation.

(ii) court cases recognising the existence and extent of Aboriginal rights and Aboriginal title in Canada which culminate in the decision of the supreme court in *Delgamuukw v British Columbia* [1998] 1 C.N.L.R 14 (S.C.C)

(iii) The Constitutional amendment in 1982 inserting section 35(1) which protects existing and future Indigenous treaty rights

(iv) The federal government policy on self-government and the making of regional agreements for self-government in the Nisga'a Agreement.

As is the case in most nation states, at present Indigenous people of Canada have sought protection for Indigenous heritage, particularly traditional knowledge, from the intellectual property system.

Canada's intellectual property system bears a lot of similarities to the Australian intellectual property system, however, it is beyond the scope of this paper to provide a detailed comparison of the intellectual property systems of the two states.

A recent Canadian government report on the Canadian intellectual property system and Indigenous knowledge of biodiversity, noted that intellectual property rights do not adequately correlate to Indigenous knowledge for a number of reasons. These included the focus of intellectual property laws on individual authorship. Rather than recognition of communal ownership, the requirement for patents of novelty, (which can be problematic for Indigenous knowledge) has been in the public domain. The main difficulty is in identifying economic damages in relation to infringements (Mann, 1997). These difficulties are strikingly similar to the problem faced by Indigenous people seeking heritage protection under the Australian intellectual property system.

Batiste and Henderson provide a detailed review of the Canadian legislative intellectual and cultural property regime, and conclude that:

> It (the regime) ignores the constitutional rights of Aboriginal peoples of Canada and their Aboriginal knowledge, heritages and rights. The existence of statutory and regulatory fines are insignificant and inadequate to prevent the misappropriation of these properties and resources by interested parties (Batiste & Henderson 2000, pp. 236–237).

The most important lesson to be learned in relation to the Constitutional recognition of aboriginal rights and title in Canada, is that this recognition has not yet impacted sufficiently on the statutory intellectual property regime to provide real protection and recognition for Indigenous Canadians. There is an important message in this experience for Indigenous Australians seeking protection for Indigenous heritage—constitutional reform without extensive legislative reform or action is no guarantee of protection of Indigenous heritage rights.

Canada has embarked on a series of regional agreements with Indigenous peoples. This is consistent with the 1995 announcement by the Canadian government of a policy structure on recognition of self-government as an inherent right of section 35(1) of the Constitution. This policy acknowledges that self-government is an inherent right recognised by the Constitution, and that Indigenous people should be able to govern themselves on matters:

> internal to their communities, integral to their unique cultures, identities, traditions, languages and institutions, and with respect to their special relationship to their land and their resources (McCausland 1997, p. 171).

However, the policy included provision for exclusion of matters which were considered to be in the "national interest". Among matters which are of national interest status is intellectual property. The jurisdiction of self-government apparently ends when it comes to matters of intellectual property.

The Canadian government policy shaped the development of the 1996 Nisga'a Agreement for self-government. A powerful example of the extent of self determination provided for by self-government under this structure is section 30 of the Nisga'a Treaty Negotiation Agreement in Principle (Nisga'a AIP) which deals with the Nisga'a Government power which states as follows:

> Nisga'a government [sic] may make laws to preserve, promote and develop Nisga'a culture and language, including laws to authorise or accredit the use, reproduction and representation of Nisga'a cultural symbols and practices, and teaching of Nisga'a language... (McCausland 1997, p. 178).

One would think that this provides the Indigenous owners with a right to manage and control their Indigenous heritage, however it is qualified as follows:

> ...provided that Nisga'a's jurisdiction to make laws in respect of culture and language does not include jurisdiction to make laws in respect of Intellectual property or the authority to prohibit activities outside of Nisga'a lands except as provided for by federal or provincial law (McCausland 1997, p. 178).

It is a serious flaw in this structure that Nisga'a laws only apply to internal matters (McCausland 1997, p. 178) and could not bind any parties outside the Nisga'a territories.

Case Study: New Zealand

The Wai 262 Claim

The Treaty of Waitangi was signed in the languages of both Maori and English in 1840. The Maori and English versions contain terms which are understood differently.

The relevant Article for Indigenous Heritage is Article 2, which is described as follows by Maui Solomon, a Maori Barrister and advocate for his people:

> Article 2 of the Maori Treaty reserved to the Chiefs and Tribes their tino rangatirtanga o ratou wenua o ratou kainga me o ratou taonga katoa. By that the Chiefs understood that their full chiefly authority to manage their own affairs in relation to their lands treasures, and people would be retained. The equivalent under the English version of Article 2 is just as robust:

> Her majesty the Queen of England confirms and guarantees to the Chiefs and Tribes of New Zealand and to the respective families and individuals thereof the full exclusive and undisturbed possession of their Lands and Estates, Forests, Fisheries and other properties which they may collectively or individually possess so long as they wish and desire to retain the same in their possession.

A lawyer could not have drafted a more watertight provision if he [sic] had tried. (Solomon 2000)

During the 1970s Maori lobbied to have this and the other provisions of the Treaty of Waitangi honoured by the New Zealand government. Maori advocacy resulted in the passing of the Treaty of Waitangi Act in 1975, which establishes the Waitangi Tribunal, and in 1985 the Tribunal was given retrospective powers to hear claims dating back to 1840. There are now over 800 claims registered with the tribunal for lands, fisheries, forests, geothermal, language, radio spectrum and the Indigenous flora and fauna claim Wai 262. The Wai 262 claim was filed with the Waitangi Tribunal in 1991, and amended in 1997. The claim was lodged by the Ngati Kuri, Te Rarawa, Ngati Wai, Ngati Porou, Ngati Kahungunu and Ngati Koata tribes. It relates to the Indigenous flora, fauna, biodiversity, genetics, Maoris symbols and designs, and their use and development and associated Indigenous, cultural and customary heritage rights in relation to such taonga. 'Taonga" in the claim refers to all elements of a tribal groups' estate, both material and non-material, tangible and non-tangible." (Solomon 2000, para 34).

The Waitangi Tribunal has the powers of a Commission of Inquiry and can order witnesses to appear before it, material to be produced, and can hold hearings on marae and follow marae kawa (protocol) during the hearing. The tribunal may make recommendations but cannot bind the Crown. The recommendations are put to the Crown. The Crown then decides whether it will put the recommendations into effect, and how the recommendations will be implemented.

As matters have become more complex, and as the jurisprudence on the Treaty has developed, hearings have become more adversarial and the Crown has begun actively defending procedural and substantive points. Procedural issues have arisen around the protections available for the evidence given by witnesses on the Wai 262 issues. The protection of traditional knowledge is at the heart of the Wai 262 claim, but the witnesses giving evidence at the hearing are subject to objections, and procedural motions which will limit the extent to which the evidence can be restricted from public availability.

Although the Wai 262 proceedings are stalling at present, and the age of witnesses means that their evidence may not be available for the whole period of proceedings, the claim is raising awareness about important ICIP issues for Maori people. For instance in 1994, the claimants successfully stopped the passage of the *Intellectual Property Law Reform Bill*. Wai 262 claimants made submissions to the recent Royal Commission into genetically modified organisms. "Maori regard the genetic modification of flora and fauna as the interference or tampering with their *Whakapapa* (genealogy). Modifying or mixing the same or different species is analogous to genetic experiments on one's own family members" (Solomon 2000, para 62).

Maori are also seeking a *Tikanga Maori Framework of Protection* (TMFP) which would have the following features:

> The system would be developed by Maori, the system would be based in tikanga Maori, reflecting Maori cultural values and ethos, inherent in this system will be the acknowledgement, protection and promotion of rights and obligations to manage, utilise and protect resources in accordance with Maori cultural values and preferences, flexibility will be very important. Whatever structures are chosen will need to be flexible enough to take account of issues that affect Maori in a national sense as well as at the regional and cultural marae level. The structure must also accommodate the rights of individuals such as Maori artists, carvers, musicians and designers. (Solomon 2000, p. 14)

Such a framework would require considerable consultation between the many Maori peak bodies. Issues of enforceability, decision-making structures and culturally appropriate policy development also need to be considered. This framework and the process of its development offer Indigenous Australians a useful model and checklist for adapting structures for protection of Indigenous heritage in Australia.

In 2001, the Maori people wrote to the Danish toy company Lego, protesting the launch of its new computer game called "Bionicle". The game features characters with common Polynesian names such as Toa, Tohunga, Pohatu and Whenua which fight for the liberation of a tropical island called Mata Nui. Maori representatives stated that the story line was very similar to traditional knowledge of Maori and Polynesian peoples.

Initially, Lego rejected the charge of "cultural and linguistic piracy," but continued negotiations with Maori representatives has resulted in Lego agreeing to develop a Code of Conduct with Maori for any further use of traditional knowledge in the manufacture of toys. Maori have made it clear that they do not wish to remove Maori culture from the international arena, but they do wish to have it treated respectfully. Mrs Roma Hippolite, the chief executive officer of Ngati Koata Trust, one of the groups at the Lego meeting stated: "If an agreement can be made and the stories and the names are used appropriately so couldn't put the name tohunga (spiritual advisor and healer) where it didn't belong, there can be a whole generation of kids around the world that get to know and understand about things Maori." (Griggs 2001).

Maori representatives have made a significant contribution in unity with other Indigenous people to setting international and domestic standards for respectful treatment of Indigenous heritage. In the instance of their dispute with Lego, the pursuit of non-legal avenues of negotiation and development of Codes of Conduct is having a very positive outcome. Lego has indicated a willingness to participate in ongoing negotiation of respectful treatment of Indigenous heritage.

Conclusion

Indigenous Australians have developed a clear rights agenda but the most effective vehicle to maximise these right is yet to be determined. The treaty discourse will make an important contribution to the ongoing development of effective rights recognition for Indigenous Australians. Indigenous heritage rights are an essential part of this rights agenda. The following rights are proposed as a checklist for any structure, law or policy which must be included in the treaty discourse, at community through to national levels.

A Set of Indigenous Heritage Rights

1. Recognition of Prior Rights: Indigenous people require recognition of their rights to their Indigenous heritage. They require recognition that the source of these rights is their status as first peoples and owners of their Indigenous Heritage. This status and the right of ownership of Indigenous heritage pre-dates any interest the nation state may have in Indigenous heritage. The nature of Indigenous heritage, including features such as communal ownership must be recognised and incorporated.

2. Self Determination: Indigenous people continue to practice the right of self-determination in relation to their Indigenous heritage.

3. Prior Informed Consent: Indigenous people require the right to be fully informed, by their own standards of any project or proposed use of their Indigenous heritage. They require the right to consent or withhold permission for the proposed use. Indigenous people require the right to an enforceable veto on proposed use.

4. Authenticity and Integrity: Indigenous people require consultation and other methods to ensure authentic use of their Indigenous heritage, complying with customary usages and protecting the integrity of the work, knowledge, sites, objects or any other Indigenous Heritage.

5.   Respect and Attribution: Indigenous people require full and respectful attribution for their Indigenous heritage.

6.   Benefit Sharing: As owners and custodians of their Indigenous heritage, Indigenous people are entitled to share equitably in any commercial or other benefits arising from the use of their Indigenous heritage.

7.   Ongoing Obligations: Indigenous people have ongoing cultural obligations to as owners and custodians. The nature of these obligations and any impact on ongoing use of Indigenous heritage must be considered.

Robyn Quiggan specialises in Indigenous cultural and intellectual property rights.

Terri Janke is a solicitor for Terri Janke and Company specialising in arts, entertainment, cultural heritage and media. She is a graduate from the University of New South Wales and has been admitted as a Legal Practitioner of the Supreme Court of New South Wales and the High Court of Australia. Terri's publications include *Our Culture: Our Future Report on Indigenous Australian Cultural and Intellectual Property Rights* (1998) and *Valuing Art: Respecting Culture: Protocols for Working with Australian Indigenous Visual Art and Craft Sector* (2001), with Doreen Mellor (ed).

Indigenous Education, Languages and Treaty: the Redefinition of a New Relationship with Australia

Lester-Irabinna Rigney

Introduction

The argument in this paper was played out on 2 June 1997, in my own Aboriginal community of Narungga, at Bookayana (Point Pearce Mission, Yorke Peninsula). A meeting was called to settle our grievances with the then South Australian Department of Education, Employment and Training (DEET). This occasion is known amongst our people as the Bookayana Education meeting. The meeting was held in the Jack Long Memorial Hall, which seemed fitting as Kauwawa (Uncle) Jack[3] was an Elder who spoke of the testimony of several Narungga people demanding self-determination at the 1915 Royal Commission into Aboriginal Affairs. My people have a strong and proud tradition in calling for our right to be self-determining. In every generation Narungga peoples have asserted our rights to sovereignty and jurisdiction over our own affairs (see Wanganeen 1987; Mattingley and Hampton1988). As a continuation of this legacy, the Bookayana education meeting called for greater Narungga control over education to improve the educational opportunities for our children. To address the crisis in education for the Narungga, there was an urgent need to resolve the following key issues:

- The recent decisions by DEET for staffing reduction and curriculum intervention in our mission school
- The lack of consultation with Narungga parents and community decision making authorities
- Lack of recognition of Narungga control and jurisdiction over the education of Narungga children
- The crisis of low retention rates of Narungga children at primary and secondary schools
- Local secondary schools curricula served the interests of farming families while educating Narungga out of a Narungga education
- The dwindling status of Narungga language and the urgent need for resources
- Addressing racism in schools

In a fiery encounter, many statements by Elders and parents centred on rejecting the total governance over our mission school by DEET. Broader criticism was levelled at the nation/state whose lack of recognition of Narungga jurisdiction and authority mechanisms was a continuing source of frustration. For many including Elder Ngarpadla Aunty Elaine Newchurch, such lack of recognition undermines the very foundations of our cultural integrity and denies our desire for self–management. Ironically, in 1966, Point Pearce mission was one of the first groups in South Australia to be self-managed. However, state legal and meta-legal recognition of Narungga jurisdiction over education has been lacking (see Wanganeen 1987; Mattingley and Hampton1988). Dr Alitja (Alice) Wallara Rigney[4] commented that the lack of recognition of Narungga authority contributed to the lack of success at school by Narungga children. She declared that the 200 years of our children's failure at 'white' controlled schools should always be balanced by the 40,000 years of successful Narungga education prior to colonisation. In short, she stated that 'our educational successes far outweigh our failures'. Dr Rigney explained that Narungga educational practices emersed in our language had stood the test of time and was extremely rigorous when our people first encountered Europeans. Equally important to our children today is English literacy and numeracy. She declared strongly, 'our love for education has not wavered'. Dr Rigney concluded that the task that lay ahead rested in Indigenous peoples re-defining a new relationship with Australia's governments for more control over education and the future of all Narungga children.

Multiply this story of the Bookayana meeting many thousand times over and a picture across Australia of Indigenous calls for self-governance and autonomy in the past 20th century begins to emerge (see Reynolds, 1987a.b, McConnochie, Hollinsworth, Pettman 1988). Real life stories of real people in real struggle summarise the complex processes needed for re-defining new relationships. Treaty and the need for a formal agreement clearly emerged from this history of unfinished business between Indigenous peoples and other Australians. The difference today is renewed calls for Indigenous rights recognition through treaty is made by Indigenous and non-Indigenous peoples alike. These people come from all sectors of Australian society and politics.

Treaty and the re-definition of a new relationship attempts to move beyond past and present injustices. The goals of social and economic justice are built on the principles of rights recognition through relationship building and reconciliation via education. Both raise questions about the nature and meaning of treaty. However, the Bookayana type meetings in Indigenous communities all over Australia offer interesting challenges for treaty. The challenge we face today is how to look at old problems with refreshed eyes. Equally, how do we address the severe conditions faced by Indigenous peoples to bring about immediate relief and long term reform? How do we build up relationships between black and white at the high levels of leadership and grassroots levels of leadership who in some ways are not like-minded, like focused nor like-situated in Australian society? The challenge is to develop genuine understanding and dialogue across the lines of division in an attempt to bring a final resolution to the citizenry rights injustices faced by Indigenous peoples. Indigenous and non-Indigenous leadership in education must develop new ways of pursuing dialogue and negotiation to build new structures to prevent further human and community devastation. In this paper I attempt to offer a dialogue of ideas for treaty and Indigenous Education toward a re-definition of a new relationship with Australia. It is not my intention to explore in depth the multiple structures, multiple activities and the multiple levels needed for treaty negotiation and implementation. Rather my intentions are modest in exploring the citizenry rights injustices in Indigenous education. I will focus on three key issues of inherent jurisdiction, Indigenous education and the status of Indigenous languages as a rationale for treaty.

Inherent jurisdiction vs. citizenry rights injustices: a history

Indigenous citizenry rights injustices have their origins in history. By citizenry rights injustices I mean the historical legal absorption of Indigenous peoples into the non-Indigenous Commonwealth system of governance. Indigenous people do not benefit equally with other Australians in the social fabric. My meaning also refers to the structural deficiencies in government service delivery that maintain Indigenous civil inequality economically, legally and politically. A brief historical analysis is needed to explore this concept further.

Prior to European arrival, Indigenous Australian nations exercised authority and jurisdiction over the culture and education of their citizens. There are jurisdictional examples that existed prior to colonisation. Jenkins (1979) highlights the complex democratic system of governance by the Ngarrindjeri peoples in South Australia, known as the Tendi council. The Tendi stood in jurisdiction over the formal education of children. Moreover this council of Elders was the 'dispenser of justice as well as the parliament' (Jenkins 1979:13). Similar, examples can be found in other Indigenous cultures in history Australia (see Edwards 1993, Berndt and Berndt 1992). Therefore, it could be argued that the inherent rights of Indigenous Australians to self-determination existed well before settler governments. In other words Indigenous inherent jurisdiction is an original source of authority not derived from a constitutional authority. The British in Canada, New Zealand and United States recognised and preserved First Nations inherent jurisdiction over their own affairs in various legal treaties. Inherent jurisdiction is a legal concept recognised and practiced in most other commonwealth countries. However, Indigenous Australian sovereignty was not afforded the same recognition as their Maori, Indigenous Canadian and United States counterparts.

Indigenous concepts of nationhood and identities were based on the ability of Elders and leaders to care for all their citizens by upholding and protecting Indigenous cultures and values, enabling all children of their nations to become contributing members. Therefore, it is understandable that Indigenous sovereignty was never ceded at first contact between Indigenous and non-Indigenous peoples. Disregarding official instructions in 1778, Captain James Cook acquired Australia for the British Crown by declaring a legal doctrine of *terra nullius*. This doctrine not only gave rise to the myths that Australia was 'peacefully settled', but that the landscape was void of 'civilised inhabitants'. Civilised in this context meant that Aboriginal peoples were categorised as not 'civil' as they possessed no means of governance that matched the halls of Westminster.

In a strange twist of fate brought about by the legal fiction of *terra nullius*, Australian nationalism, constitutional governance and identity was established without regard or inclusion of Indigenous systems of governance and inherent jurisdiction over education. The denial of Indigenous governance practices is the origins of future citizenry rights injustices for Indigenous peoples. To secure the British/Australian identity, the new colony saw a rapid growth of governmental systems controlled through extensive bureaucratic institutions. Like Canada and United States, settled Australia is an 'immigrant nation' whose colonising ethnicity was predominantly British (Hutchinson 1994:164). All those who identified with this ethnicity at this time wanted British identity and its values maintained and secured by the new Australian system of governance. Indigenous systems did not stand a chance of being legally or constitutionally protected.

Indigenous Australians up to the early 1920s have existed outside the settler colonial 'nation'. Indigenous peoples featured nowhere in the new structure of settler governance nor were they absorbed through equal citizenship rights at contact. It is simply an undisputable fact that the dispossession, colonisation and assimilation absorption occurred without Indigenous Australians consent (see Reynolds 1987a, b, Miller 1985). Strategies of including Indigenous peoples into Australian society gained strength from 1920 and gathered momentum after the Second World War Governmental strategies of civil assimilation of Indigenous peoples were commonplace between 1930–1970 (see McConnochie, Hollinsworth, and Pettman 1988:103–130). In 1962, Indigenous Australians were allowed to vote in federal elections. The assimilation period saw the end of formal exclusion of Indigenous peoples from Australian society. A majority of 'non-Indigenous Australians voted successfully in the 1967 referendum to change section 127 and 51 (xxvi) of the constitution allowing the federal government to pass laws relating to Indigenous Australians' (Lippman 1994:30–31). The referendum was not a vote specifically on citizenship rights, but to enact laws to increase the number of Indigenous peoples in civil services. The 1967 referendum saw a shift from the colonial education by missionaries that was to 'Christianise and civilise', to substantial changes in content and policy ushered in by the federal government during the assimilation era from 1940s–1970s. Lippmann (1994) suggests that the referendum vote was unsuccessful in bringing relief to the appalling conditions of Indigenous Australians.

> Undoubtedly there was a false belief among Aborigines and their white supporters about the outcome of the referendum result: that the Australian government would speedily take over Aboriginal Affairs and improve conditions … the results of the referendum victory were not as marked as Aboriginal groups had expected … the States clung to their powers where they could and another level of bureaucracy to be battled was added in the form of the Federal government. Lippmann (1994:31)

Indigenous Australians were admitted to Australian society only to find our languages, cultures and systems of education were to be assimilated and absorbed through equal citizenship rights held in trust by the federal and state governments. Despite Indigenous assimilation into settler society, many citizenry rights injustices continued through discriminatory beliefs and practices. The contradictions of such absorption are many. Indigenous identities, cultures and systems of education were absorbed into a government system whose structures were designed to secure and protect the identities and cultures of the settler government. Moreover, Indigenous people were absorbed into a government who in the past used force and legislative power to exclude people who were not ethnically British. At this time, minority dissent was overridden. There was little questioning of the legitimacy of colonial control and power via the governance system that absorbed Indigenous Australians. Nor did it seem to matter that it was settler Australians via the referendum deciding settler governance of Indigenous affairs not Indigenous people themselves.

Several questions emerge here. How were Indigenous languages and cultural structures of education going to survive in a settler government system, whose basis for governance is its loyalty to its British origins and to colonial Australia itself? How would the settler government make room for Indigenous Australian jurisdiction over their cultures, languages and education, in the absence of a treaty? Although old these questions remain relevant today. Without treaty, Indigenous peoples are forced into government care and obligation with its associated paternalistic practices, as the governance over Indigenous affairs rests with others.

Citizenry obligations

Citizenry obligations were a key aspect of the 1967 referendum. In other words, government citizenry duty refers to the responsibilities and obligations of the government in providing a high standard of care for all Australian citizens, including Indigenous peoples. Put simply, the government is to act in the best interest of all citizens of Australia including Indigenous peoples. The constitutional amendments, while removing offensive provisions aimed at excluding Indigenous peoples, provided the federal government with greater constitutionally-based jurisdiction over Indigenous civil inclusion. Despite substantial progress in government outcomes for Indigenous peoples since colonisation, Australia's governments today via its constitution, still remain in control, and exercises jurisdiction over Indigenous affairs. Paternalism remains evident in Indigenous education via infra structure deficiencies and lack of coordination between federal and state governments (see MCEETYA 1995, Commonwealth 2000). Full transition of Indigenous jurisdiction, control and authority over resources, structures and administration in Indigenous education is yet to be realised. However, government obligation over the past forty years has had some success in allowing greater access to and opportunity in education for Indigenous children. The development of the National Aboriginal and Torres Strait Islander Education Policy in 1989 championed the cause for educational access and equity.

Indigenous Australians today have greater powers than before in some areas of policy making and service delivery through the development of the1989 ATSIC legislation. However, the existence of ATSIC does not equate to inherent authority over Indigenous education. Nor does the existence of ATSIC absolve government citizenry obligations. The ATSIC mandate has an education component. However, the governance, administration and delivery of Indigenous education remain with governments. Constitutionally, the civil jurisdiction and responsibilities of Indigenous education is divided between the federal government and the state and territories. Service deliveries of Indigenous education are administered through usual civil state and territory bureaucracies. While citizenship determines the rights and abilities of Indigenous Australians to access government services in education, Indigenous jurisdiction over our education and its resources continues to remain outside service delivery policy and practice. Indigenous jurisdiction over education must be synonymous with control rather than merely with Indigenous people being consumers. Poor statistics in almost every social indicator from education and health, to imprisonment and unemployment, reflect the state of a people who have been dispossessed and left powerless. Major inquiries like the 1991 Royal Commission into Aboriginal Deaths in Custody and the 1997 National inquiry into the Separation of Indigenous Australians children from their families, highlight in various ways the widespread nature of citizenry rights injustices and discrimination. If a new relationship between Indigenous peoples and the crown is to be re-defined through treaty, I argue that issues of Indigenous inherent jurisdiction over Indigenous affairs, including education, must be finally settled. Below I highlight governance issues that a treaty might resolve.

Treaty Principles

To address the issues of *governance* and *jurisdiction* we must find ways to

- Understand that the history of colonial disruption to Indigenous inherent jurisdiction and decision making authority over education has occurred without Indigenous consent. Indigenous inherent jurisdiction must be reinstated legally to revive, maintain and protect languages and culture by law.

- Re-orientate resources to strengthen Indigenous self-governance and political leadership systems for self-management of education.

- Investigate new mechanisms, structures and institutions to allow interfacing of Indigenous systems of governance in education with other Australian federal /state/territory systems. These new mechanisms should have legal status similar to government education departments through enactment of federal/state/territory /shire legislation and or constitution recognition.

- Increase mandatory representation by Indigenous peoples (locally elected by Indigenous peoples), to all governmental educational policy making decision bodies across all levels.

To show how a treaty could potentially address issues in education, I now elaborate further on Indigenous citizenry rights injustices, in particular, education and languages.

Citizenry rights injustices: education

The Bookayana meeting highlighted succinctly the history of colonial disruption to Indigenous control of education. Similarly, the meeting reaffirmed the low retention rates of Indigenous children which lead to further social disintegration and deprivation. The lack of success in education for Indigenous students is at crisis point. The National Indigenous English Literacy and Numeracy Strategy (2000:11), states that 'in 1997, 83% of Indigenous students remained in school to year 10, but only 32% to year 12, compared to 73% of non-Indigenous Students'. Indigenous students are less likely to get a preschool education; are well behind in literacy and numeracy skills development before they leave primary school; are less than half as likely to proceed through to year 12; experience more grave health problems and have higher mortality rates than other Australians (Commonwealth of Australia 2000:1–10). These factors clearly lead to economic injustices and poverty and require urgent attention. However, as recently as 1989, Australia developed its first major National Aboriginal and Torres Strait Islander Education Policy' (NATSIEP). While Indigenous education policy has only emerged in the last 40 years, there has been some positive progression. 'Year 12 retention rates have shifted from single digits to about 32% in 1998; Indigenous participation in university courses has increased from under 100 people 30 years ago to some 7,800 in 1998 (Australians Commonwealth of Australia 2000:1–10). However, despite this progression and goodwill by individuals and government institutions, Indigenous students do not presently achieve educational outcomes at similar levels to other Australian students.

Past and present government documents, senate inquiries and State and Territory's commissioned reports are testimony to the fact that citizenry rights injustices in Indigenous education remain. Nicholls (1998:149) writes of 'the continuing and consistent failure of the state to provide the secondary education needs of Indigenous youth in the Northern Territory, particularly for secondary-aged youth who live in rural areas'. 'In 1993 in some parts of the Northern Territory, less than 25% of Indigenous youth participated in secondary school education' (Nicholls 1998:149). In the Commonwealth Schools Commission Report in 1987, found that between 10,000 and 12,000 Indigenous youth between the ages of 12–15 did not have any access what so ever to recognised school facilities (see CSC, 1987). For other Australian youth, this provision is regarded as nothing more than basic (Nicholls1998). Similarly, a Northern Territory Department of Education report, found a 'large unserviced group of Indigenous adolescence in the southern and Barkly region' (Toyne 1993: 2-3). It was found from a sample group 'of 922 school-aged teenagers in this region, that 41% of the total group existed outside of any schooling program' (Toyne 1993:2-3). Nicholls (1998:151), analysing statistics from the Northern Territory Education Department's *Indigenous Education Outcomes Report 1997–1999 Triennium*, claims in 1997, 97 Indigenous students in the Territory obtained a Junior Secondary School Certificate, compared with 1000 non-Indigenous students (a decrease of 31 Indigenous students from the previous year)'.

Several inquiries have emerged recently that offer conclusive evidence that the lack of Indigenous access to education is caused by poor health, poverty and isolation. Recommendation 4.4 of the National Inquiry into Rural and Remote Education conducted by the (HREOC) Human Rights and Equal Opportunity Commission (2000a), referred to the need to develop a national rural education policy. Specifically, recommendations 8.1 of the HREOC report seeks urgent address of Indigenous rural and remote education (HREOC 2000b:72). The Human Rights and Equal Opportunity Commission (HREOC) report (2000a, b) strongly supported similar findings of the Katu Kalpa Senate Inquiry (2000). Katu Kalpa (2000;164) acknowledged the inadequate service provision of Indigenous communities in remote regions. As a result of the HEROC report, a National Framework for Rural and Remote Education has been developed by MCEETYA (Ministerial Council on Education, Employment, Training and Youth Affairs). Despite a progressive National Framework, Indigenous access to education in rural communities remains denied by remoteness. As declared at the Bookayana meeting, English, numeracy and literacy are important to Indigenous communities. These statistics are harrowing in what they mean for continuing Indigenous citizenry rights injustices. They also have direct implications for future Indigenous leadership in the Northern Territory. Moreover, the strong correlation between level of education, income and health, indicate that the citizenry rights injustices in Indigenous education will mean more government expenditure on social problems later. Indigenous remote communities in the Northern Territory still do not have secondary high schools built in regions to enable collective access by several remote communities due to high cost. Yet government expenditure on poverty related illness, substance abuses and incarceration rates are ever increasing in the Northern Territory. The fundamental duty and citizenry obligations of the government to provide education services to Aboriginal youth are vital to the solution of this unacceptable situation. In the absence of a treaty, urgent action is needed to bring immediate relief to what Indigenous communities have been voicing for some time. I raise some Indigenous education issues below that treaty would need to address to bring about a new relationship with Australia.

Treaty Principles

To address the issues of *Indigenous Education* we must find ways to

- Increase the mutual understanding that the lack of government obligation continues in many areas of Indigenous education service delivery, particularly access and equity. News ways of educational partnership need recognition to achieve educational parity.

- Investigate ways for Indigenous governance of education to be applied through local rural and remote communities' leadership systems and organisations for decision making. This governance system through designated Indigenous educational authorities must have legal status like other government educational bureaucracies.

- Annual summer forums to discuss the educational status of remote communities.

- Increase the local Indigenous community jurisdiction of education via new infrastructure that allows local Indigenous councils or their delegated educational authorities to have autonomy and control over curriculum, educational policies, resources, management and administration, employment of teachers, program quality, community and parent participation.

- Increase local Indigenous community jurisdiction of education to represent Indigenous peoples on other educational national and state policy committees.

Major gaps exist in educational provision for rural and remote communities in schooling in the dominant skills of English, literacy and numeracy as well as Indigenous languages and culture. Significant gaps in Indigenous language education contribute to the demise of children being numerate and literate in their ancestral languages. I briefly explore these issues to understand how a treaty could bring solutions to these problems.

Citizenry rights injustices: Indigenous languages

Prior to colonisation there were approximately 250 Indigenous languages with 600–800 dialects (SSABSA 1996:7–8). Indigenous Australia was multi-lingual and multicultural, with most individuals capable of speaking five or more languages fluently. Indigenous knowledges transmitted through languages reinforce worldviews and identities, whilst reaffirming the unique relationship with lands, laws and cultures.

As mentioned at the Bookayana meeting, Indigenous communities have always recognised the importance of education and language to transmit culture. Education and language are instruments of empowerment for cultural and economic justice. However the effects of colonisation on Australian languages have been devastating (Walsh and Yallop 1993). There are approximately 50 Indigenous languages left with only a few elderly speakers remaining. This means that these languages are being lost at a rate of approximately one per year.

Indigenous peoples today are victims of past settler cultural and linguistic eradication strategies sanctioned and enacted by previous government systems. These factors have contributed to a disruption in intergenerational transmission of language and culture. Although these civil eradication strategies and their practices are now illegal, it is testimony to the courage and strength of Indigenous peoples that their languages have survived. Reversing language loss (also known as language shift) is a difficult task. Over the last decade or so there has been success by Indigenous peoples with the assistance of government services in arresting language shift, and in some cases reversing language loss. This success is attributed to Indigenous languages becoming a part of Australia's National Language policy in October 1984 via the Senate Committee's Report on National Languages policy, and later, the publication of Joseph Lo Bianco's the National Language Policy on Language in 1987(SSABSA 1996). These reports established the National Aboriginal Languages program (NALP) that led to allocation of $1million per year to community language programs. Low funding continues today that contributes to difficulties for the Indigenous community to restore and maintain their languages.

SSABSA (1996:8) attributes the success among other things, to the recent development of 'Aboriginal-run Language Centres and the teaching of Aboriginal Indigenous Languages in schools'. In 1984 the Kimberly Language Resource Centre was the first Centre in Halls Creek to be established. These centres currently receive money from ATSIC (via federal resources) through the Aboriginal and Torres Strait Islander Languages Initiatives Program (ATSILIP). This program funds around 20 regional language centres and many more community-based language projects. These centres are represented by the Federation of Aboriginal and Torres Strait Islander Languages (FATSIL). FATSIL is a national body for community based language programs.

Schools and Indigenous languages also have an interesting history worthy of inclusion here. Indigenous languages are latecomers to language learning curriculum in schools. It was only in 'the early 1970s that some schools began to receive government funding to teach Indigenous languages. By 1990, bi-lingual education programs were running in 21 Northern Territory schools. Similarly, over the last twenty years, strong support for bilingual programs flourished in Western Australia and Queensland' (SSABSA 1996:9–10). Therefore, the growth in Indigenous languages and the slowing down of language shift is a recent phenomenon. It is important to note here that the Northern Territory Government, with very little consultation with the Indigenous communities affected, axed these programs on the 1st December 1998. The result of these cuts to bilingual language programs and what they mean for the disruption of intergenerational transmission of language and culture remains to be seen.

Indeed, good examples of language recovery and revival are evident in the last 15 years. In South Australia and elsewhere, schools teach Indigenous languages as Languages other than English (LOTE) which provides programs with much needed resources and support. Without such infrastructure and support, Indigenous languages would not have achieved its small successes. A successful example is that of the Kurinal language. Similarly, I have been actively involved in the last ten years in the reclamation of my grandmother's language Kaurna[5]. Kaurna language has not been spoken fluently for well over a century. According to linguist Rob Amery (2000:1), 'Kaurna language reclamation has taken place against insurmountable odds, yet with positive results, at least according to some criteria'. Amery's (2000) longitudinal study of our language movement witnessed its reclamation from the pages of history books, and its gradual return to the vocal chords of my people. Kaurna still has a long way to go to recovering fully our language. However, as a result of hard work from several committed people, Kaurna language is now taught at an institution at every level of education from primary school to university.

As mentioned above, success is evident in all language programs from language maintenance of fluently spoken languages to the languages like Kaurna whose programs are centred on recovery and revival. In other words there are pockets of language safety areas where Indigenous languages are spoken, learned, written and heard. However, despite this success, language diversity and the number of Indigenous languages speakers continue to rapidly decline (see Amery, 2000, Schmidt 1990, Hale 1992). The peak government body in South Australia for Secondary School Assessment declared that 'despite the recognition of Indigenous languages in schools, there are Indigenous students enrolled in education that do not have the opportunity to study their language' (SSABSA 1996:11). There are many factors that contribute to this ongoing problem. Let me deal briefly with social factors.

Language hurdles

Unlike the past, it is no crime (as far as the law is concerned) to speak an Indigenous language in public. However, in some areas of Australia, there are racist attitudes that make it unsafe to speak Indigenous language in public places. Some unwelcoming and culturally insensitive government and non-government service delivery organisations (hospitals, counselling services, childcare centres, shopping malls, welfare, and prisons) create an atmosphere where people are ashamed to speak their language. These social practices marginalise the social usage of language. Equally, there are many structural and institutional obstacles in language maintenance and revival. The list is by no means exhaustive but includes the following.

- ATSILIP programs are restricted from operating directly in schools
- Indigenous language maintenance is extremely under-resourced financially
- A higher priority for languages in ATSIC mandate needed
- More resources and government interconnection for FATSIL
- In Indigenous communities languages have a lower priority than Native Title
- Lack of training and careers for language workers
- Lack of employment for Indigenous peoples in language work
- Limited availability of teachers of Indigenous languages
- No scholarships for Indigenous peoples in Linguistics
- High death rate and poor health of few remaining elderly speakers of language
- Low level of documentation of Indigenous languages
- Limited availability of literature and materials in Indigenous languages
- Limited availability of teaching materials and associated technologies
- Limited availability of interpreters in courts and hospitals
- High burn out rate for those few committed Indigenous peoples working in Languages
- The dominance of English across all sectors and levels of education and society
- No Indigenous Languages Act in Australia
- The lack of Indigenous language delivery within the university and TAFE systems
- The absence of a national Indigenous language institute.

The social, structural and institutional factors listed above directly impact on Indigenous languages survival. These citizenry injustices add unnecessary hurdles to language maintenance and revival processes. While the critical state of Indigenous languages remain in the balance, a positive feature of the Indigenous language movement is the development of powerful partnerships and collaboration between

Elders, language speakers, schools, educators, government departments, administrators and linguists. In South Australia, the public education system has been instrumental in establishing these relationships in an attempt to reverse language loss.

Multiple collaborations, multiple strategies at multiple levels are needed to stop and reverse language shift. Reversing language loss will need to be addressed in combination with efforts for better health and services for elderly speakers. Increased language activity in the home and community is needed. A greater determination of land rights and native title is required as land, language and culture are linked. Further societal integration of Indigenous languages and culture into the wider Australian society must be fostered. Fundamental to the prevention of language and cultural loss is continued collective Indigenous and non-Indigenous partnerships with both individual and organisational determination. It will also require a greater commitment of financial and human resources. The value of treaty is the ability to address multiple factors of health, education, native title and language issues in one legal document. This moves beyond current government civil strategies of addressing Indigenous matters in isolation. Moreover, treaty moves beyond addressing symptoms as important as this may be, to targeting the root causes of injustice, which is the lack of legal and constitutional recognition. As I have argued elsewhere, language and cultural maintenance activities are constrained and marginalised without having a legal status that is supported by legislation (see Rigney 2001, 2002 a.b).

Official and legal status

Indigenous languages are a fundamental part of Australian heritage. However, Indigenous languages do not enjoy legal protection or support in a manner deserving of the fact that they are First Australian languages. Currently, every other language taught in South Australian schools, excluding Indigenous languages, is an official language of other global countries. This citizenry rights injustice has been appallingly sidelined. At present there is no official or legal status recognition for Indigenous languages as national Australian languages. In the 2001, Paulo Freire Memorial Lecture, Christine Nicholls (2001:6) spoke to the current critical situation of Indigenous languages and the issue of their legal status.

> … Whilst Indigenous language rights are assumed to exist in this country by many speakers and their supporters, in fact this position has no legal force … the assumption that Indigenous languages will automatically be respected in this country is naïve, in light of past and present practices and in the present political climate. The recent axing of the bilingual education programs in the Territory, despite the stated wishes of affected communities is one case in point. (Nicholls 2001:6)

I have argued that there is no legislative protection or support at present by federal or state and territory governments (see Rigney 2002 a.b). Nor is there by-law recognition and protection at the local shire/council level. Australia's Indigenous languages remain outside the official language status of the country and therefore receive few financial resources compared with international economic languages such as French, Japanese and German. Lack of an official language status recognition result in government naming policies and practices in relation to newly formed parks and public spaces that disregard and ignore Indigenous naming practices. This civil rights injustice continues the colonial settler government practices of the past, by renaming the landscape that already has names given by First Nations Indigenous Australians. This practice has serious consequences for Native claimants who are required to prove continuous links to the land by being able to name country in language.

Indigenous languages are sites of heritage maintenance for practicing traditions that nurture cultural integrity and diversity. Indigenous languages are used for communicative and symbolic functions. Communicative functions of language are used to speak to other members of a particular community. . Symbolic languages are languages whose communicative function has been eroded due to influences of colonisation. Symbolic functions like my language of Kaurna, are used to reinforce and reaffirm my Kaurna identity and culture by reviving those traditions that have been silenced due to colonisation. Few Indigenous peoples oppose the maintenance and revival of their language. Therefore, if language maintenance activity is to succeed, there is an urgent need for legal protection accompanied by further resources that derive from such legal recognition.

There are numerous examples of specific international language Acts that give Indigenous languages legal status (see Rigney 2002b). Gaelic (traditional Irish language) was recognised as an official language in the Republic of Ireland since its independence from Britain in 1919. In the United States the Native American Languages Act in 1990 recognises and supports the teaching of Native American languages in school. In 1987 the Maori Language Bill announced Maori as an official language of New Zealand. The Bill enacted the Maori language Commission that advises the government on policies and program. It would seem that Australia is slow to incorporate the necessary legal mechanisms to maintain its own linguistic heritage. A new relationship with Australia through treaty must involve the legal recognition of Indigenous languages. I offer some factors below that treaty will need to consider in addressing the critical state of Indigenous languages.

Treaty Principles

To address the issues of *Indigenous language extinction* we must find ways to:

- Understand that the history of colonial disruption of Indigenous languages continues to cause dramatic interruption to intergenerational transmission.

- Increase the development of structures that enable the stabilisation of communicative Indigenous languages and the revival of all symbolic Indigenous languages.

- Educationally invest in the urgent need to establish local language and family cultural education enclaves in schools, with a mandate purely for cultural and linguistic language maintenance and reclamation. Attendance could possibly be in school hours to allow students from reception to secondary school to access its services cross-institutionally. Such a language and cultural school enclave would not compete but compliment existing government schools. Language and cultural enclaves in schools could also operate out of school hours to incorporate the building of Indigenous learning communities. Sessions could be facilitated by Indigenous knowledge authority holders, qualified teachers and linguists to maintain, develop, and teach Indigenous spiritual beliefs, traditions, customs, languages, and ceremonies. Such enclaves are open to all ages to promote family learning and can be located in regions that several communities can access.

- Understand that through enactment of federal/state/territory /local legislation, governments of Australia can formally recognise the legal status of Indigenous Languages by introducing a language Act to preserve and develop Australia's linguistic heritage for Indigenous peoples and all Australians.

- Increase the development of language employment with associated career paths to become language teachers.

Indigenous language is an important element of our Australian national identity. In this sense Indigenous languages are uniquely and irreplaceably Australian. Therefore treaty is fundamental for their survival. It is in the context of the need for negotiation of a final settlement through agreement making that I briefly address the concept of treaty.

Treaty

Despite the achievement of formal legal equality for Indigenous peoples in Australia, Indigenous education statistics highlight that current citizenship rights are not being shared equally by all. To prevent the continuation of citizenry rights inequality, treaty serves as a pro-active way for Indigenous and non-Indigenous peoples to redefine and rebuild a stronger relationship. New ways of Indigenous education delivery must be sought in order to address the re-establishment of Indigenous communities, economies and laws. No matter how one defines agreements, whether as compacts or treaties, such models are a way of addressing past histories whilst negotiating new futures. However, only addressing one level of social injustice (in this instance education) will not achieve systemic empowerment for Indigenous peoples. No one activity and no one level will be able to deliver and sustain the necessary reforms for Indigenous cultural, economic and social development. Therefore, building stronger communities through education and treaty offers the Australian government and Indigenous peoples a framework through agreement and partnership. This partnership could address a variety of interrelated issues that impact on each other such as addressing past injustices, improved service delivery, legal recognition of rights, native title, health, self-determination and inherent jurisdiction. It is my view that addressing these issues in isolation of each other increases the risk of further harm to Indigenous communities.

Great investment has been expended in the past to reduce and eliminate Indigenous jurisdiction and control over our own affairs. Therefore high expectations for social and economic, cultural change in Indigenous statistics is problematic without reform and transformation of the governance structures that reinforce civil injustice.

Treaty must promote the opportunity to negotiate changes in power relations within society. Treaty should not be judged by its threat to Australian harmony, but for its potential to transform the structures that continue to cause disharmony. Moreover, treaty making should not be used by non-Indigenous governments as a means of evading their citizenry obligations. The exercise of the Indigenous inherent right to self-government may alter the nature of the current fiduciary relationship but is unlikely to eliminate it. Treaty is a mechanism by which legal recognition cannot be dismissed or discounted outright. The benefits of such legal recognition would enable Indigenous Peoples to continue our relationship with our cultures and languages whilst providing the government the opportunity for final redress.

In relation to education, treaty would benefit all Australians in that all children, including Indigenous youth would have access to education at all points of entry in the system. Similarly, once within the education system all children including Indigenous youth have privileged access to English, numeracy and literacy as well as Indigenous language and culture values that support and extend Indigenous identity. As argued in the Bookayana meeting, a new relationship with Australia's governments is desired to reform and protect Indigenous education. Treaty offers a way of addressing the depressing failures and realities of Indigenous education, through the legal recognition of Indigenous rights and much needed transformation of service delivery.

Conclusion

The Australian governments (Federal, State and Territories) have assumed jurisdiction over education, over the last century or so, yet the crisis in Indigenous education still remains. It is my belief that whilst the status quo of government jurisdiction of Indigenous education with its structures of resource distribution and governance system remains, so to will the reality of crisis. Documented in statistics are the lives of Indigenous peoples who live in real struggle. Colonial interruption in language and education from older to younger generations continues to effect greatly the identities and cultures of First Nations Australians. It was for our children's sake that the Narungga called for negotiation of an agreement in education. The calls for treaty are no different. When our children engage in the journey of education that does not do violence to their culture, it teaches them to dream of possibilities and not to be a prisoner of certainty. It teaches our children to be the best they can be. Education that welcomes Indigenous governance and identities reinforces Indigenous cultural views of the world. As in the past, what was made clear at the historic Bookayana meeting was that western domination was widespread and that we as Narungga people can recognise and name this phenomenon. More importantly, we are not overwhelmed by its complexity or the task ahead to de-construct and disempower its legacy. I therefore position my writing here to follow the strong Narungga tradition of my people's struggle against domination by the Nation/state in the educational, political and economical domains. I welcome treaty toward negotiating new futures. It is the alternatives to treaty that I fear.

Acknowledgments

I cannot write without the source that gives me strength. Therefore, as is my cultural custom, I give recognition here to those who make it possible for me to speak. Thanks to my colleagues Daryle Rigney, Simone Ulalka Tur, Marilyn Wilson and Mandy Price for reading previous drafts, and for all your support. Thanks to Jo (Kurraki), Tikari and Tarniwarra whose love helps me to recover myself from my intellect. The spirit I have is your spirit. The pen I have is for our protection. To my Narungga families, Elders and people, I hope these words bring some relief from the torturous rhythm of injustice.

Lester Irabinna Rigney is a Narungga man who is a Senior Lecturer at Yunggorendi First Nations Centre, Flinders University. His areas of interest include Indigenous Education, Indigenous Knowledges, Indigenous Research Methodologies/ Epistemologies.

'Who's Your Mob?'—The Politics of Aboriginal Identity and the Implications for a Treaty

Louise Taylor

I was a young teenager when Yothu Yindi released their single 'Treaty'.[6] I remember listening to it and feeling proud that it was a song performed by an Aboriginal band. I remember hearing it on the radio and watching the film clip. I don't remember thinking too much about what the song was actually referring to. I don't remember turning my mind to what exactly 'treaty' was or what it meant for Aboriginal people. Nowadays it seems 'treaty' is on the lips of Aboriginal people for a reason totally apart from musical appreciation or popular culture. In recent times the notion of a treaty has emerged as the centrepiece of the Indigenous rights agenda. Treaty is a major talking point of current Indigenous rights political discussion and the focus of academic deliberation. How would a treaty work? Would it be a treaty or treaties? What is the constitutional framework under which a treaty would be implemented? Is it the most effective way forward for Indigenous Peoples? Treaty is so much a part of the current Indigenous affairs agenda that the peak Indigenous representative body, the Aboriginal and Torres Strait Islander Commission (ATSIC) has highlighted 'treaty' as a major priority in the advancement of the rights of Aboriginal and Torres Strait Islander peoples. Geoff Clark, the current chairman of ATSIC has said "I make no apology for placing the pursuit of a treaty at the top of my political agenda."[7] With the convening by ATSIC of treaty workshops around the country for Aboriginal and Torres Strait Islander peoples to discuss treaty issues, Mr Clark's sentiment can hardly be ignored. Undoubtedly it would seem, 'treaty' is the catch cry of future debate surrounding the Indigenous rights campaign.

In this paper I aim to examine how debates surrounding Aboriginal identity will impact upon the development and negotiation of a treaty or treaties. A treaty or treaties will potentially see these two issues collide, potentially resulting in confusion and antipathy in Aboriginal communities, kin groups, local and extended families across Australia. The relationship between these two historical, yet at the same time contemporary issues—treaty and identity—could have practical and wide reaching effects on the negotiation and execution of a treaty or treaties. The intersection of these two issues raises several complex, intensely personal, often inflammatory questions that make for passionate discussion. Who will be and who won't be party to treaty negotiations or agreements? Who will adjudicate identity challenges and conflict? How will Aboriginal identity be conceptualised, verified and ultimately authenticated?

These questions and more require the examination of one key debate—who can rightfully claim Aboriginality?

The Construction of Us

> The construction of Aboriginality in Australia has been achieved through a
> variety of processes, in various places and at various levels of society, giving rise
> to a complex interaction between the loci of construction. At the local level, the
> most striking line of tension may seem to lie between what Aboriginal people say
> about themselves and what others say about them. But crosscutting this is
> another field of tension between the ideas of Aboriginality (and non-
> Aboriginality) that people of all kinds construct and reproduce for themselves,
> and for the constructions produced at the national level by the state in its various
> manifestations, the mass media, science, the arts and so on. (Beckett 1988, p. 191).

The legal and popular construction of Aboriginality has an exhaustive legislative
and political history.[8] Enter discussions surrounding this topic and you find a
discourse packed with colonial stereotypes, urban myths, redneck attitudes and
romantic traditionalism. Historically what you won't find is the strong presence of
Indigenous voices among those arguing the toss about Aboriginality. Fortunately the
tide is slowly turning. More and more we are demanding to be heard on subjects that
are quintessentially Indigenous, subjects that only we can provide the impetus for,
and that only we should guide the discussion on. One of those subjects is quite clearly
that of our own identity.

The challenge that 'identity' presents to the notion of a treaty is complex from both
an Indigenous and non-Indigenous perspective. Firstly, and perhaps obviously, the
government will never agree to a treaty or treaties without the support of non-
Indigenous Australians. Support from non-Indigenous Australians for the idea of a
treaty will be directly influenced by the historical legacy of the notion of
'Aboriginality'. I see this historical legacy as so pervasive in current thought, that age-
old myths and stereotypes surrounding the concept of 'Aboriginality' and Aboriginal
people remain prevalent within the hearts and minds of many non-Indigenous
Australians. It seems fair to say that given the current unsympathetic political climate,
where reconciliation remains elusive, a treaty between the Indigenous peoples of this
country and others, seems quite some time away. This colonial, historical legacy
coupled with the political climate is a major hurdle that must be overcome if we
decide that treaty is the next step for us. Overcoming this hurdle on the path to a
treaty requires analysis of both the historical and contemporary construction of
Aboriginality and requires us to look precisely at what is the historical legacy that
substantially impacts, for many non-Indigenous Australians, on their perception of
'Aboriginality'?

Since white invasion we have been the subject of definition, classification and
categorisation. Who is an Aborigine and who isn't? In the past non-Aboriginal people
most often answered this question. Anderson (1997, p. 4) and Taylor (2001, p. 136)
highlight the inherent power imbalance that underpins the participation of non-
Aboriginal commentators in the dialogue on our identity. Taylor (ibid) writes:

> (Aboriginality) has been recreated endlessly by both Aboriginal and non-
> Aboriginal commentators and selectively (re)invented and (re)invoked to match a

dynamic and diverse set of social, political and other situational contexts. Until recently, however, such (re)inventions and (re)invocations of Aboriginality have overwhelmingly lain in the domain of non-Aboriginal individual and institutional constructionists. This historically accrued bias or imbalance of white over black, or etic over emic, standpoints has been noted with considerable and growing concern by the indigenous (and indigenous academic) community.

Our identity is an issue that should be adjudicated by us, not for us. There has been an assumption made by non-Aboriginal commentators that they should rightfully participate in the construction of our identity. Anderson (ibid) notes: 'It is taken for granted that non-Aboriginal Australia has the right to dissect and define Aboriginalities—a privilege that is rarely reciprocated." As I see it our right to formulate our own identities is tightly bound up in our right to self-determination. That right to self-determination is guaranteed to us all by the International Covenant on Civil and Political rights and the International Covenant on Economic, Social and Cultural Rights. The right to self definition, Dodson (1994, p. 5) asserts, "must include the right to inherit the collective right of one's people, and to transform that identity creatively according to the self-defined aspirations of one's people and one's own generation. It must include the freedom to live outside the cage created by other peoples' images and projections."

We have been and continue to be the subject of definition. We've been defined and redefined. Originally we were categorised by reference to blood—our families and communities were divided into half-castes, full-bloods, quadroons and octoroons.[9] Langton (1981, p. 17) comments that: "the implementation of the assimilation policy itself gave the quarter-caste-half-cast-full-blood classifications of Aboriginal people validity through the legislative and administrative oppression of Aborigines. These ideas did not originate with Aboriginal people nor did Aboriginal people perpetuate them…". Consequently, modern attitudes towards Aboriginality and Aboriginal identity echo strongly the sentiments of times past. Popular non-Aboriginal ideas of Aboriginality are heavily influenced by the 'caste' classifications Langton refers to. Dudgeon (2000) notes: "Australian society mostly relates Aboriginal identity to the 'real' Aboriginal people; similarly, 'tribal' people are understood to be those who are still overtly practising 'traditional culture and who look Aboriginal. In contrast, 'half-castes' and/or those living in urban situations, who have 'lost their culture' are perceived as 'unauthentic', or 'not real' Aboriginal people."

Historically the legislature, the government and the non-Indigenous community were stakeholders in definitions of Aboriginality—we unfortunately, were not. Definitions of Aboriginality stemmed from racist policy and racist people. To define Aborigines was to control them. By defining who we were, non-Indigenous Australians were also able to say who we were not, what we were not.[10] Definition of Aboriginal people was undoubtedly a blatant attempt to manipulate and disempower, a way to divide and confine, a chance to restrict and deny.[11] Definitions of Aboriginality were arbitrary and obscure often resulting in bizarre consequences— Read (1998, p. 169) captures this in his passage:

> In 1935 a fair-skinned Australian of part-indigenous descent was ejected from a hotel for being Aboriginal. He returned to his home on the mission station to find himself refused entry because he was not Aboriginal. He tried to remove his children but was told he could not because they were Aboriginal. He walked to the next town where he was arrested for being an Aboriginal vagrant and placed on the local reserve. During World War II he tried to enlist but was told he could not because he was Aboriginal. He went interstate and joined as a non-Aboriginal person. After the war he could not acquire a passport without permission because he was an Aboriginal. He received exemption from the Aborigines Protection Act—and was told that he could no longer visit his relations on the reserve because he was not an Aboriginal. He was denied permission to enter the Returned Serviceman's Club because he was. In the 1980s his daughter went to university on an Aboriginal study grant. On the first day a fellow student demanded to know, 'What gives you the right to call yourself Aboriginal?

Dodson (1994, p. 4) further highlights the arbitrary and bizarre nature of efforts to define Aboriginality which did not revolve around blood quotient but stemmed from perceptions of essential Aboriginal behaviour. This formula for Aboriginality further reiterates the inherent power relationship that underpinned much of the legislation of the time relating to Aboriginal identity. Not only was an Aborigine characterised by their level of Aboriginal blood, they were also clearly identifiable from the behaviour they displayed. Typically, and I would argue currently, this essentially Aboriginal behaviour had to include abuse of alcohol, criminal acts and/or stupidity. As Dodson (ibid) asserts a clear legislative example of this formula can be seen from the exemption certificates granted under the Aborigines Protection Act 1909–1943. These certificates allowed Aboriginal people to access the general rights afforded to all other Australians. The catch was that in order to get an exemption certificate Aboriginal people had to declare that:

(a) they had not been convicted of drunkenness in the last two years; nor,

(b) committed any offence against the Aborigines Protection Act, the Police Offences Act or the Crimes Act in the last two years.

So because, as Dodson (1994, p. 8) puts it, "the basic assumption was that Aboriginal people were incompetent to look after their own affairs and were degenerates, drunkards and criminals unable to fulfil their status as social subjects", Aboriginal people had to cease 'Aboriginal' behaviour and essentially remove themselves from their Aboriginality to be granted an exemption certificate and be permitted to access their basic rights.

In contemporary Australian society, whilst legislation such as the Aborigines Protection Act no longer exists, there remains an abundance of speculation and scepticism about Indigenous, specifically Aboriginal, identity. Non-Aboriginal Australians in the whole, continue to attach the sentiments and stereotypes held in colonial times and beyond to Aboriginal people living in 2002. Judgements are made according to a perceived authentic/inauthentic scale. Depending on factors such as skin colour, speech patterns, ostensible intelligence and popular stereotypes about

Aboriginal people, a person's Aboriginal identity or 'claim' to Aboriginality will be assessed. [12]

 If according to non-Aboriginal standards a person's outward appearance does not match up with popular perceptions of Aboriginality then a challenge will usually be issued and explanation will be required.

Aboriginal people, particularly those who are considered to have been assimilated, colonised, urbanised, educated, and/or separated[13] are frequently called upon to justify their Aboriginality. Dodson (1994, p. 2) comments "The obsession with distinctions between the offensively named 'full bloods' and 'hybrids', or 'real' and 'inauthentic' Aborigines continues to be imposed on us today." The idea that Aboriginality could evolve and change over time seems to contradict the idea of the traditional (read real) Aborigine who hunts, gathers and lives off the land in the minds of those who seek to classify us as unauthentic or fake. I say this confidently based substantially on my own experience as a fair skinned Aboriginal woman who proudly identifies as such. Non-Aboriginal people are often very confused and sceptical as to why someone who does not fit their stereotype of what an Aboriginal person looks like, talks like or acts like, would identify as being Aboriginal. I suspect this scepticism also mainly from the perceived financial benefits that accompany a claim of Aboriginality.[14] A notion of 'pan-Aboriginality' does not sit well with those who seek to freeze us in time.[15] The idea that there exists as Taylor (2001, p.135) puts it a "separate and distinct nature of urban Aboriginal identity and culture to be recognised as authentic in its own right, in the same way as the integrity and authenticity of the identity and culture of Aboriginal people who happen to reside in what is sometimes termed 'remote' Australia", significantly challenges entrenched stereotypes and popular misconceptions. Generally speaking there is little or no recognition amongst non-Aboriginal people that, as Langton (1993, p. 11) puts it: "Aboriginal cultures are extremely diverse and pluralistic. There is no one kind of Aboriginal person or community."

Of concern is the emergence in the non-Indigenous dialogue on Indigenous issues of a distinction between 'community' Aboriginal people and so called 'elite' blacks.[16] A recent feature in *The Australian* focusing on 'a new generation of well-educated, highly motivated young indigenes' stated that: "In Aboriginal and corporate Australia, there are moves to foster this emerging black elite, hoping for something new in what has become a stale degeneration of an argument." Sutton (2001, p. 7) in his review of Indigenous policy is careful to draw a distinction between those Aboriginal people who live in "outback ghettos" (2001, p. 2) and those "leading Aboriginal people, at the national level many members of such elites tend to live in the suburbs, are not normally based in Aboriginal communities among kin, choose partners who are not Indigenous, and enjoy the lifestyle of their (and my) professional class." Perhaps unintentionally this appears to be an attempt to alienate 'professional' Aboriginal people from our remote or rural (read real, authentic) brothers and sisters. Implicit in this distinction is an inference that somehow as 'professional' or 'elite' Aboriginal people we are removed from an authentic Aboriginal experience.

To my mind this distinction, like the exemptions provided during the era of the Aborigines Protection Act, equates a move away from a traditional Aboriginal experience[17] to a denouncement of our Aboriginality and weakens our ability to authoritatively speak on those subjects considered 'classically' Indigenous—particularly those subjects which are of major significance in rural or remote communities. For mine, this unhelpful distinction continues and perpetuates something of a full-blood-half-caste dichotomy—an archaic dichotomy that provides the basis for much of the misunderstanding and myth that accompanies 'Aboriginality'.[18]

Nowadays we use a three pronged approach viewed as the 'test' for Aboriginality that was developed in the 1950s:

i)   Aboriginal descent; and

ii)   Self identification as an Indigenous person; and

iii) Recognition by the relevant Aboriginal community[19]

In contrast with past legislation this test, accepted by the federal government and generally by Aboriginal people and our organisations, allows for Aboriginal people to influence and to an extent control the identification of Aboriginal people.

The reality of Aboriginal identity is that the process of colonisation, compounded by the impact of racist assimilation policy and the devastation of the removal of children, has resulted in significant diversity amongst Aboriginal people. Diversity in terms of appearance, presentation, location and lifestyle is clearly reflected in the diversity between those who currently identify as Aboriginal. The nature of the colonisation process in Australia has inevitably resulted in a multiplicity of Aboriginal identities—no longer are we able to be solely represented as the traditional nomad, if we ever were. Common assumptions made by non-Aboriginal people surrounding Aboriginality and Aboriginal identity continue to ignore the existence of this prevalent diversity. It is this ignorance surrounding diversity of Aboriginality and a reluctance to recognise the existence of that diversity, fuelled by the present political climate, that presents a major hurdle in any campaign for a treaty.

The (black) Politics of Identity—The Challenge for Treaty

> I have come to the conclusion that I am who I am. I readily accept my culture in its present form and I am happy with who I am. I firmly believe that if more Aboriginal people accepted their Aboriginal culture in its current form they would not have feelings of incompleteness. Along with this, I am happy to accept all Aboriginal people for who they are. Hence this raises a very pertinent question—'Who am I to question other Aboriginal people's identity?' (Kickett 1999, p. 47).

A very pertinent question indeed. Assuming that a treaty proposal is accepted by Indigenous and non-Indigenous Australians and the government of the day as the next step in Indigenous affairs, the challenge then becomes one of representation and treaty membership. In terms of negotiation with the government for a treaty or treaties, the reality is that Indigenous peoples would be represented as a group rather than as individuals. Whether this representation would be provided by ATSIC remains to be seen. Firstly ATSIC would have to ensure that it has a mandate to negotiate on behalf of Indigenous Australians. Secondly ATSIC (or whoever the representative body or bodies would be) would have to be sure who made up their constituency and obviously given that they would be negotiating on behalf of Indigenous peoples, that there constituency was, in fact, Indigenous. This is where the issue of identity potentially impacts on the development of a treaty or treaties.

To my mind the only way a treaty could take practical effect in this country is if something akin to the Regional Agreements provided for under the Native Title legislation were implemented. This would allow communities to negotiate on their own behalf with either a larger Indigenous representative body or directly with the government. Similarly, organisations that would serve a function like that of the existing Native Title Representative Bodies may have to be established in order to facilitate the negotiation and implementation of the rights and obligations articulated in a treaty or treaties.[20] Whilst individual Aboriginal identity, where treaty is concerned, becomes subsumed into a broader notion of a common, national Aboriginal identity—it is the credibility or authenticity of an individual that will be the litmus test for the legitimacy of an Aboriginal representative organisation. So to confirm the legitimacy of those representative bodies (whether they be ATSIC or a local land council) the question must be asked: how do we ensure the authenticity of the Aboriginal identity of those individuals on whose behalf the representative body speaks or negotiates?

The final arbiter of individual identity is ultimately the Aboriginal community from which a person originates, and the role that community plays in authenticating identity is pivotal to treaty membership.

There is a somewhat secret, internal dialogue ongoing in our own communities reflective of the increasingly important role 'identity' plays in our relationships with one another. 'Where you from?' Who's your mob?' What's your last name?' These are some of the questions asked in order to establish that someone is indeed a blackfella in order to verify a claim to Aboriginality, links with an Aboriginal community and ultimately, in order to establish Aboriginal descent.

In the light of racist assimilation and separation policies these are questions not always easily answered. Like Native Title, Treaty has the potential to see Aboriginal v Aboriginal in the quest for inclusion, negotiation and recognition. This raises extremely provocative and emotional issues that ideally must be settled by Aboriginal people and their communities if a successful treaty process is to be ensured.

Moving from how we are defined by others to how we define ourselves raises uncomfortable questions. In recent years the politics of identification in the context of contemporary Aboriginal communities have risen to the fore in internal debate and discussion. It is a painful and confusing issue for many—it requires the examination of family histories and perhaps family secrets. Nevertheless we must navigate, direct and debate, among ourselves, the questions to be answered in the labyrinth that is our identity. To my mind, this is a specifically and to an extent, an exclusively Indigenous issue that must ultimately be adjudicated by Indigenous voices. It is our vision that must guide the direction of this critical debate. Situations that present the biggest challenge to our communities on this issue of identity arise in the context of the Stolen Generation, long histories of denial of Aboriginality, inadequate record keeping and genuine cases of mistaken identity.

This somewhat uncomfortable question of identity forces us to examine our own identity and to look closely at how our own concept of Aboriginality and the impact of those same stereotypes and racist preconceptions that we continue to fight against today. It is our internal debates on identity that will test the integrity and authenticity of what we consider essential Aboriginal criteria for being Aboriginal. The elements and/or characteristics that we see as at the heart of what constitutes Aboriginality go directly to the fundamental question—who has the right to claim Aboriginality?

This fundamental concept raises other equally important topics that have to be canvassed in the identity debate. We must be honest with ourselves and with each other in our analysis of this delicate issue. How is it that we as Aboriginal people are able to recognise or authenticate Aboriginality without reference to external characteristics or essentialist behaviour? What are our reference points for identity? Are we guilty of reverse racism in our analysis of a claim of Aboriginality? What do we see as essential to authenticate a claim of Aboriginality?

For myself and undoubtedly for many other Aboriginal people descent is the key for the right to claim Aboriginality.[21] It has to be the starting point upon which a claim is founded. Without it, a claim to identity must ultimately fail.[22] The three pronged test referred to earlier that we now apply and seem comfortable with, is undoubtedly better than what we have faced in the past. Though by no means is this three-tiered approach fool proof.

Will the real blackfellas please stand up?

> ...there has become, in recent years, the practice of non-Aboriginals claiming, or assuming, an Aboriginal identity in order to gain money, awards and fame as Indigenous writers and artists. These cheats are stealing Aboriginal identities from the Indigenous people....in the past we've had everything stolen from us, our land, our culture and our children—now Aboriginal people are having their very identities stolen from them. (van den Berg 1997, p. 5)

There have been several infamous and controversial instances whereby non-Aboriginal people have wrongly claimed and been attributed Aboriginality. The circumstances surrounding these mistaken identities bring sharply into focus the difficulties associated with authenticating Aboriginality.

There are those cases that can only be described as deliberate misrepresentation. For example, the Wanda Koolmatrie/Leon Carmen debacle which saw Aboriginal publishing house Magabala Books publish *My Own Sweet Time* in 1994. The book was meant to be the life and times of Aboriginal woman 'Wanda Koolmatrie'. In fact, the manuscript was written by a 47 year old white male taxi driver from North Sydney,

Leon Carmen.[23] Likewise in 1996 several paintings were entered into the *Native Title Now* contest in Perth—a contest only open to Indigenous artists. The artist was 'Eddie Burrup' and three of 'his' paintings were selected for the national exhibition associated with the contest. Mr Burrup's work was accompanied by a biography and photos of his country. Eddie Burrup was in fact the creation of 81 year old, non-Indigenous, Elizabeth Durack's imagination.

Then there are those cases on the margins. These are the cases that I would argue present the biggest challenge to our community. The case of Gordon Matthews provides a poignant example of the difficulties of establishing identity. Hailed as Australia's first Aboriginal diplomat, Matthews was adopted as a child and was an active member of the Aboriginal community where it was generally assumed that he was a member of the stolen generation. In fact Matthews' father was a Sri Lankan and with that discovery Matthews could no longer claim to be an Australian Aboriginal—an identity he had lived since childhood.[24] For dark skinned children growing up in Australia, Aboriginality was an identity readily attributed to them, clearly for some this may not necessarily have been the case.[25] Ironically many Aboriginal children were schooled by their family to deny their Aboriginality and attribute their physical appearance to some other ethnicity other than Aboriginality.[26]

Mudrooroo Narogin, Colin Johnson enjoyed success and international recognition as one of Australia's premier Aboriginal writers. In 1996 Johnson's sister publicly exposed their family history—a history that she says does not include Aboriginal ancestry. Mudrooroo (1997, p. 263) poignantly articulates the magnitude of the crisis he faced as a result: "When, in 1996, it was declared that Mudrooroo was of Negro ancestry, thus negating thirty years of being an Aborigine, it necessitated some identity searching: what did this mean to me? I had discovered that identity is a fragile thing and can be taken away, just as it can be given. As I had not confronted such a crisis before, did it mean that through a genetic oversight I had lost my culture and had become unauthentic?"[27]

Pybus (2002, p. 4) captures the dilemma we now face: "Genetic markers that caused so much trouble for Aborigines in the colonial context now re-emerge as the hallmarks of authenticity, with Aboriginal people themselves articulating the case for unique characteristics carried by the genes. This racial essentialism may be necessary to overcome the long history of identity denial. It has become crucially important for Aboriginal Australians to demonstrate a biological link to a unique cultural heritage which only they can be said to have." With treaty looming on the Indigenous affairs horizon who will be and who won't be included in the membership of parties signatory to treaty agreements is a vitally important question. We must ultimately answer this question by reference to our own concepts and ideas of 'Aboriginality'.

Authenticating Identity—Secret Blackfella Business?

> It is unfortunate that the determination of a person's Aboriginal identity, a highly personal matter, has been left by a Parliament that is not representative of Aboriginal people to be determined by a Court which is also not a representative

of Aboriginal people. Whilst many would say that this is an inevitable incident of political and legal life in Australia, I do not accept that that must always be necessarily so. It is hoped that one day if questions such as those that have arisen in the present case are again required to be determined that that determination might be made by independently constituted bodies or tribunals which are representative of Aboriginal people (Justice Merkel, Federal Court of Australia, 20 April 1998).

Authenticating Aboriginal identity is rife with difficulties. Difficulties associated with but not limited to, long histories of denial, poor record keeping, the removal of Aboriginal children from their families and the attempted process of assimilation. Nevertheless in the face of a proposed treaty we are faced with the dilemma: how do we authenticate identity and who will adjudicate conflict? For mine, this is a dilemma that we cannot shy away from. The recent Federal Court case of *Edwina Shaw & Another v Charles Wolf & Others*[28] emphasises this dilemma. The case underscores the significant problems establishing a right to Aboriginal identity can present and highlights the substantial challenge faced by a party seeking to contest a person's right to claim Aboriginality.

The case revolved around the identity of eleven Tasmanian people who claimed Aboriginality and stood as candidates for election under the *Aboriginal and Torres Strait Islander Commission Act 1989* (Cth) ('the Act') to the Regional Council. The principal allegation was that each of the eleven were not Aboriginal and accordingly were not entitled to stand for the election. James (2002), a petitioner in the case, cites her motivation for bringing the action:

> The first ATSIC elections in TAS saw the elected members as being people our community did not know or even know where they came from. The community decided to just ignore it and hoped, I think that they would go away. The next election saw these same people elected as well as other Johnny come latelys or pop up Blacks. The Chairperson position was held by people we did not know or who knew nothing about what our community needed. We went to the Aboriginal Legal Service who agreed to support us and the 18 month battle began.[29]

The decision is interesting from several perspectives. Firstly it stands for the proposition that it is the person or persons challenging the identity of another who bears the onus of proof. That is, it falls to the party who calls another's right to claim Aboriginal identity into question, to establish that the person they are challenging indeed has no foundation for that identity.[30] The petitioners in this case contended that upon establishing a prima facie case the onus then shifted to the eleven respondents to establish that they were Aboriginal persons. Merkel J disagreed. Applying the principal in *Briginshaw v Bringinshaw*[31] his honour found that "given the serious consequences for the defending respondents of an adverse finding in the present case, good conscience and principle require that the Court should not lightly make a finding on the balance of probabilities, that any of those respondents is not an Aboriginal person as defined in the Act."

Each respondent, save one who did not appear, were examined according to the formula prescribed by the well established three-pronged test. The respondent's identities were challenged on the basis of their bona fide self identification, lack of community recognition and inability to establish descent. Justice Merkel, examined the ability of each individual to satisfy the three pronged test and subsequently found that nine of the eleven were Aboriginal people. Leaving aside the somewhat unique nature of Tasmanian Aborigines, this case clearly articulates the complexities this issue presents to the entire Aboriginal population.[32] Similarly this case is one of the few examples of a very public challenge to individual Aboriginal identity. In my experience the Aboriginal identity, or lack thereof, of an individual is usually only subject to speculative innuendo and grapevine gossip—gossip, which is usually substantiated by a lack of community knowledge regarding the person's family and/or links with the Aboriginal community.

The upshot of the case is that upcoming ATSIC elections in Tasmania will be held under a new regime—namely the trial of an Indigenous Electoral Roll to be held in this years round of ATSIC elections. James (ibid) is sceptical about the implementation of the Electoral Roll and provides a timely reminder that this is not simply a uniquely Tasmanian issue: "Maybe the Tasmanian trial election process will work—who knows?—but I hope our brothers and sisters on the big island realise that we are their future in this situation. As our people do become fairer skinned and choose to live in the cities and towns this will happen in other places." ATSIC Chairman, Geoff Clark (2002) had this to say in relation to proposed eligibility measures: "The primary goal of the trial was to ensure all voters, and indeed those elected to office, were truly representative of the Tasmanian Aboriginal and Torres Strait Islander community. There has been ongoing controversy in past ATSIC regional council elections, particularly in Tasmania, involving eligibility questions."

So where does this leave us? The Federal Court judgement of Merkel J expressed a clear reluctance to become involved in such matters. Surely then the Parliament, considering the low representation of Aboriginal people in government, is equally unqualified to determine identity conflict—clearly this is an issue best confronted by Aboriginal people. The question remains as to the process by which Aboriginal people can resolve these challenges with integrity and authority.

The Australian Law Reform Commission (2001) in the course of compiling an issues paper examining the Protection of Human Genetic Information heard suggestions that genetic material could or should be used as a means of establishing or proving Aboriginal or Torres Strait Islander identity for the purposes of establishing:

i)   eligibility for membership or voting rights in Indigenous organisations; and

ii) eligibility for the provision of entitlements and services reserved for Indigenous people; and

iii) in the case of Native Title and Treaty, the right to negotiate or to be party to an agreement.

If this were possible, some might argue that introducing DNA testing could result in conclusive evidence of identity and become the determinant for treaty membership.

Personally I am uncomfortable with this argument—going down this path would see us treading in dangerous territory. We might agree that descent is an essential criterion for authenticity and credibility but should we leave verification to genetic material alone? Are we willing to say that genetic information truly captures the essence of Aboriginality?

In the aftermath of court action, with proposals for DNA testing and in the face of treaty, what are we left with? The dilemma remains for us Aboriginal people, both as individuals and as a community. I feel confident to say only this much. I do not believe that our individual and collective identities should be left to the non-Indigenous court system or to the predominantly non-Indigenous legislature to adjudicate—these two forums, to my mind are unacceptable and entirely inappropriate for the resolution of Aboriginal identity issues. To this end we must assert ourselves as the gatekeepers of our culture and our identity. The construction and resolution of our individual and collective identities are distinctly Indigenous areas and must remain exclusively ours. We must attempt to confront issues surrounding Aboriginal identity with compassion and honesty, recognising that there are those cases in the margins that will present the biggest challenge to us as Aboriginal people. For mine, the final thought is best left to Dudgeon: "there will never be one solution, one resolution to this debate/dialogue on identity, and perhaps there should not be."

Louise Taylor is an Indigenous lawyer with the Department of Public Prosecutions in Canberra.

At the annual Barunga festival in the NT in June, Prime Minister Hawke receives a list of Indigenous demands including for a treaty. Hawke signed a document that committed his government to 'work for a negotiated Treaty with Aboriginal people'.

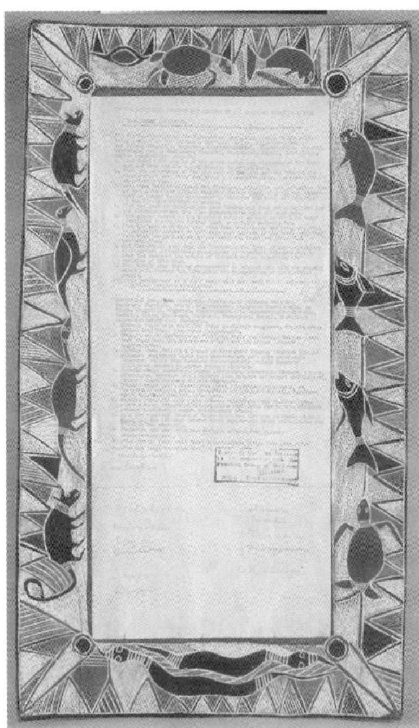

Yirrkala Bark Petition, 1963

The Yolngu people of Yirrkala sent the bark petition to the House of Representatives in protest against the Commonwealth's granting of mining rights over 380 square kilometres of land excised from Arnhem Land. In response to this petition the parliamentary enquiry found that the Yolngu were entitled to compensation. In 1972 court case the Yolngu people were not granted native title under the common law for their land.

Kev Carmody launches the first National Treaty Conference in August 2002.

Professor Mick Dodson and ACT Chief Minister John Stanhope talk treaty at the National Treaty Conference, August 2002.

ATSIC's Chair, Geoff Clark gives a keynote address at the National Treaty Conference.

Professor Marcia Langton, ATSIC Treaty Think Tank Member.

Mr Ruddock, Minister for Immigration and Multicultural and Indigenous Affairs addressing the National Treaty Conference in August 2002, where he talked about the new culture of agreement making as an alternative to a treaty.

ATSIC Commissioner Rodney Dillon.

Glenn Shaw, ATSIC Treaty Think Tank Member.

Gregory Phillips, National Indigenous Youth Movement of Australia spokesperson.

Professor Larissa Behrendt, ATSIC Treaty Think Tank.

Michael Mansell, ATSIC Treaty Think Tank.

National Treaty Support Group and Think Tank at one of the first meetings.

ATSIC's Treaty Ambassador, Nova Peris with daughter Destiny and Elders Angus Wallam and Wilma Williams. Nova spoke about Treaty at the opening of the Waitjen Cultural Trail.

A Story of Emergence: Niyma's View on a Treaty

Gregory Phillips, Timothy Goodwin, Dameeli Coates, Seleneah More and Mark Yettica-Paulson. On behalf of NIYMA

Story

Aunty Lilla Watson, respected Elder of the Brisbane community, has shared with us the following story. We believe this story is critical to our place and time in history as Aboriginal and Torres Strait Islander Peoples.

> ...See the impact of colonialism has been huge...we Aboriginal people are spiritual people and we are still recovering because of colonialism... There's not a lot of understanding about that on the part of white Australia because they have this misguided belief that colonialism doesn't affect them. Of course it does! It's made them into the people they are today, which means they cannot hear what Aboriginal people are telling them... Many are trying to run away from their own history... As they get older and more mature [chuckles], hopefully they'll have a better understanding... You see, that mouth of the snake... our people are in pathological grieving. Our people have retreated into the belly of the snake... it's our consolidation of our Aboriginality, a renewing of our identity. Only recently have we begun emerging from the mouth of the snake with renewal and consolidation of who we are...

This story of emergence helps us to understand that we can be ourselves, and conceptualise ourselves as being in renewal, and now emerging as strong, vital and rich Peoples and cultures again. This story tells us of survival, of renewal and of a freedom to go through our own spiritual process of living regardless of what the white man does or does not do. In this story, we are sovereign because in this story, we choose our own destiny and live it out. We do it in an innate and instinctive way. The story also speaks to us about the reality of our situation in a non-political and non-reactive way. This is a broad life process that is not only about white politics or structures or funding. It is about spirit. It is about collective senses of renewal and survival—about our belief that we already have cultural stories that tell of our emergence. The story tells us that in our planning and efforts to bring about political change, we sometimes miss or minimize our cultural and spiritual ability to just be in process, and know that everything will be alright. The story does not tell us to stop our efforts, but to make peace with broader life processes, and to incorporate our cultural and spiritual values and beliefs into our work.

We need stories that explain ourselves to ourselves—not stories that explain ourselves according to (or in reaction to) whites. That to us is the essence of what we need to survive. What we need to survive is to know who we are without white oppression. That is our vision. What follows are our thoughts (in progress) about how we might get there.

Background

This paper will act as a discussion paper on certain ideological and practical aspects of proposals for a treaty, and we acknowledge that NIYMA will continue to develop our views and strategies with time.

Young people are critical to the development of a treaty for two reasons:

a)   approximately two-thirds of Aboriginal and Torres Strait Islanders are under the age of 25 years; and,

b)   we will be the people who negotiate and implement any treaty in the future.

These two key facts represent the primary motivation for the National Indigenous Youth Movement of Australia (NIYMA) of being involved in this process.

This paper is written *about* the issues which affect young Indigenous peoples, and it is also a paper written *by* young Aboriginal and Torres Strait Islanders about Black affairs in general, and about national and international issues. NIYMA does not seek to represent the views, needs and aspirations of *all* young Black people. What we are doing is putting forward our vision for the future of the whole country—a vision sorely lacking at present.

We are concerned with understanding, respecting and learning from the past; with the current state of play in the nation; and with the efforts and contributions we have to make to Australian and global society now and in the future. But most importantly, we are concerned with the survival, strength and *emergence* of future generations of our countrymen and women.

We are of the belief that any treaty must engender both agreement *and* fundamental change to the nature of Australian society for it to be a worthwhile pursuit. Any treaty must inspire all young people in Australia (particularly young Indigenous people) to believe that there is a worthwhile future in this country. It is naïve to simply assume that young Black people believe that a treaty could deliver us the changes and/or agreements needed in this country, or that we even want to pursue a treaty in the first place. A treaty is only one vehicle for agreement between parties, and there are no guarantees that it will be implemented. Therefore, NIYMA is asking critical questions about a treaty, such as, will a treaty help our situation? What can it realistically deliver? Is it the only option we have at our disposal?

Further, NIYMA believes that before Black Australia negotiates a treaty with its white counterparts, we must know what we need and want in life in general. Or at the very least, we must undertake the identification of our needs separate from any specific treaty agenda—we see this as a critical step in becoming independent, and of following the 'natural' process of emergence. What does Black Australia need and want for the survival and strength of future generations? We believe we must ask ourselves this question first, otherwise we might be asking for something they haven't got—we might ask for things white Australia can not or will not deliver. If we start negotiating a treaty without knowing what we need for survival—that is, to work to our own agenda—we run the risk of always being reactive, not proactive, and of denying our own ability to do some things for ourselves now.

To truly appreciate what we need and want for survival, strength and emergence, Aboriginal and Torres Strait Islander Peoples must also acknowledge what we have got already. NIYMA believes in focusing our attention on what we do have, and building from within on that core.

The issues outlined above are some of the philosophical underpinnings of both our Movement and this paper. We use this foundation/grounding, as a starting point for our analyses and the proposals we put forward to answer some of the questions we pose about the usefulness, role and process of a treaty in the overall agenda of emergence and fundamental change for Black Peoples in Australia.

Issues regarding young people that need to be addressed

The multitude of issues that affect young Indigenous people today cannot be easily summarised in a few hundred words; thus, this paper will therefore not attempt to present a checklist of the problems in the community faced by our young people. Instead, some of the major issues facing young Indigenous people are identified in order to question how a treaty may or may not address these problems or be appropriate format for resolving some of these issues. It is also important to point out that a treaty will not solve all the problems for young Indigenous people either immediately or fully.

The current federal government's concentration on the ill-conceived 'practical reconciliation' agenda comes as a result of the many tangible problems that are faced by our communities. Such problems as education, health, housing and employment need attention, as do the systematic causes of such problems, and we will address both these aspects here.

Education outcomes for Indigenous people are far below national 'mainstream' standards, with retention rates requiring urgent attention. Young Indigenous people need to be in a learning environment accepting of their unique identities as Aboriginal and Torres Strait Islander students, instead of one that promotes conformity. Education needs to promote the learning of human, child and Indigenous rights as much as it does maths and biology. Cultural studies can no longer be based only on our pre-1788 societies, but also needs to teach the truth of our harsh colonial history, and how the men, women and children whose spirits are seemingly lost have reached the positions today they now find themselves in.

Each Indigenous family has the right to adequate health and housing services. The pathetic political discussion over the 'mainstreaming' of Indigenous medical services ignores the issues of community privacy and 'shame' that may exist in the Indigenous community about attending mainstream clinics. When the life expectancy of Indigenous people is so low that 50% of Black men and 25% of Black women will be dead by the age of 50, it is irrelevant to discuss the eradication of Indigenous specific services. What should be discussed is how best to deliver these services. Indigenous people also need to be employed in areas that provide them with a future, instead of growing up with the complacency of joining their uncles and aunties and brothers and sisters in CDEP.

Under these tangible problems lie systematic issues that must also be dealt with within the Indigenous community. The sense of hopelessness that exists in the young community is unbearable for some, leading to suicide and substance abuse. Young Indigenous people need role models and most importantly and simply, love, in order to grow with support and self-esteem. Young people need to know that our culture is based on respect and love, not drugs, alcohol and violence. Parents, aunties/uncles, grandparents—many who consider themselves to be 'leaders'—need to lead the way in this respect, because a young person's first perspective on life is given to them by such guardians, and that responsibility needs to be maintained.

Young Indigenous people also need to be able to be involved in youth and community affairs in their local communities and on larger levels. It is essential that young people are properly involved in decision-making, program implementation, and the monitoring and evaluation of programs, particularly those that are of significance to the future well-being of themselves and their communities. This is in essence an important step in encouraging young people in the self-belief that they are valued and important, and not isolated and alone.

The isolation that consumes many of our young people leads to the problems our community has in the juvenile justice system. Obviously this paper supports the repealing of mandatory sentencing, and we agree with the espousal by the Royal Commission into Aboriginal Deaths in Custody that detention needs to be the last resort. Healing camps should be established as alternatives to detention in order for our young people to realise their place in this country and their culture—in order for them to journey through life unburdened by the mental barriers built as a result of a history of pain, suffering and confusion.

Finally the identity of our young people is a major issue that underlies all the problems already discussed. Other young Indigenous people need to know that their identity as a Black person is based on their spiritual connection to their culture, and spirituality, not the pigmentation of their skin. Both the Indigenous and non-Indigenous community need to know that it is not true that only 'real' Indigenous people live in the Northern Territory or Western Australia. Indigenous young people have the self-evident right to be proud of who they are, and need to be able to decide for themselves what it means to be Black in a changing world.

What does Black Australia need and want?

As stated in the introduction, NIYMA believes that at this critical juncture Indigenous Australia must put energy into asking and deciding on what we need and want as a group of Peoples so that we can be fully alive, vibrant and strong again. There have been very few occasions to date where Aborigines and Torres Strait Islanders have sat down together and systematically asked, what do we need for survival? What do we want? This is not to say that we have never had any planning or strategic thinking at all. Further, every community meeting, every protest, every program is in some way a response to a need and an attempt to solve the issues that confront us. We have usually responded to our needs in an instinctive way—fighting for our lands, services and equality. We have done our best. Yet the circumstances of history, politics and economics have also ensured that at best this planning has been ad hoc and reactive to our needs—the generations before us mostly never had the opportunity to ask in any proactive, strategic and collective way what we need and want for regeneration, survival and the strengthening of our Peoples and cultures. The Federal Council for the Advancement of Aborigines and Torres Strait Islanders and their role in strategically bringing about fundamental change is a notable and honourable exception.

NIYMA believes we must undertake this strategic development regardless of whether or not we engage in the process of negotiating a treaty. If these steps are not taken won't it just be Blacks begging for something from the machinery of government, thus falling short of our responsibilities to future generations? As previously stated, a treaty is only one vehicle for agreement. Maybe some other option will help us more effectively. Why not a Bill of Rights for all Australians which also guarantees Indigenous rights and responsibilities? Why not regional agreements? Maybe a treaty will help us with certain things we need for survival, but not others. Maybe we can do some of this ourselves, now, without agreement from white Australia.

For Black Australia to be able to talk with each other and identify our needs there must be some level of *collective sense of purpose*. We believe we can work together in an overall general direction of emergence while still respecting regional and cultural diversity.

What follows is the result of a general brainstorming exercise between some of our Members that needs to be replicated on a national level, free of the limitations of focusing on a treaty. A treaty or any similar instrument may or may not factor in at some stage of this process. Here we answer the question 'what does Black Australia really need and want?' by outlining the process we believe Australia must embark upon in order for fundamental change to take place. We acknowledge this process is not linear, and some things may need to be undertaken simultaneously. We also acknowledge this is a work in progress, and we are committed to its continual development.

Phase 1

Healing and Basic Equality of Outcomes

Healing will entail establishing truth and reconciliation commissions, healing and trauma recovery centres for Black Australia, and truth and healing circles for whites, including general education and awareness. By 'basic equality of outcomes' we do not mean equality of treatment, because equality does not mean sameness. More spending per capita on Indigenous affairs is required to achieve equality of outcomes given two centuries of colonisation. However, at this stage, we believe that the same spending per capita as on other Australians would make a difference. This must be applied to the health, education, justice, infrastructure and other sectors in culturally appropriate manners. Full repeals of mandatory sentencing in both Western Australia and the Northern Territory is also necessary.

Phase 2

Foundation Building

Preparing Black and white Australia for Black self-governance would include on-going development of a collective sense of purpose and action among Aboriginals and Torres Strait Islanders, establishment of structures, legislative changes, training and education and public relations exercises. This cannot be a government or institution led exercise only—it must engage people and communities so that fundamental change will be a reality.

Phase 3

Realisation

Where Black self-governance, dual national governance (including resources), and a treaty or agreements to guarantee equality and respect between the two parties are realised.

In order for the above to proceed, clarification of the following points will need to occur:

- Definition of sovereignty (to whites it's control over land and to us it's about spiritual responsibility to land and self);
- Decision on do we want self-governance or governance in general?
- Definition and structures for self-governance;
- Definition of citizenship.

These points can be agreed on, but we must invest in occasions for deliberation free of government/white interference. Essentially, NIYMA believes Aboriginal and Torres Strait Islanders must ask and solve these questions for ourselves with a common sense of purpose so we might be more effective in achieving fundamental change on our terms.

Why would a treaty help and what could it realistically deliver?

A failed treaty will only provide the critics of the Indigenous community with an opportunity to attack Indigenous people and exploit the fear in the non-Indigenous community about Indigenous rights and sovereignty. Considering what we believe Indigenous Australia needs and wants to move forward as a culture, we now outline our thoughts on why and what a treaty could realistically deliver. As has been mentioned, no one can believe that a treaty will solve all Indigenous Peoples' issues as well as solve the problems it *can* address immediately or completely. If we are complacent with that belief then our treaty will fail because it will have been founded on unrealistic expectations.

Firstly if a treaty is to be successfully implemented it must be negotiated between two equally sovereign parties, or at least parties who act like they're sovereign. If not, it will set up an apparent position of inferiority that hands the non-Indigenous community a position of power over us. This position of power will be used to degrade our efforts to achieve real social justice for our people on *our own* terms.

In order to understand how a treaty can benefit the community we must be willing to learn from the experiences of the past. Rights to native title negotiated following the High Court's decision in *Mabo (1992)* have not benefited the community in the way that it was hoped it would. The legislature has hi-jacked the process and complicated native title recognition in order to halt Indigenous peoples' assertions of basic rights. Native title has also divided the Indigenous community, and the focus on native title in the Indigenous rights debate has ignored the fact that Indigenous cultures and survival are based on much more than only land, though this is obviously central. Many Indigenous people have, as a result of history, lost their greater connection to their land through separation and death, and we need to include this as part of our identity as Indigenous peoples. We must address all the needs of our communities, not just those that are land-based. Further, the RCIADIC's recommendations have never been fully implemented by either the federal or state/territory governments. Considering these past experiences, a wariness among some young people that a treaty could potentially further water down our power and produce insubstantial outcomes is highlighted. Thus, we must negotiate a treaty on our terms and be vigilant against potential pitfalls.

A treaty must focus on a rights and responsibilities agenda between two equal parties, without being simplified to purely land-based agenda, financial-based or a symbolic paper-signing agenda. A treaty must be entered into with real intentions and real belief. Considering this statement, a treaty must ultimately be a legally binding instrument, recognised in national and international law. Aiming for 'second-best' in negotiating a treaty will only reinforce doubt and a lack of belief in the genuineness of the process and undermine the principle of equality between the sovereign parties.

Any treaty would need to not only recognise and protect Indigenous rights pre-1788, but the continued rights of Indigenous people now and in the future. Therefore part of the protection a treaty should deliver is to ensure that the rights and responsibilities between both parties are guaranteed not only in a treaty but also in the Constitution of Australia and in legislation passed by the federal and state/territory governments. Such legislation could then include as a schedule the negotiated treaty that western domestic law would be required to adhere to. This in turn would ensure that the treaty did not remain a symbolic document, but would be enforceable.

A treaty must also provide constitutionally guaranteed resources for Indigenous self-governance. We argue that approximately 2.1% of the GDP must be negotiated for a treaty to be realistic, useful and workable. Given that we are the fastest growing group of people in Australia, this figure would need to be adjusted in line with growth in the Indigenous population. This proposal will require further research to make sure it is sustainable, yet the basic intention is to create an independent, guaranteed share of the nation's wealth proportional to population and subject to it being adequate.

A treaty must act as a document to inspire young Indigenous people into believing they have a worthwhile future. A treaty has the potential to be evidence for young Indigenous people they are significant elements of Australian society, and that their cultural heritage is valued and recognised. A treaty should also be evidence for non-Indigenous people, especially its young people, that co-existence is possible, and that assimilation should not be valued but instead rejected. A treaty must *transcend* barriers of identity between Indigenous and non-Indigenous people in order to promote understanding of the importance of diversity, and that diversity does not necessarily equal adversity or disagreement.

Importantly a treaty must be protected regardless of the possibility that Australia will one day become a republic. Ideally a treaty will be negotiated and implemented before a republic is established, or as the first and most central issue in the formulation of a new constitution and republican governance framework. In any case, whichever governance structure the nation takes, a treaty's validity and significance should be guaranteed and protected.

We suggest that a treaty be a multi-level document that is negotiated at a national level with the support of the various States and Territories. Therefore a treaty could be an over-arching national document to include foundation principles, enshrine rights and responsibilities, and include benchmarks for implementation. The treaty could then be implemented by all political and social levels of Australian society (ensuring the flexibility, recognition and protection of regional and cultural diversity) so that it has substance and is owned by every person in this country, most especially Indigenous people.

What a treaty can't help with

As stated, for a treaty to be useful and workable, the general foundations outlined in phases One and Two above must firstly be laid, or at least begun. We need to achieve all we can today, with the power we currently have. If not, all a treaty will be doing is 'playing catch-up' in terms of the fight for Indigenous rights and responsibilities. By understanding and achieving what we can now, we can understand more clearly how and what a treaty can help us with.

It is imperative that Indigenous and non-Indigenous people are reminded, in the media and throughout the negotiation process, that a treaty will not be the 'magic wand' many are hoping it will be. Indigenous Australia can learn from the experiences of our brothers and sisters from other countries, such as the Maori in New Zealand and the Native Peoples of Canada and the United States. Their treaties have accomplished some positive outcomes for their people, with recognition of land, constitutional rights, and opportunities for young people. Many problems have been left unmet, but have been overcome, therefore we can learn from the experiences of those Indigenous people and so gain a clearer understanding of exactly what a treaty can and can't accomplish.

NIYMA's views on how to process a treaty

Preparation

We need to start from our cultural and spiritual stories that define who and what we are and where we are going. We need to go inside and ask ourselves who we are without white people and oppression. These beliefs and values must guide our path of emergence. Then we need to prepare our needs and wants, advance our own agenda slowly but surely, prepare ourselves for self-government or government, prepare our claims from white Australia, and decide when the political and economic environment is most favourable and realistic.

Timeframe

We believe at least a ten–twenty year perspective is needed. We need to be prepared to be in for the long haul, and to advance an overall agenda (of which a treaty may or not be a large part) incrementally over a long period of time. We need to do what we can now, stick steadfastly to our own agenda, and prepare for the right time and place to negotiate a treaty and other major changes.

Process—Where to Start?

We believe Phases 1 and 2 above, or steps approximating them, need to be begun before a treaty can be truly effective or useful. This is not to say we expect the government to apologise for the stolen generations before we can proceed, for example. What we are saying is that if we want self-government, we have to clean up our act and prepare ourselves. That is one thing the South Africans say they forgot— Dr Ramphele, a key intellectual figure in the struggle against apartheid, has made the observation that they were so focused on liberation that they forgot to prepare themselves to actually govern. We have the privilege of hindsight and space to learn from this experience.

Process—Getting Parties to the Negotiating Table

For Indigenous Australia, we believe by beginning Phases I and 2 above first, we will give ourselves some strength and robustness to fully engage in negotiations with whites as equal parties. We are equal as human beings now, but we have to work to restore our self-governance structures, including the way we treat each other in the decision-making process. Respectful and respected Elders must lead the process of emergence (including negotiating any treaty), in conjunction with the vital roles played by women, men and young people.

For white Australia, education and some process of engaging and persuading the masses must be undertaken. We must convince them it is advantageous for Australia as a whole that Black emergence and self-governance is needed for the nation to truly mature. If we can achieve this, then it makes it politically favourable for governments to fully engage in a true process of healing, agreement and fundamental change.

Parties

We need to decide who the parties are. Is ATSIC the best-placed organisation to negotiate any treaty on behalf of Indigenous Australia? Perhaps a community-based organisation will be best suited, or an especially created agency charged with the responsibility of negotiating on behalf of Indigenous Australia. Similarly, is the federal government the best-placed agency to be the party to a treaty representing whites? Perhaps a bi-partisan committee of Parliament in conjunction with direct input from citizens would be more representative and favourable to our cause.

NIYMA believes an especially created agency should be resourced to consult and negotiate on behalf of Indigenous Australia. We believe white people should be represented by an independent agency that includes representatives of all federal, state and territory and local governments, churches, business corporations, the judiciary, and the community. Any agreement must be made with full endorsement from the people, both Black and white.

Guarantee of currency and effectiveness

The treaty/agreement requires constitutional and legislative protection, regardless of whether Australia is a constitutional monarchy or a republic at the time. It will also require that the Australian people are involved through a process of mass engagement where education and an analysis of the level of support for a treaty are undertaken. Further, we believe an independent adjudicating body needs to be set up so that representatives of both parties can resolve any potential conflicts or breaches of the treaty/agreement. Structural and resource issues must also be addressed in the document and Constitution so that the treaty is not only about *agreement*, but implementation and fundamental *change* as well.

Vision

We are at a critical turning point in history, and this is one of emergence of our Peoples as who we really are. NIYMA believes we must conceptualise our move forward as a spiritual process of emergence rather than in purely political and legal terms. This will allow us to strengthen and focus on our own values and beliefs. Of course political and legal changes are needed, and we must continue to fight for them, yet we must not let that fight become the sole basis of our identity.

We must acknowledge the gifts and strengths we have now, do what we can, decide what we need and want, and strategise for those changes. In doing so, we prepare ourselves to govern ourselves in our own right, including the establishment of organisations that reflect our cultural and spiritual emergence. We must act sovereign if we want to be recognised as sovereign—and this includes treating each other with respect, diligence and love in our families, organisations and events.

In negotiating with white Australia, we must stick to our own agenda, and identify the parts we are flexible with and the parts that are not up for negotiation. Then we must begin the process of education of the masses and the turning of the political tide. We must wait for our opportunity to negotiate and call the parties to the table when it is most advantageous for us.

Australia's first Black professor, Professor Eric Wilmot has hypothesised in his book, *The Last Social Experiment*, that perhaps Australia is the last continent on Earth with the chance to get race relations and human harmony right. He suggests that the struggles of Aboriginal and Torres Strait Island Peoples is a key aspect of the maturation process for Australia as a whole. Similarly, NIYMA believes that if Australia is to truly mature, the emergence of Black Australia must be a key priority—including negotiating and implementing fundamental change.

We believe a treaty may play an important part in Black Australia's emergence, but only if it is supported with adequate preparations, foundation building and guarantees of effectiveness. Young Indigenous peoples are critical to this process, and NIYMA accepts and is committed to the responsibility that this entails.

Our vision is for two equal parties to live in this country in a system of dual sovereignty and governance. Ultimately, Black Australia must hold steadfast to our own agenda and our belief in our emergence from the belly of the snake if this is to be a reality.

National Indigenous Youth Movement of Australia is a non-government organisation focussed on representing the views and aspirations of Indigenous youth. NIYMA (pronounced nigh-mah) is an independent national trust established by five young Aboriginal and Torres Strait Islander people.

Native Title, 'Tides of History' and Our Continuing Claims for Justice—Sovereignty, Self Determination and Treaty

Hannah McGlade

The Australian common law's recognition of native title by the High Court in the *Mabo* case of 1992 signalled a 'retreat of injustice' from which no turning back seemed possible. This recognition of Aboriginal and Torres Strait Islander peoples' rights as the first peoples of this land contrasts sharply with the history of the common law which was marked instead by a blatant infringement of human rights: the colonial parliaments and legislatures effected many discriminatory laws aimed at the 'natives', laws that were shaped by official policies such as segregation and assimilation. These laws would appear abhorrent in Australian life today: laws that prohibited the intermarriage and association between Aboriginal and white or Asian, laws that permitted the theft or removal of children from their mothers, laws that allowed for the 'indenturing' or slavery of men, women and children to the burgeoning pastoral and pearling industries.

This paper surveys the developments following the 1992 recognition of native title by the common law, and also highlights the importance of Indigenous people's fundamental claims to justice: sovereignty, self-determination and treaty.

Native Title and 'Tides of History'

Up to 1992 this country was said to be 'terra nullius' and Indigenous peoples had no rights to the lands our Ancestors had cared for since time immemorial. The course of Australian history was changed by a group of Torres Strait Elders and their lawyers who took their case all the way to the High Court of Australia. The case of *Mabo v Queensland (no2)* (1992) 175 CLR 1 signalled the end of the Australian common laws denial of Indigenous rights in Australia and the victory was received with great joy and hope by the peoples and nations of the islands and mainland. The decision, known simply as *Mabo*, not only set important legal precedent, it promised to influence and shape a new future for race relations in this country. According to the sovereignty leader, Kevin Gilbert, the *Mabo* case was 'the turning point for justice for Aboriginal People and indeed the turning point to lay the firm foundations and a vision for the whole of this country' (Gilbert 1994:336). It was embraced by the then Prime Minister, Paul Keating, who considered that 'Mabo establishes a fundamental truth and lays the basis for justice' (Keating 1994: 379).

The High Court in *Mabo* accepted that Aboriginal and Torres Strait Islander people have legal entitlement to traditional lands—a unique form of property rights they described as 'native title.' The court also rejected the offensive legal doctrine of terra nullius that claimed Australia as 'empty land' there for the taking by the British in 1788. Although the doctrine was originally said to apply to lands that were truly unoccupied, it was later expanded in a racially discriminatory manner to justify the appropriation or theft of Indigenous peoples lands. In *Mabo*, Justice Brennan rejected this expanded doctrine of terra nullius as contrary to 'international standards and the fundamental values of our common law'. The common law could not continue to accept a 'discriminatory rule which, because of the supposed position on the scale of social organisation of the indigenous inhabitants of a settled colony, denies them a right to occupy their traditional lands' (30).

The issue of Aboriginal rights to land had only been argued once before in Australia in 1971 before a single judge of the Northern Territory Supreme Court in *Millirpum v Nabalco* (1971) 17 FLR 141. Although the judge in this case accepted the Yolgnu people had a complex and evolved relationship with land, he found this relationship could not be recognised because it did not 'fit' the English common law notions of property. Under the leadership of Prime Minister Malcolm Fraser, the Federal Parliament later overcame the *Millirpum* decision by enacting the *Aboriginal Land Rights (Northern Territory) Act 1976 (Cth),* establishing a land rights process for the Northern Territory. Although most of the other states subsequently passed some form of land rights legislation, Western Australia, one of the largest states with a significant Aboriginal population, refused to. When the Hawke Labor government came to power in 1983 they promised national land rights legislation, but the intense hostility generated by the mining industry in WA subsequently resulted in the abandonment of this commitment (Nettheim et al 1997:163-193).

The history of colonisation in this country had been highlighted nationally and internationally by the insensitive bicentennial commemorative 'celebrations' of 1988. An Indigenous political movement that acknowledged the injustice of Aboriginal dispossession, and celebrated instead our survival, took place as peoples from across Australia, and hundreds of thousands of people of all nationalities took to the streets of Sydney demanding the nation remember that 'White Australia has a Black History' (Harris 1994: 138). During this time the tragedy of Aboriginal deaths in custody and the politicising of the issue by Aboriginal peoples and organisations resulted in the Royal Commission into Aboriginal Deaths in Custody who examined both the deaths and the broader 'underlying issues', especially the harmful legacy of colonial history (ATSIC 1997).

There was some commitment to improving Indigenous and non-Indigenous relations under the 1991 legislative establishment, by Prime Minister Paul Keating, of the Council for Aboriginal Reconciliation (CAR). Patrick Dodson Chairperson of the CAR was to describe reconciliation as 'the need to recognise the essential dignity of every person '(CAR 1993). He considered *Mabo* and the High Court's recognition of native title to right a 'distortion in the history of Australia', one that gave Australia an 'opportunity to set right the relationship in a way that was not possible in the beginning' (Dodson 1993:7).

The High Court's recognition of native title in *Mabo* resulted in legislation being passed by the Keating labor government, the *Native Title Act (Cth) 1993*. This legislation established the National Native Title Tribunal to administer and process claims of native title and non-native title claimants. Additionally, the government made a commitment to the land needs of the many people dispossessed of their traditional lands, by way of the Indigenous Land Fund and its administering body, the Indigenous Land Corporation. The third response to *Mabo* was a commitment to the broader and fundamental 'social justice measures' for Indigenous Australians. The Aboriginal and Torres Strait Islander Commission (ATSIC) was requested to consult with Aboriginal communities Australia wide and report on the further measures government should consider to 'address the dispossession of Aboriginal and Torres Strait Islander people' (ATSIC 1995). Also during this period (1994–95), the Council for Aboriginal Reconciliation (CAR) and the Aboriginal and Torres Strait Islander Social Justice Commissioner of the Human Rights and Equal Opportunity Commission, undertook their own consultations into Indigenous social justice measures. According to Peter Jull these events were 'an internationally unprecedented 'Indigenous social justice' exercise [which] brought Australian Indigenous policy into modern times' (2000:21).

The promise of social justice for Indigenous Australians was not respected by the Liberal National government first elected in 1994 and led by Prime Minister Howard who soon dismissed the emerging historical accounts of Indigenous dispossession as 'black armband history' and claimed that he could 'sympathise fundamentally with Australians who are insulted when they are told that we have a racist bigoted past' (cited in Fletcher 1999:337). Relations between the Howard government and Indigenous communities and leaders deteriorated seriously with the passage in Parliament of the *Native Title Amendment Act 1998 (Cth)*, which extinguished further the native title rights of Indigenous land holders. There was no Indigenous involvement in the legislation, not even that of ATSIC, the statutory body established by the Keating government as the principal Indigenous advisor to government. The legislation was brought to the attention of the United Nations Committee on the Elimination of Racial Discrimination who found that it was racially discriminatory and in breach of our binding treaty obligations. As a result, Australia was named the subject of an 'early warning/urgent action' procedure, invoked by the United Nations where there is real cause for concern with respect to racial discrimination—it is the first western country to be named under this serious procedure (McGlade 2000:1000).

How could relations have deteriorated so seriously after the High Court's *Mabo* decision, which was applauded for discarding a racist history and according a long overdue recognition of Indigenous peoples human rights? As Noel Pearson surmised, 'Mabo should have meant negotiation for the first time in this country's history but the prevailing colonial reality is that no-one is talking about that' (1994: 158–159). Perhaps the answer can be found from within the case itself, possibly it was not the victory that many initially assumed it was. There were some (almost lone) earlier criticisms, for example, Michael Mansell was to strongly reject the restrictive nature of native title and the reluctance of the Court to consider the original sovereign status of Aboriginal and Torres Strait Islander nations (1992).

The recognition of native title could have resulted in comprehensive negotiations, a process of regional agreements or settlements, modern day treaty-making such as that pursued in neighboring Aotearoa New Zealand. A negotiating process aimed at achieving lasting settlement and underpinned by a respect for Indigenous rights under international law was certainly urged by the many Indigenous representatives who met at Eva Valley in the Northern Territory to consider the proposed native title legislation. (Tickner: 153). The government rejected this approach and claimed that a response based on negotiated settlements was not 'a practicable approach for dealing with immediate land use issues' (Bartlettt 1999: 419). Richard Bartlett has outlined the intense lobbying of the state and territory governments and industry that occurred after the *Mabo* decision and argues that the *NTA (1993)* is a legislative compromise that 'has put non-Aboriginal interests to the fore by providing a regime of dispossession as much as of protection of native title' (1999:426).

One of the most disappointing aspects of native title as recognised by the High Court concerns the finding that the extinguishment (or wiping out) of the title by the Crown (or government) is lawful and does not give rise to a claim for compensation. It is only the extinguishment of native title that takes place after the enactment of the *Race Discrimination Act (RDA)* in 1975 that can give rise to a claim for compensation under the *NTA (1993)*. And yet much of the dispossession of Indigenous peoples lands occurred before 1975—and it was this dispossession, the High Court acknowledged, that 'underwrote the development of the nation' (Brennan J 89–90). Mick Dodson informed the United Nations that our common law's recognition of native title did not therefore 'recognise equality of rights or equality of entitlement: it recognises the legal validity of Aboriginal title until the white man wants the land. For the vast majority of Indigenous Australians the Mabo decision is a belated act of sterile symbolism. It will not return the country of our ancestors, nor will it result in compensation for our loss' (Cited in Nettheim 1993:23). Kent McNeil's comprehensive study of the common law's development of native title has also shown that this aspect of native title is contradictory to the common law rule that requires the Crown to respect the property rights and interests of its subjects (1989). However, it was only Justice Toohey in *Mabo* who was prepared to treat native title in a non-discriminatory manner and limit the ability of government to extinguish native title to circumstances where it would be able to acquire any legal title (193–195).

Another questionable aspect of native title relates to the evidentiary requirement of proof—native title claimants must show not only the continuing occupation of the land, despite the widespread removal and dispersions practices of past governments, but also the continuation of ties that are based on traditional laws and customs (Brennan J 59-60). This continuation of laws and customs is to be judged within and by the non-Indigenous legal system, a system that has shown little respect for Indigenous laws and customs. For example, in 1984 the Australian Law Reform Commission undertook extensive inquiries into the existence of Indigenous customary laws and called for its recognition within the non-Indigenous legal system, yet this was never to occur (Reynolds 1999:138). And although the legal system now requires quite extensive proof of our customs and law as part of the native title claims process, it still does not allow for the recognition of these laws and customs in their own right.

In the *Mabo* case it was commented that 'when the tide of history has washed away any real acknowledgment of traditional law and any real observance of traditional customs, the foundation of native title has disappeared' (Brennan J 59-60). This finding was relied upon in *The Members of the Yorta Yorta Aboriginal Community v The State of Victoria* [1998] 1606 FCA where Justice Olney was to decide that the 'tide of history' had defeated the Yorta Yorta claim to native title over their ancestral lands. The oral evidence provided by the Yorta Yorta apparently required corroboration by way of white 'official records' and the archival records of a European settler were relied upon in preference to the contemporary evidence given by the Yorta Yorta people themselves (Case 1999:18). The High Court of Australia, who not so long ago rejected the racist legal fiction of terra nullius and denounced it from the Australian common law, went on to uphold this discriminatory and offensive decision against the Yorta Yorta people: *Members of the Yorta Yorta Aboriginal Community v Victoria* [2002] HCA 58 (12 December 2002).

The *Yorta Yorta* case illustrates the serious problem of bias that operates within the Australian common law, a system that purports to be neutral and free from racial discrimination (Strelein 2000). Bias was no doubt a concern of Indigenous representatives at the Eva Valley meeting who in commenting on the proposed native title structure recommended that 'the majority of Mediators, Assessors and Tribunal Members should be Aboriginal and Torres Strait Islander persons' (Eva Valley Working Group Fact Sheet 1993). This has not occurred, and the body established and charged with legislative responsibility for native title negotiations, the National Native Title Tribunal, has developed as a predominantly non-Indigenous body with little Indigenous representation. This imbalance has been reflected in the development of this new area of law, as reflected by an examination of the early decisions of the Tribunal by Bartlett 'After three years of operation, there has not been a single determination of native title in favor of claimants' (1999:422). More disconcertingly, Bartlett was of the view that the Tribunal, in its first decisions actually 'discounted and diminished the protection that the Act extended to native title' (423).

Recently the New South Wales Aboriginal Lands Council denounced the *NTA (1993)* as 'discriminatory and flawed', the Chairperson Rod Towney declared that the Act had 'been a disaster' that had 'created a lot of division amongst us' the only people who had appeared to benefit being 'lawyers and anthropologists'. The Council noted that only one agreement in the whole of NSW had actually recognised native title, and although there had been some other agreements they did not acknowledge the existence of native title and in fact were considered to 'go a long way to avoid it'. The acquisition of lands was seen as more viable by way of the state land rights legislation, under the *NSW Aboriginal Land Rights Act of 1983* there are no onerous evidentiary requirements of proof and traditional connection, compensation is allowable for past dispossession and successful claims result in freehold title and full ownership (Sydney Morning Herald 14 March 2002 p7).

Litigation as an appropriate native title strategy has now been firmly rejected by the Indigenous political leadership who once negotiated and agreed to the *NTA* as a legislative response and who now urge agreement making, for example the adoption of Framework Agreements based on the concepts of recognition, negotiation and commitment (WAANTWG:4). This approach is more consistent with that called for by many Indigenous peoples and representatives at the historic Eva Valley meeting of 1993 which rejected the proposed native title legislation and called for a 'negotiating process to achieve a lasting settlement between government and indigenous peoples' (Tickner 2001: 153). Important recent framework agreements, such as the Wotjobaluk agreement in Victoria, have gone outside of the NTA to hand back Crown land and involve people in land management and cultural heritage protection issues, affirming the 'deep spiritual connection that continues to exist between Wotjobaluk peoples and their lands' (ATSIC October 2002).

Sovereignty

Australia may be the only country in the world where Indigenous people were not recognised at all and where the land was claimed as *terra nullius* (Wallace-Bruce 1994:42). In 1776 the British colonial office instructed Captain Cook 'with the consent of the Natives to take possession, in the name of the King of Great Britain, of convenient situations in such countries as you may discover' (Reynolds 1999:130). However, Cook treated Australia as if it were terra nullius, an empty land. The accepted practice under international law was that the European powers were to take possession of lands with the consent of the Indigenous peoples, and treaty agreements were the means by which consent was gained. Why was the situation so different in Australia? Joseph Banks, who accompanied Cook on his expedition, simply declared that 'there was no probability while we were there of obtaining anything either by cession or purchase as there was nothing we could offer them they would take except provisions and those we wanted for ourselves' (Reynolds 1999: 131).

Indigenous peoples sovereign rights to their own lands and territories was recognised under international law by the United Nations International Court of Justice (ICJ) in 1975 in the *Western Sahara* case (1975) ICJ 12 where it was found that Western Sahara, being inhabited by Indigenous tribes, could not be regarded as terra nullius. The ICJ made it clear that 'whatever differences of opinion there may have been amongst jurists, the State practice of the relevant period indicates that territories inhabited by tribes of peoples having a social and political organisation were not regarded as terra nullius' (39 According to international law, as established by the ICJ in *Western Sahara*, it was thus clearly wrongful for Australia to have ever been regarded as a terra nullius country open to acquisition by occupation and 'peaceful' settlement.

Nonetheless, the British claim to Australia was justified in 1889 by the English Privy Council in the case of *Cooper v Stuart* (14 AC 286) when Australia was said to have been lawfully acquired by 'settlement', and New South Wales was considered 'practically unoccupied, without settled inhabitants or settled law at the time when it was peacefully annexed to the dominions.' Henry Reynolds has argued this view did not receive the support of the British Colonial Office and that concern about the rights of Aboriginal people resulted in the establishment in 1837 of a parliamentary committee who declared that it should have been obvious 'that the native inhabitants of any land have an incontrovertible right to their own soil; a plain and scared right, however, which seems not to have been understood' (Reynolds 1993).

There were some early challenges to the denial of Aboriginal sovereignty in the Australian courts, such as the 1836 New South Wales case of *R v Murrell* (1 Legge 72, however, the Court said 'although it might be granted that on the first taking possession of the Colony, the Aborigines were entitled to be recognised as free and independent, yet they were not in such a position with regard to strength as to be considered free and independent tribes. They had no sovereignty' ((Bartlett 1993:4). In the 1841 case of *R v Bon Jon* (Unreported) this same court found that Aboriginal people were a sovereign people who must be considered as 'distinct, though dependant tribes' entitled to govern themselves according to their own laws and customs (Bartlett 1993: 5). This latter judgment clearly drew from a series of decisions of Chief Justice Marshall of the United States Supreme Court which recognised the Indigenous peoples as 'domestic dependent nations' entitled to a degree of sovereignty, albeit one subject to the legislative powers of Congress (Williams 1991: 51).

The issue of Aboriginal sovereignty has been placed directly before the full court of the High Court of Australia only in the 1979 case of *Coe v The Commonwealth* (1979) 53 ALJR 403 where the Koori lawyer, Paul Coe, argued that Aboriginal nations were 'entitled not to be dispossessed thereof without bilateral treaty, lawful compensation and/or lawful international attention'. This case was rejected on the basis that Aboriginal sovereignty claims are not 'justiciable'—they cannot be considered by the court as the 'annexation of the east coast of Australia by Captain Cook in 1770 … were acts of state whose validity cannot be challenged' (408).

Coe's case also attempted to characterise Aboriginal people as a 'domestic dependant nation', consistent with the approach of the United States which has allowed Indian nations to exercise a considerable degree of self-government (Cassidy 1998: 106-109), one never accorded to Aboriginal and Torres Strait peoples of Australia. However, our High Court stated that the history of the relationships between white settlers and the Aboriginal people had differed from the United States and Aboriginal people were not, apparently unlike the Indigenous peoples of the US, organised as a 'distinct political society separated from others' they had no 'legislative, executive or judicial organs by which sovereignty might be exercised' (408).

The classification of Australia as a settled colony was maintained by the High Court in *Mabo*, despite the fact that the acquisition of Australia by settlement was supported by the racially discriminatory terra nullius doctrine—as only lands truly unoccupied could properly be acquired by way of 'peaceful settlement'. As Justices Deane and Gaudron explained 'the annexation of territory by 'settlement' came, however, to be recognised as applying to newly 'discovered' territory which was inhabited by native people' (77). It was the expanded and discriminatory doctrine of terra nullius that allowed for this to occur and yet *Mabo* rejected that doctrine as part of Australian law, and condemned it strongly. In the words of Justices Deane and Gaudron:

> The doctrine of terra nullius ... provided the legal basis for the dispossession of the Aboriginal peoples of most of their traditional lands. The acts and events by which that dispossession in legal theory was carried into practical effect constitute the darkest aspect of the history of this nation. The nation as a whole must remain diminished unless and until there is an acknowledgement of, and retreat from, those past injustices ...The lands of this continent were not terra nullius (109).

Although the issue of sovereignty was not argued before the court, Justice Brennan described the annexation of the Murray Islands to the Colony of Queensland as a prerogative act 'the validity of which is not justiciable in the municipal courts'. He also considered that challenges to sovereignty would 'fracture the skeleton of principle which gives the body of our law its shape and internal consistency' (43). Notwithstanding this analogy, Justice Brennan still acknowledged that under international law sovereignty could only be acquired over another territory by way of conquest, cession or occupation and settlement of lands that were properly terra nullius (32). In Australia an absence of either formal warfare or a treaty agreement meant that Indigenous sovereignty was not acquired by conquest or cession. The High Court now agrees that the occupation and settlement of our lands by way of the terra nullius doctrine was wrongful, however it still maintains that Australia is a country acquired by settlement and relies on the 'act of state' doctrine to avoid answering the question of how Aboriginal and Torres Strait Islander peoples were ever dispossessed of sovereignty. In *Isabel Coe on behalf of the Wiradjuri Tribe v The Commonweath* (1993) 68 ALJR 110, Chief Justice Mason said that *Mabo* is 'entirely at odds' with the 'notion' that any sovereignty resides with Aboriginal peoples although he does not explain his argument in any way and it is not a convincing claim—*Mabo* overturned the terra nullius doctrine that operated to deny both land title and sovereignty. A limited form of sovereignty that could recognise Indigenous peoples as 'domestic dependent nations' was again rejected.

The dismissal of Indigenous sovereignty by the High Court in the *Mabo* case has drawn strong criticism, Michael Mansell arguing that 'political conveniences' were relied upon 'to shut the door to any Aboriginal hopes for arguing Aboriginal sovereignty in the courts' (1992). Garth Nettheim agreeing that 'The fiction of terra nullius has thus been discarded in relation to Indigenous people's property rights though it remained intact in relation to their 'sovereignty' rights' (1998: 73). Irene Watson has argued that there is now a new myth—that terra nullius is dead, 'The

High Court has merely closeted terra nullius, and to replace it, the court has taken off the hanger the 'act of state' doctrine. The legal theory of terra nullius has remained intact. The real death of terra nullius would have dismantled the Australian legal system' (1997:48).

Canadian commentator Patrick Macklem points to the direct relationship between the racist legal fiction of terra nullius and the failure to recognise Aboriginal sovereignty 'The principle that the discovery of land inhabited by an indigenous population vests sovereignty in the discovering nation, is based on the proposition that indigenous people are insufficiently civilised or Christian to merit being viewed as competing sovereign powers' (1993:27). In *Mabo*, Justice Brennan criticized the principle that the Crown became the absolute beneficial owner of the whole continent, commenting that 'judged by any civilized standard such a law is unjust', and it is equally unjust, Macklem argues, to assert that the Crown can acquire the sovereignty over land inhabited by an Indigenous population by the mere act of settlement (27).

The International Court of Justice's Advisory Opinion in *Western Sahara* shows that the *act of state* doctrine referred to in *Mabo* does not act as a bar to international litigation, however, the rules of the ICJ are such that only states may be parties in cases before the court. Indigenous peoples throughout the world have been denied sovereignty and the associated status of statehood through the colonisation processes. Although there is the possibility of the General Assembly or the Security Council of the United Nations requesting the ICJ to give an advisory opinion on such a matter, this is highly unlikely as it is a most political and controversial act (Cassidy 1998:9). In *Thorpe v Commonwealth of Australia* (Unreported M15/1997) Robbie Thorpe from Victoria sought a court order that the Commonwealth take steps to obtain an advisory opinion from the ICJ on the issue of Aboriginal sovereignty. Justice Kirby was to decide that the claim raised 'purely political matters' and not legal issues that could be reviewed by a court of law (Indigenous Law Bulletin 1997).

In 1983 the Australian Senate Standing Committee on Constitutional and Legal Affairs considered the issue of Aboriginal sovereignty and found that it was defeated by the legal doctrine 'prescription' (1983: 45-46). For a claim of prescription to be substantiated the possession of territory must have been acquiesced or agreed to, and such possession must have been of a 'peaceful and uninterrupted' nature, however, Julie Cassidy describes the doctrine as a dubious one that it has never been conclusively supported by a decision of an international tribunal (1998:76). The Senate Committee did not point to any evidence to support their argument that the Australian continent had remained under the 'continuous and undisputed' sovereignty of the Commonwealth, many would argue that it was not and the frontier violence extensively documented (Reynolds: 1982) undermines this claim. The resistance of Indigenous peoples and opposition to British sovereignty can be evidenced by historical and political events such as the establishment of the Aboriginal Tent Embassy outside of Parliament House in Canberra in 1972 and the formation of the Aboriginal Provisional Government in the 1980's. There have been many statements of rights affirming our sovereignty including the Day of Mourning and Protest resolution (1939), the Yirrkala bark petitions (1963), the Barunga statement (1988), the Eva Valley statement (1993) and the Kalkaringi statement (1998).

Under the international law doctrine of reversion it is possible that sovereignty not ceded (given up) or extinguished may again become operative (Cassidy 1998: 65) and it has been argued that this original sovereignty remains and 'still adheres in the Aboriginal people of this land: it has never been extinguished by cession, by treaty, nor by formal purchase, nor by conquest; neither was it acquired by the invaders, the British/Australians, by peaceful settlement of an uninhabited land' (Gilbert 1993: 27). Still, the doctrine of reversion requires recognition by the United Nations membership and that is a political matter, not a question of law. Although colonialism was a principal concern of the UN there is serious resistance to the recognition of the sovereignty of Indigenous peoples on the part of UN states whom Irene Watson notes maintain that 'colonialism no longer exists' despite the fact that 'millions of Indigenous peoples still live a colonised existence' (1997: 56).

The most fundamental barrier to the recognition of a 'shared' sovereignty between Indigenous and non-Indigenous Australia derives from the traditional English view of sovereignty: it is indivisible and deriving from 'one supreme, irresistible, absolute, uncontrolled authority' (Reynolds 1998: 209). However Henry Reynolds has argued that 'the concept of sovereignty is undergoing intense scrutiny in many parts of the world' (1998: 209) and there is a move away from the concentration of sovereignty that occurred with the creation of strong centralised states. Reynolds describes the Australian federation as a division of sovereignty and precedent for the recognition of a level of Indigenous government (209).

Certainly the international treaty making that took place in accordance with international law can be seen to have allowed for a sharing of sovereignty between Indigenous and non-Indigenous peoples and governments. International law consistently acknowledged the sovereign rights of Indigenous peoples by way of treaty agreements such as the 1840 Treaty of Waitangi, which guaranteed the Maori peoples of New Zealand Aotearoa continued respect for their tino rangatiratanga or sovereign like authority (Durie 1998:177). Many such treaties were also signed in the United States and Canada and they were extensively considered by the United Nations in the 'Study on treaties, agreements and other constructive arrangements between states and Indigenous populations' (1999). Relevant to Australia, the study questioned how Indigenous peoples who did not enter into treaties with non-Indigenous States could possibly have been legally deprived of their international legal status? (288)

Self Determination

Like sovereignty, the right to self-determination is a human right of the utmost importance and is enshrined in the Treaty establishing the United Nations, the United Nations Charter, Article 1 which provides that 'All peoples have the right to self determination. By virtue of that right they freely determine their economic, social and cultural development.' The right to self-determination is also enshrined in Article 1 of the *International Covenant of Civil and Political Rights* (ICCPR). Australia is a signatory to, and bound to abide by, both these international instruments. Indigenous peoples' right to self-determination is currently being developed at the United Nations Commission on Human Rights in its consideration of the *Draft Declaration on the Rights of Indigenous Peoples* (the 'Draft Declaration').

The claims of sovereignty and self-determination are distinct and yet related: self-determination can be seen as a process or means by which the original sovereign powers of Indigenous peoples are in some way re-established (Nettheim 1993: 236). Lowitja Lois O'Donoghue, the first ATSIC Chairperson, described self-determination as 'the right to make decisions. These decisions affect the enjoyment and exercise of the full range of freedoms and human rights of Indigenous peoples' (1994: 5). Self-determination has also been adopted as policy by past governments and was considered to have underpinned the establishment by the former Labor government of the Aboriginal and Torres Strait Islander Commission (ATSIC). However, the limitations of ATSIC as a self-determining body have been visible, and were evidenced by the exclusion of ATSIC by the Howard government in the negotiations that resulted in the *Native Title Amendment Act 1998 (Cth)*. This legislation has been found to be racially discriminatory by the United Nations Committee for the Elimination of Racial Discrimination, who also condemned the Australian government over the 'lack of effective participation by Indigenous communities' in the legislative process (McGlade 2000).

The right of self-determination is provided by the *Draft Declaration on the Rights of Indigenous Peoples*. Article 3 adopts the language of the Human Rights Charter and the ICCPR, also expressing that the right is one belonging to Indigenous peoples. The position of the Australian Indigenous representatives is that Article 3 and the right to self-determination is of the utmost importance and 'fundamental to the integrity of the Declaration' (ATSIC 1996: 23). However, Indigenous people's right to self determination has not yet been accepted by the Commission on Human Rights (CHR), which is representative of governments, and a number of representative states have expressed opposition or serious reservations to Article 3. This stems from the fact that traditionally the exercise of self-determination included, as one option among many, secession or separation from the nation state. In 1998 the Australian government urged the United Nations to abandon self-determination in favor of 'self management' or 'self empowerment', terms noted by Mick Dodson and Sarah Pritchard to be 'without any basis in political theory or international law' (Dodson and Pritchard 1998: 6). The Australian government has since rejected the inclusion of 'self-determination' in the Draft Declaration, declaring that it 'implied the establishment of separate nations and laws' (Pritchard 2000: 31).

The issue of Indigenous peoples right to self-determination under international law is a complex one related to a number of international law instruments and decisions of the expert United Nations human rights committees. It was clarified in 1996 by the *Committee on the Elimination of Racial Discrimination* (General Recommendation No 27) who emphasised that the internal and external aspects of the right to self-determination must be distinguished. The internal aspect refers to the right of all peoples to 'pursue freely their economic, cultural and social development'—their right to take part in public affairs. This right means that governments must represent the whole population without discrimination based on race, colour, descent or national or ethnic origin. The external aspect refers to the right of peoples to determine their political status and place in the international community and includes the liberation of people under colonialism. Importantly the Committee called upon governments to fully implement the *International Convention on the Elimination of All Forms of Racial Discrimination* and confirmed that while a state has the right to the utmost respect for its 'territorial integrity' or boundaries, this was only so providing the government was a representative one without distinction as to 'race, creed or colour'.

It has been said that the right to internal self determination 'is best viewed as entitling a people to choose its political allegiance, to influence the political order under which it lives, and to preserve its cultural, ethnic, historical or territorial identity' (per Madam Daes cited in CAR 1993: 54). Internal self determination is embodied within the *Draft Declaration*, in particular Article 31, which provides that Indigenous peoples have 'as a specific form of exercising their right to self determination' the right to autonomy or self government in matters relating to their internal or local affairs (ATSIC 2001: 181-182). This shall include matters relating to culture, religion, education, information, media, health, housing, employment, social welfare, economic activities, land and resources management and environment.

Concern has been expressed that an internal/external dichotomy of self-determination may be misleading because some Indigenous peoples still live under non-self-governing territories and therefore have the full right to self-determination under international law (Pritchard 1994: 6). Also there are 'external' aspects or dimensions of the right to self-determination that allow for Indigenous peoples important international connections and opportunities, including attendance at the United Nations itself. And further, self-determination is positioned as an inevitable threat to territorial integrity even though many Indigenous peoples do not actually seek independent statehood. Secession also implies that Indigenous people originally submitted to the sovereignty of colonial powers and now seek to reassert their own sovereignty, as one Indigenous representative informed the CHR 'Indigenous people's homes and lands have been invaded and occupied and [yet] the accused is trying to create a crime of secession' (UNPO: 1997).

There is also a serious issue as to whether any limitation on the right to self-determination ('internal') specifically with respect to Indigenous peoples would itself amount to racial discrimination, as ATSIC informed the 1997 CHR Working Group 'To proclaim self-determination as a right of all peoples, and at the same time to deny or seek to limit its application to Indigenous peoples, surely offends the prohibition of racial discrimination'. (ATSIC 200: 57). Nonetheless, there is concern that Indigenous people's attainment of the right to self-determination may be hindered by the use of the term as a 'synonym' for secession (Pritchard 1994: 5). James Anaya views secession therefore as a remedial option available in 'limited contexts', in particular where 'substantive self determination for a particular group cannot otherwise be assured' (1996: 200).

The Commission on Human Rights has come no closer to the necessary agreement or consensus concerning the application of the right of self-determination to Indigenous peoples. A resolution recently adopted by the Sub-Commission on the Promotion and Protection of Human Rights on the International Decade of the World's Indigenous People appealed to the CHR to consider ways and means to accelerate the *Draft Declaration* (E/CN.4/2000/84). It was originally intended that the *Draft Declaration* be adopted no later than the end of the International Decade of the World's Indigenous People in 2004, however, international lawyer Megan Davis noted following the 2002 UN session that 'Progress remains slow and almost deliberately hindered' (Davis 2002: 9) and most troubling, there has been rapid progress on an alternative Draft Declaration text being drafted by states parties 'without transparency or consultation with Indigenous peoples' (Davis :9).

Treaty

The Indigenous claim to sovereignty, based on a wrongful acquisition of Australia by the British in 1788, and the emerging international Indigenous human right to self-determination, underpins calls for the reform of the Australian legal system—in particular, there have been and continue to be proposals for a treaty, and this has been linked to the need for constitutional reform.

In 1979 the National Aboriginal Conference (NAC) passed a resolution requesting that a 'Treaty of Commitment is executed between the Aboriginal Nation and the Australian Government' (Mosiadis: 24). The government, led by Prime Minster Fraser, indicated it was willing to consider the proposal and join discussions, however, they were opposed to a 'Treaty' on the basis that this may imply 'an internationally recognised agreement between two nations' (24). The NAC resolution was supported by a group of prominent non-Aboriginals led by HC 'Nugget' Coombs who formed a high profile organisation, 'The Aboriginal Treaty Committee', which aimed to raise awareness and support for a Treaty by way of media campaigns and political lobbying (Harris 1979). The government's position resulted in suggestions for the negotiation of a 'Makaratta' or 'compact' and the issue was referred to the Commonwealth Parliament's Senate Standing Committee on Constitutional and Legal Affairs. In 1983 the Committee released their report that also rejected the use of the term treaty, concluding that Aboriginal people were not a sovereign nation. However, they expressed support for a compact agreement on the basis that Aboriginal people have legitimate claims as 'recognised prior owners of the Australian continent' (125).

Treaty then appeared to have lapsed, possibly as a result of the disagreement over terminology, and also as a result of opposition from some Aboriginal people such as Pat O'Shane who rejected a treaty reasoning that it deflected 'collective attention from the basic demands for social justice' (1991: 147). In 1988 the Northern and Central Aboriginal Lands Council were to raise treaty at the Barunga festival in the Northern Territory and Prime Minister Bob Hawke was issued with the Barunga statement calling upon the Commonwealth 'to negotiate with us a Treaty or Compact recognising our prior ownership, continued occupation and sovereignty and affirming our human rights and freedoms' (Tickner 2001: 41). The Prime Minister acknowledged that there was a need for 'real and lasting reconciliation and honest negotiation between Aboriginal and non-Aboriginal citizens of this nation, leading to an agreement with the Aboriginal people—a treaty, a compact, call it what you will' (Brennan & Crawford 1990: 55). However, the Federal Opposition Leader, John Howard described treaty as 'utterly repugnant' claiming that it would 'increase rather than diminish hostility among some white Australians towards Aborigines' (Mosiadis: 49).

According to the then Minister for Aboriginal Affairs, Robert Tickner, the lack of progress on treaty was due to the 'implacable opposition' of the coalition party and resulting 'deep political divisions' (2001: 28). One of the last official acts of Prime Minister Hawke was to hang the Barunga statement on the walls of parliament house, and in doing so Hawke spoke not of treaty but of 'reconciliation' that could possibly be 'embodied in a document' (Tickner 2001: 42). It was this concept of reconciliation that was then promoted by the Government, despite the acknowledgment that it had no 'substantial base of support' on the part of government, the opposition, nor the Aboriginal and Torres Strait Islander peoples (Tickner: 28). Legislation establishing the Council for Aboriginal Reconciliation (CAR) was passed in 1991 and the ATSIC Board of Commissioners made it clear to government that treaty not be excluded from this possible agenda of Indigenous aspirations (Tickner: 38). Under the *Council for Aboriginal Reconciliation Act 1991 (Cth)* the CAR was required to seek views on whether any 'document of reconciliation' would benefit the Australian community as a whole.

Despite the CAR's mandate to consider some formal agreement with Aboriginal people the government's ambivalence was clear and the Council was instructed to 'concentrate on the process of reconciliation and not on an instrument which might become an outcome of that process' (Kelly 1993:10). Loretta Kelly noted the primary focus on the education of non-Indigenous Australians, 'whether or not an agreement or treaty were to result' (1993: 10). ATSIC was to subsequently advise the CAR that the development of a document of reconciliation become a 'focus point' and that such a document include 'a statement of indigenous rights and provide a basis for their entitlement' (CAR 1994b:178).

The Council presented the 'Australian Declaration Towards Reconciliation' to the Prime Minister at the Corroboree 2000 event, which signified the end of the Council's statutory term. The Declaration has importance as an educational and awareness-raising measure, but it is still a symbolic statement that does not require legal or substantive recognition of Indigenous peoples' rights. However, the CAR's Final Report to Government importantly recommends that each government and parliament:

- recognise that this land and its waters were settled as colonies without treaty or consent and that to advance reconciliation it would be most desirable if there were agreements or treaties; and

- negotiate a process through which this might be achieved that protects the political, legal, cultural and economic position of Aboriginal and Torres Strait Islander peoples (2000:106).

The Australian Parliament was also called upon to enact legislation in order to put in place a process to unite Australians by way of agreement or treaty, through which the unresolved issues of reconciliation could be resolved (106). There has, however, been no implementation of these recommendations of the Council that has now dissolved.

At Corroboree, the ATSIC Chairperson, Geoff Clarke, publicly confirmed the importance of treaty and the need for the reconciliation process to 'lead us into a new era of constitutional consent'. This position was consistent with the ATSIC recommendation to the CAR in 1994 that the development of a treaty must be linked to the process of constitutional reform (CAR 1994b: 176) and the 1995 consultations into social justice measures that found widespread support for treaty which they said must 'forge the ground rules for relationships between indigenous and non-indigenous Australians based on justice and equity and the proper recognition of indigenous rights' (1995: 64).

The constitutional developments of 1900 were exclusionary toward the Indigenous peoples and that aspect of history was condemned by Patrick Dodson who explained that 'our Constitution was drafted in the spirit of terra nullius. Land was divided, power was shared, structures were established, on the illusion of vacant possession. When Aboriginal people showed up—which they inevitably did—they had to be subjugated, incarcerated or eradicated: to keep the myth of terra nullius alive' (cited in CAR 1993: 6).

Indigenous peoples were referred to twice in the new Constitution, and both instances were exclusionary. Section 51(26) gave the Commonwealth powers to make laws with respect to 'The people of any race, other than the aboriginal race in any State, for whom it was deemed necessary to make special laws'. The 'races power' as s. 51(26) is known, was crucial to the government's white Australian policy that discriminated against Asians and other coloured peoples. Indigenous people were originally excluded from the scope of s. 51(26) and were considered a State responsibility. Also, under section 127 'aboriginal natives' were, for the purpose of being excluded from the national census, not to be counted in the reckoning of the peoples of the Commonwealth or a State. Sustained pressure from Aboriginal organisations and the prospect of international scrutiny influenced by the signing of the International Convention on the Elimination of all Forms of Racial Discrimination (ICERD) by the Australian government in 1966, led to the federal referendum of 1967 which saw the reference to Aborigines in s. 51(26) being removed and s.127 removed altogether (Williams 2001). However, section 25 of the Constitution, which permits discrimination on the basis of race with respect to voting, was not removed.

The Commonwealth Constitution today does not provide for the adequate protection of human rights, and this has led to considerable debate concerning the adoption of a Bill of Rights—a constitutional document that would entrench human rights in the Australian domestic legal system. Larissa Behrendt has described Australia as a 'human-rights wasteland'—the United Kingdom, Canada, New Zealand, South Africa and the United States have all now enacted, either constitutionally or legislatively, a Bill of Rights (2000: 24). The prohibition against racial discrimination required by the ICERD is implemented domestically in Australia by the Race Discrimination Act (RDA) 1975 (Cth). However, the RDA, despite its impressive effect in invalidating discriminatory state native title legislation, is still Commonwealth legislation that may be repealed, amended or 'suspended' by subsequent Commonwealth legislation and this has effectively occurred as a result of the 1998 native title amendments (Trigg 1999).

There are a number of possible ways in which Indigenous rights can be recognised and protected by the Commonwealth Constitution. Such reform is consistent with international human rights development where it has been proposed that 'the existing State has a duty to accommodate the aspirations of indigenous peoples through constitutional reforms designed to share power democratically' (per Madam Daes cited in Barsh 1994: 190). Firstly, the Constitution's preamble could be amended to refer to the Aboriginal and Torres Strait Islander peoples. As it now stands it is an outdated reference to some of the colonies (not all) agreeing to form a Commonwealth federation. According to Lowitja Lois O'Donoghue 'It says very little about what it is to be Australian. It says practically nothing about how we find ourselves here—save being an amalgamation of former colonies. It says nothing of how we should behave towards each other as human beings and as Australians' (cited in Brennan 1994: 18).

A new preamble was agreed to between the Prime Minister and Senator Aden Ridgeway as part of the 1999 unsuccessful republic referendum. This proposed preamble included a reference to 'honouring Aborigines and Torres Strait Islanders, the nation's first people, for their deep kinship with their lands and for their ancient and continuing cultures which enrich the life of our country'. ATSIC, who expressed concern over the limited consultations concerning this proposed preamble and the use of the term 'kinship', arguing that it failed to recognise Indigenous peoples continuing custodianship of the land, had previously proposed the following preamble:

> Whereas the territory of Australia has long been occupied by Aboriginal peoples and Torres Strait Islanders whose ancestors inhabited Australia and maintained traditional titles to the land for thousands of years before British settlement (Constitutional Centenary Foundation 1999: 7).

Secondly, the Constitution could be amended to guarantee non-discrimination:

> Everyone has the right to freedom from discrimination on the ground of race, colour, ethnic or national origin, sex, marital status, political, religious or ethical belief (Constitutional Centenary Foundation 1999: 5).

This issue has become pressing following the decision of the High Court of Australia in *Kartinyeri v The Commonwealth (1998)* 183 CLR 337, a case concerning the Constitution's 'race power' under s.51(26). The question raised by *Kartinyeri* was whether this power could support laws that discriminate negatively against Aboriginal peoples—only two judges were prepared to limit the scope of the power and confine it to laws made for a beneficial purpose. Justice Kirby did so by examining the history of the 1967 referendum, arguing that it was clearly aimed at redressing the discriminatory nature of the Constitution, and allowing for the Commonwealth, with the States, to act in the best interests of the Aboriginal people of Australia (Williams 2001: 10). However, the majority of the Court either did not agree or did not address the question—thus failing to resolve the issue of whether the Commonwealth possesses the power under the Constitution to enact racially discriminatory laws (Williams 2001: 11). The need for a further constitutional referendum was also supported by the CAR in their final report to government in 2000 whereby they recommended that the Commonwealth Parliament prepare legislation for a referendum that seeks to

- recognise Aboriginal and Torres Strait Islander peoples as the first peoples of Australia in a new preamble to the Constitution; and

- remove section 25 of the Constitution and introduce a new section making it unlawful to adversely discriminate against any people on the ground of race (CAR: 106).

Thirdly, the body of the Constitution could be amended in some way to recognise Indigenous rights, possibly by the incorporation of a treaty itself. This has been supported by Patrick Dodson who called upon the 'Aboriginal unfinished business' to be addressed by a formal agreement recognising and guaranteeing our rights within the Australian Constitution (2000: 29). There has also been support from a summit meeting of Indigenous leaders hosted by ATSIC where it was agreed that the Constitution's preamble was not the 'right section of the Constitution to deal with Aboriginal peoples and Torres Strait Islanders rights'. Rather, the body of the Constitution should be amended to 'ensure proper recognition of Aboriginal peoples and Torres Strait Islanders status' (ATSIC 1999b: 23).

The possibility of a treaty agreement being supported by the Constitution was considered by the Senate Standing Committee in their 1983 report in which they noted that there were two possible ways of providing a specific constitutional basis for such an agreement. Firstly, the inclusion within the Constitution of the full text of an agreement once it is settled. Secondly, the amendment of the Constitution by the assertion of a broad enabling power granting specific constitutional power to negotiate an agreement between the Commonwealth and Aboriginal people based on certain principles. Such a power could be similar to the existing s.105A, which gives effect to financial agreements negotiated between the States and Commonwealth. It was this option that was preferred by the Committee who recommended that:

> The Government should, in consultation with the Aboriginal people, give
> consideration, as the preferred method of legal implementation of a compact, to

the insertion within the Constitution of a provision along the lines of section 105A, which would confer a broad power on the Commonwealth to enter into a compact with representatives of the Aboriginal people. Such a provision would contain a non-exclusive list of those matters which would form an important part of the terms of the compact, expressing in broad language the types of subjects to be dealt with (xii).

Mick Dodson has supported the treaty making option of section 105A stressing that this power makes agreements binding on all Parliaments thereby giving them 'Constitutional force' (Dodson 2001). A 'national framework agreement' protected by the Commonwealth Constitution could provide for regional negotiations and agreements, which may also attract a level of constitutional protection. The national treaty could deal with matters of national relevance, such as the entrenched prohibition of racial discrimination, and also importantly provide local agreements (or 'treaties') with agreed standards or negotiating principles.

Negotiations for a treaty or treaties in Australia may require the establishment of an independent Treaty Commission (Dodson 2000: 19). There are international models that may be considered in this respect, most obviously the Waitangi Tribunal of Aotearora New Zealand. Any such model must be a bicultural one that is properly representative of Indigenous peoples. Treaty negotiations in Australia must also be informed by a commitment to reconciliation and to the ongoing and developing nature of Indigenous and non-Indigenous relations. The work and future of the Canadian British Columbia Treaty Commission has apparently been seriously impeded by an attitude to treaty making underpinned by notions of claims extinguishment and 'final agreements'. Taiaiake Alfred has described this process as being 'designed to solve the perceived problem of indigenous nationhood by extinguishing it and bringing indigenous peoples into Canada's own domestic political and legal structures with certainty and finality (2002).

In Aoteaoroa New Zealand the concept of the 'partnership' between the Crown and the Maori peoples that derives from the *Treaty of Waitangi 1840* has required treaty negotiations be conducted in the utmost good faith, and this has resulted in significant treaty settlements (Durie 1998). Nonetheless, it also appears that Government concerns with 'finality' and 'fiscal envelopes' have impeded what Paul McHugh describes as the necessary 'establishment of mechanisms to manage the ongoing relationship between Crown and tribe, from which exit is not an option' (1999: 461). McHugh has been very critical of the Australian legal process in this respect describing the *NTA (1993)* as 'geared towards establishing and extinguishing Aboriginal title over Crown land and [making] scant provision for the establishment of a comprehensive framework of relationships between the Crown and the owner group' (1998: 119).

Conclusion

In 1992 the High Court of Australia, with the Indigenous peoples, applauded the overdue recognition of native title and many people truly believed that the decision signified the 'retreat from injustice' that it purported to be. There was hope that the Australian common law could further develop in a non-discriminatory manner toward Indigenous peoples, and the strong rejection of the racist doctrine of terra nullius strengthened that hope. A decade later and the same cannot be said to be true, the developments of native title under the law have been discriminatory toward Indigenous peoples. The native title fiction of 'settlement' remains embedded in the Australian law, and continues to support the denial of the fundamental justice claims to sovereignty, self-determination and treaty that have been outlined in this paper.

There has been much discussion within Aboriginal and Torres Strait Islander communities about the need for treaty and constitutional reform and in encouraging debate, ATSIC has identified the 'mistake of terra nullius', reminding that the British acquisition of Australia in 1788 was wrongful, it has questioned our lack of 'place under the Constitution' and asked whether a 'treaty may be one way of achieving some of the things that the Constitution fails to do' (ATSIC 2001). The Reconciliation process and the recommendations of the CAR also highlight treaty as central to reconciliation between the Australian people as a whole (CAR 2000).

Indigenous laws and customs have survived many tides of history—old and new— and our rights and responsibilities as the first peoples of the land continue. A spirit for justice—and our claims to sovereignty, self-determination and treaty—will never be relinquished.

> Our title to land is spiritual
>
> And man made laws can never take that away
>
> That law has been in place many thousands of years
>
> It began in the Dreamtime
>
> It is with us today
>
> It will be forever
>
> *Wadjularbinna*
>
> *Elder of the Gungalidda Nation 2002*

Hannah McGlade is an Indigenous lawyer who is currently completing her PhD at Murdoch University.

International Human Rights Law and the Domestic Treaty Process
Megan Davis

Introduction

The international law of human rights will play a vital role in any domestic dialogue regarding the development of a treaty for indigenous Australia. The international human rights framework established through the United Nations provides a valuable source of human rights standards and jurisprudence that could be used in the discussion about the content of a treaty. These international human rights standards will be useful in relation to many potential areas of negotiation such as the right to equality, an entrenched prohibition of racial discrimination, and issues of resource and access capacity in key areas of concern for indigenous people like education, employment and health. Such standards are even more authoritative considering the developments of the past three decades of an emerging body of international law relating specifically to indigenous peoples.

In this paper I initially summarise some key concepts in international law, providing a basic outline of the international human rights framework and emphasise the importance of Australia's international obligations and ongoing commitment to the United Nations human rights system. These are basic concepts that all Australian citizens must understand to be able to participate in an informed debate of not only indigenous peoples issues but also about international human rights law in general and the relevance of the United Nations to Australia. This will be followed by a discussion of indigenous people in the context of international human rights law, surveying in particular recent developments of indigenous involvement at the United Nations. The United Nations has provided an important forum in which indigenous peoples have been able to discuss grievances from within their state, develop international human rights standards and has successfully promoted the specific concerns of indigenous peoples throughout the world. This overview is essential in illustrating the impact of indigenous voices at the United Nations and its contribution to a growing body of customary international law pertaining to indigenous peoples.

Ultimately I hope to impress upon the reader the relevance of importing internationally developed human rights standards into a domestic treaty document. Recourse to such international standards is even more vital at a time when the Australian government is hostile to external influence in the ongoing debate over Australian human rights protection. Indeed it is true that many indigenous peoples are yet to be convinced of the value and relevance of international conferences at the United Nations, international law and to a far greater degree, a treaty. Yet even if they are not convinced of the value of international law or indeed a treaty, most people would be concerned that indigenous peoples and a growing number of Australians have to look outside of Australia to supranational institutions to argue for protection of their most fundamental human rights. This is damning evidence of the lack of rights protections in Australia. This inadequate protection of rights and freedoms is unusual in the modern common law world as Canada, New Zealand, South Africa and even the United Kingdom all have a Bill of Rights. With most of these countries also having some form of treaty with their First Peoples perhaps it is time for Australia to actually become the modern inclusive participatory democracy it claims to be. A domestic treaty for indigenous Australia could be a first step in the right direction.

International Law

International law is a body of both unwritten and written rules and laws designed to regulate and govern the relationship between states and indeed the conduct of subjects within those states. States generally consider this law to be binding upon them. A treaty is the most common form of international law that is considered to be a formal agreement between states in a written form that is governed by international law. Treaties are also sometimes referred to as 'conventions' or 'covenants'. How laws in relation to treaties are interpreted and governed can be found in the primary document regulating treaties at international law: the *Vienna Convention on the Law of Treaties 1969* ('VCLT'). The VCLT defines a treaty as 'an international agreement concluded between states in written form and governed by international law' (Article 2 (1)(a) VCLT 1969).

For an international treaty to have effect in domestic Australian law, it first needs to be signed by the Executive, which in practice in Australia are the Prime Minister and Senior Ministers. Technically, they have the final decision as to whether to sign and ratify a treaty however prior to any substantive decision being taken most treaties are tabled in both Houses of Parliament after their initial signing for at least 15 sitting days. In Australia, there is also the Joint Standing Committee on Treaties (JSCOT) that examines tabled treaties. The purpose of the Committee is to review and report on all treaty actions proposed by the Government. Treaty action means bilateral and multilateral treaties in all areas from trade to human rights including amendments to treaties, withdrawals from treaties and new treaties. The establishment of the Committee is to increase transparency of the treaty making process in Australia.

It is important to note that the initial step of signing a treaty does not give that treaty or its provisions effect in Australian domestic law. To have effect in Australian domestic law there also needs to be an act of transformation or enabling act that implements the treaty into the Australian legal system.

Another significant aspect of international law is 'customary international law'. Customary international law does not derive from any written treaties or written documents. It is law that has derived from the practice or custom of states and their usual behaviour. This means the 'usual' way in which states consistently behave in relation to a particular law. The important thing about customary international law is that it binds all states. It cannot be limited in the way that treaties are in that they apply only to those states that ratify or accede to them. There are two considerations that are attributed to customary international law, firstly that there should be consistency in state practice and secondly there should be a belief in the obligation of the custom being practiced (opinion juris).

The principle of *jus cogens* also exists at customary international law. *Jus cogens* reflects a pre-emptory norm or rule that is considered by the international community to be of such importance that it cannot be derogated from or limited in any way (such as through a treaty). The only way to modify *jus cogens* is through the development of another general principle at international law of the same nature. This is outlined in article 53 of the VCLT. For indigenous peoples important examples of *jus cogens* are the prohibition of slavery, genocide and racial discrimination.

The debate so far: the law of treaties

The international law of treaties is significant for indigenous people in the treaty debate because of the position held by the Aboriginal Torres Strait Islander Commission (ATSIC) that there can indeed be other forms of treaties such as a domestic treaty between the government and the Aboriginal and Torres Strait Islander people. This is not the position of the Australian Commonwealth government currently led by John Howard who has rejected calls for a treaty arguing primarily that a nation cannot make a treaty with itself. However as Ivan Shearer has pointed out the VCLT does 'expressly recognise that there can be other forms of agreement' (Shearer, 2002). This could potentially be 'between states and other subjects of international law, the legal force of which is to be determined by applicable rules of international law independent of the Convention'. There are many possibilities that can be explored by indigenous peoples however, as Shearer does recognise, there is no general 'recognised capacity of non-state entities to enter into treaty relations' (Shearer, 2002).

To adequately understand the main objections and resistance to a treaty in Australia, it is important to outline the dominant theory of 'state sovereignty' as organised at international law. Sovereign states are entitled to fully govern their own affairs without undue influence from other states. States are considered to be legal entities if they have all the characteristics of statehood that are outlined in the *Montevideo Convention on the Rights and Duties of States 1933*. Under this Convention, for a state to be legally recognised as a state at international law, four elements must be satisfied. There must be a defined territory, there must be a permanent population, there must be an effective government and there must be the ability to enter into international relations. Nations like Australia or New Zealand are considered to be sovereign states.

The Australian government relies upon this dominant international notion of state sovereignty. Nevertheless at international law, many groups, for example, indigenous peoples, people of West Papua, Palestinian people, the Basque people, contest this dominant notion. Clearly, for some Australians, a domestic treaty process in the 21st century challenges this approach to sovereignty.

'From the United Nations perspective the strong category of group claims is especially sensitive and problematic and is seen as threatening the territorial integrity of important members' (Falk 2000, p. 128).

This is one explanation of why Australia argues internationally and domestically that indigenous sovereignty claims and the domestic treaty process could represent or characterise a weakening or derogation of that state sovereignty.

Human rights

Human rights can be defined as claims to fundamental dignity and respect that result from one's membership of the human race. That is to say human rights are a right or claim of all human beings by virtue of their humanity alone (Levin 1981, p. 15) and they are inalienable and cannot be derogated from. They are 'the conditions necessary for people to live lives of dignity and value' (Charlesworth 2002, p. 41). The United Nations also claims human rights as an attempt to define basic dignity and worth of the human being and his or her most fundamental entitlements. Such entitlements are universal and range from civil and political rights like the right to freedom of speech or right to peaceful assembly, to economic, social and cultural rights such as the right to food and water, the right to shelter and the right to education. These claims or rights to dignity and respect have been translated over the course of the past century into international agreements and institutions that are now commonly known as international human rights law and the international human rights system.

Collective rights: A challenge to individual human rights system

A legitimate challenge to the Western human rights framework is the historically 'individual' nature of rights in its discourse and structures. This is to the exclusion of claims to 'collective rights' as asserted by indigenous peoples around the world. Collective rights mean the rights of the group or community collectively as opposed to merely the rights of an individual.

Western human rights discourse has promoted the individual as being paramount within the system yet this is at odds with indigenous communal and collective cultural practices. Group rights have therefore been determined restrictively:

> Protection of group identity, whether involving religious, cultural or gender has generally been approached as a matter of individual freedom to engage in group activity. (Falk 2000, p.127)

Collective rights are recognised in numerous international human rights law instruments, for example *the International Convention on the Elimination of All Forms of Racial Discrimination (1969)* affirms collective rights in Articles 1(a), 2, 4(a) and 14. *The International Labour Organization Indigenous and Tribal Peoples Convention 1989*, Convention 169 uses the term 'indigenous peoples' throughout the convention. *The 1986 African Charter on Human and Peoples Rights* provides recognition of indigenous peoples claims to collective rights (Art 19, Art 20, Art 21, Art 22, Art 23 and Art 24) and the *1978 UNESCO Declaration on Race and Racial Prejudice* also affirms collective rights (Article 6(1)).

The progress of the United Nations Working Group on the Draft Declaration on the rights of Indigenous Peoples' has been controversial partly due to its focus on collective rights. States' reluctance to acknowledge collective rights informs the slow progress. The dominance of the individual notion of human rights at international law translated into universal standards and supranational structures has undoubtedly hampered indigenous peoples attempts at seeking redress and ultimately survival in the modern world.

'Historically, the refusal to recognise non-European peoples as 'sovereign' greatly constrained their capacity to shape the development of rules of international law. This brings into question the capacity of international law to achieve justice today. The ongoing struggle by indigenous peoples to be recognised as peoples entitled to self-determination and as subjects of international law is one of the contemporary manifestations of this history.' (Anne Orford 2000, p 19)

For indigenous peoples, Orford raises a very astute consideration of how international law has developed and continues to develop. Historically the unique interests and culture of indigenous peoples have not been considered in terms of the development of international rules and principles. This was quite deliberate and has heavily influenced the development of municipal legal systems. In terms of collective rights, their incorporation and recognition in the treaty dialogue alongside fundamental civil and political, economic, cultural and social rights allows some of the imbalance and injustice to be addressed.

The International human rights framework

The primary institution of international law in contemporary world law and politics is the United Nations. It was in 1945 that representatives of 50 countries met in San Francisco at the United Nations Conference on International Organisation to draw up the United Nations Charter. The United Nations officially came into existence on 24 October 1945. It was in the United Nations Charter that the first reference to the rights of individuals and the role of the states in promoting universal respect for human rights emerged. The United Nations currently has a membership of 191 states.

The United Nations has also become the primary facilitator of international human rights discourse. While human rights as a discourse had been developing for centuries, following the devastation wrought by the Second World War and the tragedies of among many, the Jewish people in Nazi Germany, the international community moved toward a formal articulation of the principles and values that must guide every state in its conduct toward individuals within their own domestic jurisdiction.

'Ever since the end of the Second World War promoting the respect for, and observance of, human rights and fundamental freedom everywhere in the world has been a major concern of he international community.' (Van Boven 1997, p. 3).

Today, the international human rights framework is constituted by the major covenants and treaties, which were drafted by and have been agreed on by the nation of states at the United Nations. The principle statement of fundamental human rights as alluded to in the United Nations Charter is the Universal Declaration of Human Rights, which was unanimously adopted and signed by the United Nations General Assembly on the 10 December 1948. *The Universal Declaration of Human Rights* ('UDHR') along with *the International Covenant on Civil and Political Rights* ('ICCPR') and *the International Covenant on Economic Social and Cultural Rights* (ICESCR) form what is commonly referred to as the 'International Bill of Human Rights'. The guiding principles of human rights that were articulated in the UDHR have also been reflected in the other United Nations human rights instruments. Some of these international instruments include:

- The Convention on the Elimination of All Forms of Racial Discrimination (CERD)
- The Convention on the Elimination of All Forms of Discrimination Against Women (CEDAW)
- The Convention on the Rights of the Child (CROC)
- The Convention Against Torture and Other Cruel, Inhuman or Degrading Treatment or Punishment (CAT)

In Australia some of these treaties have been incorporated into the Federal domestic legal system through legislation. For example the *Racial Discrimination Act 1975 (Cth)* incorporates the Convention on the Elimination of All Forms of Racial Discrimination. The *Sex Discrimination Act 1984 (Cth)* translates some aspects but not all of the obligations under the Convention on the Elimination of All Forms of Discrimination Against Women 1979 into domestic law as well as certain aspects of the International Labour Organisation Convention 156. These Acts are monitored and administered through the Human Rights and Equal Opportunity Commission (HREOC) established by the *Human Rights and Equal Opportunity Commission Act 1986 (Cth)*.

The major human rights conventions mentioned above also have accompanying Committees that oversee the commitment and implementation of states. The mandate of each committee differs, however generally they address and review the conduct of states that have signed their respective treaty as well as respond to individual complaints through an individual complaint mechanism. The Committees provide negative and positive general comment and observations about each state's commitment to the specific obligations of the treaty. They also make recommendations and comments on the various articles or provisions of a relevant convention. This is to provide states like Australia with guidance and information on how to most effectively fulfil their obligations under the Convention.

Australia and the International Human Rights system

Australia's respect of indigenous rights and commitment to eliminating racial discrimination were called into question when the CERD committee commented on the racially discriminatory conduct of Australia in legislating away native title. In signing the treaty and giving effect to it in legislation, Australia was agreeing to:

> pursue by all means and without delay a policy of eliminating racial discrimination and to amend, rescind or nullify any laws and regulations which have the effect of creating or perpetuating racial discrimination (CERD).

The committee's criticism centred on the conduct of the Australian Commonwealth government led by Prime Minister John Howard with respect to the amendments made in 1998 to the *Native Title Act 1993(Cth)*. These amendments allowed for the discrimination against indigenous native titleholders in favour of the rights of non-indigenous landholders through the suspension of the RDA. The CERD committee found that the government failed to negotiate and consult adequately with indigenous peoples over the amendments. An interesting comment the Committee made related to the ease in which parliament can override important legislation like the RDA that was suspended by the 1998 amendments.

'The Committee is concerned over the absence from Australian law of any entrenched guarantee against racial discrimination that would override subsequent law of the Commonwealth, states and territories'. (CERD/C/304/Add.101 at 6).

The Committee was highlighting an issue that is significant for indigenous Australians in that there are too few rights and freedoms protected by Australian law. This again raises the importance of entrenching rights in a statutory or constitutional form beyond the reach of populist whims of governments of the day.

Indigenous peoples at the United Nations

According to the United Nations there are more than 300 million indigenous people worldwide in 70 different countries. The past three decades have seen indigenous peoples make enormous inroads into the consciousness of the United Nations and international law. This has occurred through improved access and transparency of the UN structures and more importantly, the employment of human rights discourse in the course of ongoing relationships with the state. Through the UN indigenous peoples have been able to highlight the injustices that have been suffered and the inequity that has been entrenched as a result of successive waves of imperialism, colonisation and now trade liberalisation. The demand for increased awareness of indigenous peoples' issues led the United Nations Sub-Commission on the Prevention of Discrimination and Protection of Minorities to enlist Martinez Cobo of Ecuador to conduct a comprehensive study of discrimination against indigenous peoples in 1971. (E/CN.4/Sub2/1986/7) As a result of this study the United Nations has come to define indigenous peoples as:

> … those people having an historical continuity with pre-invasion and pre-colonial societies who consider themselves distinct from other sectors of the societies now prevailing in those territories or parts of them. They form at present non-dominant sectors of society and are determined to preserve, develop and transmit to future generations, their ancestral territories, and their ethnic

> identity, as the basis of their continued existence as peoples in accordance with
> their own cultural patterns, social institutions, and legal systems.

Since the time of the Martinez Cobo study, indigenous participation in the United Nations system has increased dramatically. Currently there are fifteen indigenous non-governmental organizations that have gained United Nations Economic and Social Council (ECOSOC) consultative status. This consultative status is vital to the capacity of indigenous peoples to attend certain meetings or working groups within the system. Article 71 of the Charter of the United Nations, states that 'NGO's with concerns falling within the competence of the Economic and Social Council and its subsidiary bodies may be granted, if they so request, consultative status with this Council'.

Australia's indigenous peoples, particularly ATSIC, have a strong record of participation at United Nations meetings on indigenous issues in Geneva. International human rights law is an important aspect of ATSIC's work and this is highlighted in the ATSIC preamble that acknowledges the importance of Australia's obligations under United Nations human rights treaties. Past participants have included ATSIC Chairpersons from Lois O'Donoghue and Gatjil Djerrkura to Geoff Clark. The Foundation for Aboriginal Islander Research Action (FAIRA) has also forged a strong reputation in lobbying at the United Nations and was the main organization responsible for the communication to CERD concerning the discriminatory derogatory impact of the Native Title amendments as well as repatriation of human remains. The National Aboriginal Islander Legal Services Secretariat (NAILSS) is a regular participant as well as Torres Strait Islander organizations.

There are many important initiatives that the United Nations have undertaken specifically to address and improve the human rights of indigenous peoples. In 1982, a United Nations subsidiary body, the Sub-Commission on the Promotion and Protection of Human Rights was authorised to establish the United Nations Working Group on Indigenous Peoples (UN WGIP) to monitor developments of indigenous peoples. Its function is to gauge the major concerns relating to indigenous peoples and human rights (ECOSOC resolution 1982/34) and develop standards for indigenous rights. Although the WGIP cannot hear specific grievances about states it has allowed indigenous peoples to voice major issues of concern including human rights violations. The WGIP attracts the highest number of participants for a UN working group, more than any other in the entire United Nations system.

In the ECOSOC resolution establishing the WGIP, there are two key roles identified for the WGIP. The first role is to review developments pertaining to the promotion and protection of the human rights and fundamental freedoms of indigenous populations. The second important role is to give special attention to the evolution of standards concerning the rights of such populations. The WGIP also has a thematic mandate and each year explores different issues of concern for indigenous peoples for example education and children and youth.

On 21 December 1993, the General Assembly of the United Nations passed a resolution (48/163) declaring the International Decade of the World's Indigenous People for the years 1995-2004. The United Nations often proclaim dedicated decades in an attempt to celebrate or bring to the attention of the world important themes or issues that are facing the people of the world. The indigenous decade was proclaimed with a view to strengthening partnerships and increasing awareness of the issues of indigenous people around the world, its slogan being: 'Indigenous People: partnership in action'.

Recently, the Commission on Human Rights ('CHR') decided to appoint a Special Rapporteur for indigenous issues (resolution 2001/57) and this appointment is a significant development in indigenous affairs at the United Nations. The Special Rapporteur has a particular mandate as defined by the CHR and the role is to collate and exchange information with relevant sources such as Governments, indigenous communities and non-governmental organizations. The Special Rapporteur will make proposals and recommendations to the CHR for appropriate measures to take in remedying and improving the status of indigenous peoples, their freedoms and human rights. The first Special Rapporteur, Mr Rudolfo Stavenhagen from Mexico has now been appointed and it is expected he will work closely with both the WGIP and the Permanent Forum.

Draft Declaration on the Rights of Indigenous Peoples

Currently a Working Group of the Commission on Human Rights is attempting to seek agreement on a draft of the Declaration on the Rights of Indigenous Peoples (United Nations Doc E/CN4/Sub2/1994/2/Add1/). The original Draft Declaration was written by the WGIP in consultation with indigenous peoples who had participated in the development of the text since 1985. The participation of indigenous people in its drafting is unique and was an outcome of the role of the UN WGIP as a standard setting body.

The Draft Declaration will not create any binding obligations under international law. If passed it will be an aspirational document on the rights of indigenous peoples. There are two potential ways in which the Draft Declaration when adopted could have effect in law. Firstly it could become binding if rights contained in the Draft Declaration were elevated to the level of a convention in which those states that sign become legally bound by the instrument. Secondly it could become binding by virtue of customary international law:

> Draft declarations ... may not be legally binding but are evidence of evolving standards and form a crucial part of the process by which guiding statements of principles become binding law (Triggs 1999, p. 375).

The Draft Declaration is important as it relates to the setting of international standards on the protection of the rights of indigenous peoples and for this reason has been very controversial for State parties that have large indigenous populations such as Australia, Canada and the United States. There are 7 sections of the Draft Declaration and the following is a brief summary of each section:

Self-determination, equality and freedom from adverse discrimination

Sections 1 to 5 deal with general principles and rights to nationality, self-determination, equality and freedom from adverse discrimination. Article 3 of the declaration is consistent with common article 1 of the ICCPR and the ICESCR that deal with self-determination stating that: 'Indigenous peoples have the right to self-determination. By virtue of this right they freely determine their political status and freely pursue their economic, social and cultural development'. The issue of Self-determination is an extremely controversial and contested concept at both domestic and international levels. Indigenous people at the Draft Declaration often draw attention to the fact that the right to self-determination is protected by both the ICCPR and ICESCR. Indigenous people also employ Western liberal rhetoric in arguing that the notion of self-determination is inextricably linked with democratic participation, 'the denial of self-determination is essentially incompatible with true democracy. Only if the people's right to self-determination is respected can a democratic society flourish' (Stavenhagen 1996, p. 8). In Australia because of the minimalist form of participation at the ballot box every 3 or 4 years, minority interests such as the unique needs and aspirations of indigenous Australians are dwarfed by the needs and aspirations of the majority who are predominantly all white Australians. Yet the growing link between self-determination and democracy in international law clearly cogitates for greater control by indigenous Australians over the decision-making and management of our own affairs and greater participation in Australian democracy. Such a link can clearly inform any future treaty dialogue.

Life, integrity and security

Sections 6–11 deal with principles and rights to life, integrity and security. This includes genocide (Article 6), collective and individual rights to maintain distinct identities (Article 8), the right not to be forced or relocated from lands (Article 10) and the right to special protection in armed conflict (Article 11). Some examples of difficulties for states in passing these articles arise in relation to emergencies. Some states believe that they do not have to gain indigenous consent prior to removal or relocation in circumstances of emergency such as natural disaster, public health and safety, public order or public works.

Culture, spirituality and linguistic identity

Sections 12–14 deal with culture, spirituality and linguistic identity. Article 12 expresses the right to practice and revitalise cultural traditions and customs as well as the right to maintain, protect and develop past, present and future manifestations of indigenous culture which includes archaeological and historical sites, artefacts, performing arts or literature. This section then goes on to highlight the right to maintain and protect and have access in privacy to religious and cultural sites and the right to repatriation of human remains. It includes the right to restitution for cultural, intellectual or spiritual property that was taken without consent. Currently, indigenous Australians are in constant negotiation with overseas institutions, particularly in the United Kingdom over the return of indigenous human remains.

Education, information and labour rights

Sections 15–18 deal with specific issues pertaining to education, information and labour rights. For example Article 15 states that all children have the right to all levels and forms of education of the state including to establish and control their own educational systems and institutions. This section of rights also includes the right of indigenous children living outside their community to be provided with access to education in their own culture and language. The importance of this standard is magnified when considering the controversy over the decision of the Northern Territory government to progressively phase out and abolish bilingual education in 1998.

Development and other economic and social rights

This section of rights (Article 19- 24) is known as participatory rights and deals with development and other economic and social rights. This extends to indigenous people participating fully at all levels of decision-making in relation to matters that affect their own lives. This section empowers indigenous people with the right to special measures for immediate, effective and continuing improvement of their economic and social conditions, including in the areas of employment, vocational training and retraining, housing, sanitation, health and social security.

Land and resources

One of the most important sections, Articles 25 – 30 deals with land and resources. This section remains a highly controversial group of articles, particularly for states like Australia that are rich in natural resources and have exploited these resources for the benefit of the national economy. The competing rights of indigenous peoples create a difficult situation in the balancing of interests. Interestingly, the United Nations Human Rights Commission in April 2003 voted to engage Dr Erica Irene-Daes to embark on research into indigenous peoples permanent sovereignty over natural resources.

Another extremely important recent development for indigenous peoples at international law that will impact upon this section of rights is the decision of the Organisation of American States, Inter-American Court of Human Rights in the *Case of the Mayagna (Sumo) Awas Tingni Community v Republic of Nicaragua*. The case contributes to the growing body of customary international law in affirming indigenous peoples collective rights to the communal land and natural resources that they have traditionally used and occupied.

> This is the first legally binding decision by an international tribunal to uphold the collective land and resource rights of indigenous peoples in the face of a state's failure to do so. It strengthens a contemporary trend in the processes of international law that helps to empower indigenous peoples as they press their demands for self-determination as distinct groups with secure territorial rights (Anaya, 2, 2002).

The Court found that the international right to property, recognised by the American Convention on Human Rights, does include the right to the protection of customary land and resource tenure for indigenous people. The Court was unanimous in finding that the Republic of Nicaragua:

> must adopt legislative and administrative measures to create a mechanism to ensure the effective and official recognition of traditional indigenous community land in accordance with the customary law, values, usage and customs of the communities (Mayagna (Sumo) Awas Tingni Community v. Nicaragua).

The *Awas Tingni* case provides emphatic support to one of the most important articles of the entire Draft Declaration, Article 26, which states that Indigenous peoples have the right to own, develop, control and use the lands and territories, including to total environment of the lands, air, waters, coastal seas, sea-ice, flora and fauna and other resources which they have traditionally owned or otherwise occupied or used. This includes the right to the full recognition of their laws, traditions and customs, land-tenure systems and institutions for the development and management of resources, and the right to effective measures by States to prevent any interference with, alienation of or encroachment upon these rights.

The exercise of self-determination

Articles 31–36 deal with the exercise of self-determination, the right to autonomy and self-government in matters relating to internal local affairs such as culture, education, information, media, housing, employment, social welfare, economic activities, land and resources and the environment. This section also deals with matters of citizenship and the capacity to determine ones own citizenship in accordance with customs and tradition. It empowers the right of indigenous peoples to promote and maintain traditional judicial customs, procedures and practices.

Problematic progress of the Working Group

As the summary above illustrates the Draft Declaration is an important document, a vital source of human rights standards that have been drafted in consultation with indigenous peoples and drawn from existing human rights instruments. The provisions of the Draft Declaration will provide valuable guidance to indigenous Australians engaging in a domestic treaty process. The problematic issue now facing the Declaration is the state's objections and resistance to the document that is a barrier to the necessary consensus and co-operation of the states in attendance. The United Nations is in effect a states body and as such it limits the capacity of indigenous peoples to negotiate on many important matters such sovereignty or access to natural resources. The continuing difficulties surrounding the drafting of a Declaration on the Rights of Indigenous Peoples have sharply illustrated the limited horizons of the official human rights system.

The Working Group seems to have reached an impasse between indigenous people and the states affecting the passage of the text in its current form. Since its inception

But it has established processes that are alienating and disempowering for most Indigenous people because the *Act* remains centred around a reliance on litigation to achieve a final settlement of claims, or to answer the more intractable questions that the *Native Title Act* did not foresee or failed to address.

Our interests in the land and the associated cultural rights and responsibilities are forced to take a back seat to complex, esoteric legal questions about extinguishment. At the end of the day, the onus of proof always rests with the traditional owners to prove decent and ongoing, unbroken connection to country, guaranteeing that many Indigenous people will never 'qualify' as traditional owners in the legal sense of the word.

The amendments to the *Native Title Act* in 1998, following the *Wik* decision, have rendered it non-beneficial in its effect on Indigenous peoples.

All the High Court determined in *Wik* was that some elements of native title might have survived the grant of a pastoral lease. Where this is the case, and there is some overlap in the exercise of those rights, the court found that the rights of the pastoral lease-holder prevail over those of the native title holders.

However, these amendments effectively licensed governments to racially discriminate against the interests of Indigenous peoples by elevating the property rights of non-Indigenous Australians.

Politicians were able to rationalise this latest compromise of Indigenous rights as being in the interests of economic development and by citing the vague but highly emotive concept of 'certainty' while providing no certainty to Indigenous people. It was a reminder to Indigenous people of just how vulnerable our statutory rights are, and how expendable the principle of equality before the law is, if enough money is involved.

Viewed in terms of actual native title outcomes, it is hard to argue the *Act* has been anything other than a spectacular failure:

- 31 successful determinations in ten years,
- 590 claims still unresolved;
- 54 Indigenous Land Use Agreements (NNTT 2002).

There is a clear need for these 590 unresolved claims to be fast-tracked so that people can get on with their lives.

However, I also acknowledge that it is primarily because of the *Mabo* decision that Australians have begun to take a much more honest look at the past and have started to realise we have a black history that sits uncomfortably with the national ethos of 'a fair go' for all.

Ordinary Australians—black and white—have had to grapple with native title issues at the local level. People who were historically on opposite sides of the fence have had to open a dialogue and give each other a voice in decisions about land and natural resource management.

This wasn't happening ten years ago because there simply was no imperative for non-Indigenous people to even contemplate the possibility of a native title right existing in their backyards or that it could deliver outcomes that were good for the entire nation.

Nevertheless, coupled with other revelations from our nation's past, such as arose in the Royal Commission into Aboriginal Deaths in Custody and the National Inquiry into the Separation of Aboriginal and Torres Strait Islander Children from Their Families, the *Mabo* and *Wik* decisions have given rise to an unprecedented outpouring of community action in support of native title and reconciliation. This culminated in the bridge walks in 2000 and the release of the *Documents for Reconciliation* by the now disbanded Council for Aboriginal Reconciliation that same year.

Practical reconciliation—or historical denial

Yet for the vast majority of Australians, Indigenous Affairs remains a 'problem', and predominantly, one that can only be addressed if Indigenous people get serious about putting their own house in order.

This is a very convenient situation for any government. If most of the country thinks the problem lies with Indigenous people themselves, a government doesn't have to try too hard—and it certainly doesn't have to set the historical record straight.

This is precisely what the current policy of practical reconciliation enables the present Government to do.

Over the last twenty years, Aboriginal people and Torres Strait Islanders have been studied, analysed and probed about every aspect of our lives in excruciating detail.

Governments have had report after report, consistently advocating the same principle: ie *Indigenous disadvantage can only be improved when Indigenous people are given greater control over the decisions that impact on their daily lives.*

However, the current Government's approach to Indigenous disadvantage is founded in its conviction that better economic opportunities and individual initiative alone will help to integrate Indigenous people into 'mainstream Australia', and deliver real equality.

The Prime Minister made it very clear earlier this year, that in his mind, the measure of success in terms of the reconciliation process, will be when Indigenous Australians blend into the wider community and no longer stand out as an embarrassing statistical anomaly.

Underpinning the Government's vision for a reconciled Australia are a number of simplistic, and in my view unsubstantiated, assertions that do not stand up to intellectual rigour or historical reality.

These assertions divorce the experience of Indigenous people in this country from any historical context and they assume that all Australians have the same life opportunities: that it is all a question of individual motivation and choice.

Among the assertions are the following:

- focusing on Indigenous health, housing, education and employment (basic citizenship rights) alone will overcome Indigenous disadvantage and achieve lasting reconciliation

- symbolic aspects of reconciliation, like an apology to the stolen generations, or a treaty, will do nothing to address Indigenous disadvantage and are socially and politically divisive

- the so-called 'rights agenda' that has sought to incorporate international standards of human rights into the Australian legal system, has been tried and failed

- there has been too much focus on Indigenous rights at the expense of Indigenous responsibility, and there is more to be gained by encouraging and supporting *individuals* to become *self-reliant* and

- by 'turning off the grog', and tackling 'welfare dependency', Indigenous communities will be able to address family violence, alcohol abuse and social dysfunction.

A few prominent Indigenous commentators have developed and advocated aspects of these assertions as part of a broader analysis of the way forward in Indigenous Affairs policy.

But by using the language of neo-liberalism, and consequently being seen to be of a similar mindset to the Howard Government, they have been cast in the media as legitimising the practical reconciliation agenda.

Now, rather than being acknowledged as a critical turning point in Indigenous Affairs in Australia, the 1967 referendum and the attainment of equal citizenship rights that it once symbolised, is being recast as the beginning of the era of Indigenous welfare dependence and social dysfunction.

Many in the Indigenous leadership now find themselves in the invidious position of being labelled 'part of the problem' and disciples of the 'rhetoric of victimhood' that underpins Indigenous dysfunction (Ruddock 2002).

The reality is however, that you cannot treat the symptoms of dysfunction in isolation from the historical causes.

Good public policy can only emerge where there has been an honest and accurate analysis of past errors and omissions, and a genuine commitment to meeting the needs and aspirations of the people affected by any new policy.

The Howard Government may be determined to address Indigenous disadvantage through practical reconciliation measures, but their record to date is not even measuring up to the rhetoric.

Just in the area of health alone only about 74c of *direct* Commonwealth health funding is spent on each Indigenous person for every $1 spent on a non-Indigenous Australian.

This remains the case even after the 2001 Commonwealth Grants Commission Report recommended that the poorer health status of Indigenous people and their greater reliance on the public health system, would justify at least a doubling of the average per capita government expenditure on non-Indigenous people, just to achieve parity in expenditure on health care for all Australians.

However, there was no recognition of this in this year's Federal Budget. Instead we saw the Government proposing a winding back of the Pharmaceutical Benefits Scheme, which will have adverse financial and health outcomes for Indigenous people, as well as many other disadvantaged Australians.

This budget also offered no extra funds for violence against women and sexual abuse of children, yet the Government has made much political mileage out of these issues. Verging on the indecent, is the same Government's under-spending of last year's allocation by some $4.5m.

We have to have a mechanism that will make governments accountable. And we have to hold the current government to account to ensure it delivers—even if it is only on its limited promises of practical reconciliation.

That is why I acted on the recommendation by Dr Bill Jonas, the Aboriginal and Torres Strait Islander Social Justice Commissioner, to establish a Senate Inquiry into the Government's progress on reconciliation. This Inquiry is due to report in March 2003.

Setting the historical record straight—the Australian Constitution

Many Australians do not realise that the current high levels of Indigenous social and economic disadvantage have their roots in the exclusion and blatant racism that was enshrined in the Australian Constitution.

Up until the 1967 referendum, s. 127 of the Constitution prevented the Commonwealth from counting Indigenous Australians in the national census. Consequently, no Commonwealth Government could even purport to know the scale of Indigenous disadvantage in comparison to the rest of the population, let alone do anything to address the dire need that existed.

Instead, Indigenous Australians became a statistical non-entity in our own country, and the reluctant responsibility of so-called 'welfare' boards, punitively administered by the States.

The recent exposure of the Queensland Government's policy of withholding and underpaying the wages of about 16,500 Aboriginal workers over an 80-year period, is just one example of how exploitative and overtly racist the Indigenous Affairs policies of the States were for much of the last century (Kidd 1997).

The reality at the federal level was not significantly different. The Constitution and the men who drafted it, guaranteed the exclusion of Indigenous people from the legislative program of Commonwealth Governments for most of the last century. What other Australians have taken for granted, we were excluded from, including:

- Commonwealth Franchise Act 1902 & Electoral Act 1918
- Invalid and Old Age Pension Act 1908
    - Maternity Allowance Act 1912
    - Child Endowment Act 1941
    - Widows' Pension Act 1942
    - Unemployment & Sickness Benefit Act 1944.

Full access for Indigenous Australians to social security benefits did not occur until the late 1970s and in some remote communities, not until the early 1980s. (Jonas 2001)

Prior to the 1967 referendum, Commonwealth expenditure on Indigenous Australians was zero. It is only as a result of the referendum that the Commonwealth was given legal power to intervene in Indigenous affairs.

And it was only after the Whitlam Government took office in 1972 that over $100 million was spent on Indigenous Affairs in one year. To give some idea of just how incremental the Commonwealth's involvement was in these early years of responsibility—the *total* Commonwealth expenditure on Indigenous Affairs to 1987— the first 20 years of Commonwealth responsibility—was just on $3 billion.

In comparison, the federal government now dedicates $2.5 billion annually to the Indigenous Affairs budget.

This historic overview of the Commonwealth's role in Indigenous Affairs provides some indication of just how recent its relationship with Indigenous people really is. We remain in a phase of relationship building—taking one step back for every two steps gained.

Building up strong, accountable and sustainable Indigenous governance structures

Astoundingly, a majority of Australians continue to believe the popular myth that Indigenous Affairs is the land of milk and honey, where organisations have endless resources.

Take ATSIC for example. It has long been the whipping boy of Indigenous Affairs, even by its master, the federal government. But few Australians are aware that ATSIC is not an independent body—even though it has an elected board—with complete authority over the expenditure of the Indigenous Affairs budget.

Less than half of this year's trumpeted 'record' $2.5b Indigenous Affairs budget is allocated to ATSIC ($1,132 billion) and of that, the Government requires that two-thirds is spent in just three areas:

- employment programs (similar to work for the dole schemes),

- housing and infrastructure, and

- settlement of native title claims.

That leaves less than $400 million for some of the key planks of the Government's practical reconciliation agenda, including measures to combat family violence and drug alcohol and other substance abuse in communities. Also, ATSIC is still managing the fallout from the $470m cut in the Coalition's first budget.

It is important to emphasise that identifiable Commonwealth expenditure on Indigenous specific programs is not simply 'on top of' the general government expenditure that benefits all Australians.

For example: Close to *one-third* of Commonwealth expenditure on Indigenous people directly *substitutes* for expenditure on mainstream assistance programs.[6] The Indigenous-specific programs deliver virtually the same outcomes, but the way in which services are structured or accessed is different on account of the cultural and other needs of the Indigenous people who use them.

To name a few:

- Abstudy is a substitute for Youth Allowance

- Community Employment programs substitute for Newstart Allowance

- Aboriginal Medical Services substitute for Medicare supported services, and so on.

At the same time, a lot of Commonwealth assistance flows to other groups within Australian society, such as veterans and farmers, which have a disproportionately low number of Indigenous members (DPL 2001).

But what the Commonwealth Grants Commission found in its national Report on Indigenous Funding is that despite the entrenched levels of disadvantage experienced by Indigenous people across all of the key economic and social indicators, we access mainstream services at very much lower rates than non-Indigenous people— regardless of whether we are in urban or remote areas.

Some of the prime examples of where Indigenous people under-utilise the mainstream services include the Pharmaceutical Benefits Scheme and Aged Care services.

As a consequence, the Indigenous-specific services that were only designed to supplement mainstream services, are struggling with levels of demand that they are simply not equipped to meet. And more often than not, it is the most disadvantaged Indigenous people who miss out.

The more recent Commonwealth Grants Commission Report also clearly recognises that the Indigenous Affairs budget has to be more wisely spent and directed to areas of greatest need. It made some very valuable recommendations about the need for greater Indigenous "control of, or stronger influence over, service delivery expenditure", particularly at the regional and local levels (CGC 2001).

However, one issue which has been absent from these discussions is the question of the number of Indigenous organisations that are already in existence, and whether by their sheer numbers, they are a drain on the already overstretched funds available.

Indigenous communities need to ask this question at the local and regional level. Many need to make some cold, hard decisions about which Indigenous organisations are delivering beneficial outcomes and operating cost-effectively, and which ones are not.

We have to start rewarding the successful and accountable organisations, rather than treating all of the good, the bad and the ugly organisations, in exactly the same way.

When you look at just how many Indigenous corporations have been established over the last 30 years of fragmented program delivery, the need for rationalisation and consolidation is obvious.

According to the Registrar of Aboriginal Corporations, who administers the *Aboriginal Councils and Associations Act*, there are about 2,188 registered Indigenous corporations nationally. This translates into a national average of one corporation for every 187 Indigenous people, using the 2001 census population figure of 410,000.

I regard this figure as a conservative estimate for the following reasons:

- not all Indigenous-owned and controlled corporations are registered under the *Aboriginal Councils and Associations Act* or (ACA Act).

- In fact, about half of all Indigenous organisations in Australia are incorporated under other laws, usually to avoid the strict requirements on the structure of corporations and their decision-making processes that exist under the ACA Act. Many are incorporated under general State legislation, which does not separately identify Indigenous organisations.

- Just looking at NSW, there is not a significant variance between the number of corporations funded under ATSIC's Regional Council Program Expenditure in NSW (425) and the number of corporations listed for NSW with the Office of the Registrar of Aboriginal Corporations (391)—a variance of only 33.

In any case, it provides some indication of the level of duplication and the administrative over-servicing that is occurring in many Indigenous communities.

I am also mindful of the extent to which the *Native Title Act* and the Indigenous Land Corporation have contributed to this plethora of Indigenous corporations and prescribed bodies corporate.

Both *Acts* provide that only prescribed bodies corporate can hold title to land or act as agents for native title holders. In addition, the NTA has given rise to the establishment of numerous Representative Aboriginal and Torres Strait Islander Bodies in most States, which have a pivotal role in the operation of the Act, particularly in terms of the services and advice they provide to their Indigenous clients.

These corporations are the latest contestants to enter the increasingly competitive arena that is frequently, and disparagingly referred to in the national media as 'the Indigenous industry'.

These organisations follow in the footsteps of the many community-based organisations that began to spring up in the 1970s as Indigenous communities around Australia were mobilised in the struggle for land rights, self-determination and basic citizenship rights.

I think it is important to recognise that this so-called 'industry' has come about as a result of legislation by our nation's parliaments, and social agitation by Indigenous people themselves. Its emergence was motivated by the recognition that Indigenous Australians have a right to good health, legal representation, a decent education, adequate housing, equitable employment opportunities, and land—and that they will not achieve these outcomes if they are not given the extra assistance required to put them on the starting blocks with the rest of Australia.

I am in no way suggesting that we should try to wind the clock back to the 1960s when few Indigenous owned and controlled organisations existed. On the contrary, I regard the prevalence of a network of Indigenous controlled organisations as a highly desirable development that is just as necessary today as it was back then.

So, whilst we should respect and pay tribute to those Indigenous leaders who have battled to achieve this institutional and economic platform for their communities, we also need to look at how well this vast and expanding body of Indigenous corporations is serving the community in 2002 and what reforms can be undertaken to make them work more efficiently for indigenous people.

Some Indigenous leaders have publicly acknowledged that the plethora of organisations has become a significant drain on many of the communities they were set up to serve, both in terms of human and financial capital.

These organisations are subject to a number of accountability checks and balances as is any similar organisation.

However, I believe we must honestly examine the existence and operations of these organisations against service delivery expectations, community expectations and performance. A series of national benchmarks should be set up as performance measures for all Indigenous community organisations to meet.

Although some communities have developed innovative ways of incorporating traditional authority structures and governance procedures into the operation of their boards of management, others have an uphill battle in managing the general administrative and reporting requirements. Often these day-to-day responsibilities have been added to the load borne by our Elders, or worse still, the day-to-day decision-making is contracted to outside consultants at great financial cost, and often at the expense of the community retaining real control over important business decisions.

Recent moves in the Northern Territory have seen that Government biting the bullet and creating regional health partnerships between Government and Indigenous organisations and communities.

All Indigenous health money—that is Territory and Federal money—for a particular region, will be pooled and administered by a community-controlled health board.

This will not only put Indigenous people in charge, it will also cut down on duplication, bureaucracy, and the general complexity and over-administration, with which most people working in the delivery of Indigenous services, are only too familiar.

While the Territory Government's action is not about rationalising the operations of Indigenous community organisations, it does attack part of the problem at its source.

That is; streamlining funding so it is directed, effective and most importantly, Indigenous-controlled.

The demographics of Indigenous Australia

We need to remind ourselves that there are only 410,000 Indigenous Australians—the largest total since Indigenous people were included for the first time in the national census in 1971.

Even though this is a quite manageable number to deal with, many Australians are still prepared to accept the stereotype of Indigenous affairs as being a terminal case of public policy failure.

How is it possible that 410,000 people should overwhelm our imagination or our ability to formulate responses to familiar challenges within community development?

Indeed, there are some additional aspects to this demographic that are quite important to remember:

- Of the 410,000, about two-thirds are under the age of 25. This is a marked contrast to the broader Australian population where the profile is very much the reverse.

- This means that 240,000 are under the age of 25 and most of them under the age of 18.

- 40% of the nation's juvenile detention population is Indigenous, as is 20% of the nation's prison population.

- Less than half of young Indigenous people aged 15 to 19 are attending secondary school, and consequently, only about 10% are completing their HSC.

- These figures contrast with those for non-Indigenous Australians, of whom 70% are attending secondary school and about 30% are completing their HSC (ABS 2001).

In my mind, the education statistics for young Indigenous and non-Indigenous Australians are both of concern. But in the case of young Indigenous people, they highlight just how much ground has to be made up if all Australians are to have equal life opportunities.

It would seem apparent to me that these statistics have significant implications for how policy initiatives should be structured and delivered over the short, medium and longer term.

It is clear that in the longer-term, inroads have to be made in relation to Indigenous educational opportunities to ensure that a new generation of leaders is able to emerge and be nurtured. The cost of failure in this regard is the possibility that current problems of high unemployment, community violence, family breakdown, and general lack of life opportunities will be compounded in generations to come.

Similarly, a group of 410,000 people should no longer tolerate the *"poor bugger me"* attitude and focus more of our energies in growing our organisations and sponsoring our young.

Despite the gloom of the present, we have every reason to be optimistic in recognising the presence of an emerging class of young Indigenous leaders to open a new phase in defining black/white relations.

In this vein, I can only hope that this round of ATSIC elections gives us new outcomes, fresh blood and new ideas. Not because the others haven't done their job—because I think they have—but because those who fall into the 30% club need to make room for the majority, indeed, it is time that, that 70% are reflected in our leadership make-up and not confined to juvenile detention centres or our nation's gaols.

We must also refute the notion that all Indigenous people live in the remote outback. Only 30% of the Indigenous population live in remote locations.

The other 70% live in the towns, regions and cities of Australia. There are Torres Strait Islanders living in Canberra and Sydney. There are plenty of the mob living in Adelaide, Darwin, Townsville, Katherine and Kalgoorlie.

These are people who for the most part have a telephone, watch TV and listen to radios in their own homes. The postman goes past everyday. The whole infrastructure of government remains within their day-to-day reach.

But for the Indigenous people of rural, regional and urban Australia, isolation is not a factor of distance, but a matter of prejudice. Overt and institutional racism are the underlying causes of our contemporary isolation, more so than any geographic realities.

If we are to tackle the scourge of racism, we first have to overcome the ignorance and misinformation that is recycled—sometimes by our political leaders, but also by friends and family.

Conclusion

It is clear that our current circumstance is derived from the dominant position of government in Indigenous affairs and the failure to see Indigenous rights as a crucial plank in changing the status quo.

No Australian Government has ever wholeheartedly embraced the right of Aboriginal and Torres Strait Islanders to self-determination, and the associated inherent rights that flow from it.

Recognition has only ever been partial—the Mabo decision is a testament to that—and then, given begrudgingly and in a compromised form. Leadership has been more forthcoming in the law than it has in Parliament because at least the law has remained 'colour-blind' in recognising Indigenous rights.

Far too much energy has been expended trying to contain and restrict the application of any rights that are recognised, and invariably more energy is consumed in manoeuvres to limit the application of those rights once they are recognised, native title, being the prime example.

Reconciliation is about the next generation. It is about giving our young people the opportunity to take up the challenges and develop the skills to avoid that pathway to gaols and unemployment queues.

Issues such as education, capacity building, leadership, and sustainable models of community development must be addressed as our top priorities. And as a community, we should be more willing to celebrate and learn from our successes.

I believe, that despite the gloom of the present, we have every reason to be optimistic in recognising the presence of an emerging class of young Indigenous leaders to open a new phase in defining black/white relations.

410,000 is not a lot of people. We can turn our future around.

We have the guidebook in the form of our cultures—the stories and wisdom that our Elders have passed on to us. These survival skills are as relevant today as they were thousands of years ago. We just need to learn new ways of applying that knowledge to our own lives so that there is a better match between institutions and people, and between resources and needs.

Governments may come and go, but we will always be here, so long as we continue to nurture our young so they can take forward our stories, our memories and our future.

Senator Aden Ridgeway is from the Gumbayngirr people of northern New South Wales, the Australian Democrats Senator for New South Wales and the only Indigenous member of the Federal Parliament. Aden has extensive experience in policy and administration, a long-time involvement in national Indigenous politics, a passionate commitment to human rights and an ongoing interest in philanthropic and arts organisations. His portfolio areas are Arts and Sport; Consumer Affairs; Forestry; Indigenous Affairs; Industry, Small Business and Tourism and Trade and Overseas Development.

Sorry Day Speech, Melbourne 2003
Nova Peris

I am ATSIC's Treaty Ambassador and I believe in a treaty because without one there is no true recognition of Aboriginal interests in this country.

Without a treaty Australia is not a truly democratic nation.

Everywhere I speak about a treaty people turn off when I use the words Constitution or Native Title.

I think this is so because there is such bad will towards Aboriginal people in the present Constitution and in the system of proving Native Title.

Australia's Constitution is an ill-adapted mix of symbolic power and the practice of government.

It is ill-adapted because it does not recognise Aboriginal culture as important or influential on the government of this land..

As a result government is about winning or losing land.

It is about establishing an economic base from which social interaction and property build the 'life of the nation'.

Because Aboriginal people are not recognised in the Constitution we have no symbolic power in this land.

There are also no overarching government practices that incorporate the practice of Aboriginal culture into the 'life of the nation'.

For example the Constitution can operate to allow the government to extinguish Native Title.

Native Title to this land cannot be put out.

The *Mabo* decision was a first step in the historical struggle for our recognition as a people.

My goal is to see the advent of a treaty that recognises us as many peoples.

At the moment the government operates in this country as massive, uniform and undifferen-tiated.

A treaty would not allow Aboriginal peoples or interests to be excluded from government.

A treaty is about goodwill.

It is not about blocking Aboriginal people.

It is not about Aboriginal people taking over.

A treaty is not massive or uniform.

A treaty is not undifferentiated.

Government laws could not exclude Indigenous laws.

People from both sides would decide on how to incorporate the interests of both parties into the 'life of the nation'.

At the moment the exclusion of Aboriginal people from government creates racism, which creates conflict, hatred, distrust and threat.

The racism that causes disease, poverty, abuse, disgust or tokenism can be directly linked to a constitutional framework that excludes Aboriginal culture from democratic processes.

We have had to fight for the right to vote.

We have had to fight for land and for centres like this.

We have had to fight for the right to be recognised as peoples.

We have survived impossible odds.

Every step of our way has been a struggle for recognition and acceptance.

Without symbolic recognition and acceptance of us as peoples we are still fighting for a place in our own country.

The democracy that we are now part of does not recognise us while democratic processes lack the symbolism of a treaty with us.

Through a treaty we could gain acceptance of the historic religions and spiritual laws of our people.

Through a treaty our peoples and our culture would be recognised for all time.

Over time a treaty would counteract discrimination against us on all social levels.

The health of Aboriginal people is the focus of my energy,

The energy of Aboriginal people is important for this country.

A treaty is the symbol that will recognise and accept our place in the power of this country.

Our power in the places in this country needs to be recognised.

Without this recognition the symbol of our nation,. Australia is disunity, conflict and unreconciled difference.

A treaty is a symbol of goodwill.

Through the symbol of goodwill we can become a truly democratic nation.

Nova Peris OAM is a Hockey World Cup Gold Medallist; was the first Aboriginal person to win a gold medal at an Olympic Games (Atlanta 1996—hockey); received an Order of Australia Medal and was named Young Australian of the Year in 1997; won a gold medal in the 200m at the Commonwealth Games, Kuala Lumpur in 1998; was the first torch bearer at the Sydney Olympic Games 2000; and is ATSIC's Treaty Ambassador.

Bibliography

Aboriginal Provisional Government, December 1992, *The Australian Provisional Government Papers* Vol. 2, Aboriginal Provisional Government, Canberra.

Aboriginal and Torres Strait Islander Commission (ATSIC) 1995, *Recognition, Rights & Reform. A Report to Government on Native Title Social Justice Measures*, AGPS, Canberra.

Aboriginal and Torres Strait Islander Commission (ATSIC) 1996, *The United Nations Draft declaration on the rights of Indigenous peoples: an analysis*, Aboriginal and Torres Strait Islander Commission, Canberra.

Aboriginal and Torres Strait Islander Commission (ATSIC) 1997, *The royal commission into Aboriginal deaths in custody, an overview of its establishment, findings and outcomes*, Aboriginal and Torres Strait Islander Commission, Canberra.

Aboriginal Torres Strait Islander Commission (ATSIC) 1998, *As a Matter of Fact: Answering the Myths and Misconceptions about Indigenous Australians*, Office of Public Affairs, Aboriginal and Torres Strait Islander Affairs, Canberra.

Aboriginal and Torres Strait Islander Commission (ATSIC) February 1999a, *Aboriginal and Torres Strait Islander Peoples and Australia's Obligations under the United Nations Convention on the Elimination of all Form of Racial Discrimination*, A report submitted by the Aboriginal and Torres Strait Islander Commission to the United Nations Committee on the Elimination of Racial Discrimination, Aboriginal and Torres Strait Islander Commission, Canberra.

Aboriginal and Torres Strait Islander Commission (ATSIC) 1999b, *Focus 2000 and beyond. emerging issues in Indigenous affairs*, report on Indigenous summit, Canberra, September.

Aboriginal and Torres Strait Islander Commission (ATSIC) 2000a, *Aboriginal and Torres Strait Islander Peoples and Australia's Obligations Under the International Covenant on Economic, Social and Cultural Rights*, Aboriginal and Torres Strait Islander Commission, Canberra.

Aboriginal and Torres Strait Islander Commission (ATSIC) June 2000b, *Report on Greater Regional Autonomy*, National Policy Office Policy Paper Series, Canberra.

Aboriginal and Torres Strait Islander Commission (ATSIC) May 2001, *Treaty, Lets Get It Right*, National Treaty Secretariat, National Policy Office, ATSIC, Canberra.

Aboriginal and Torres Strait Islander Commission (ATSIC) 2002, *Review of Electoral Systems*, u.p.

Aboriginal and Torres Strait Islander Social Justice Commissioner 1999, *Social Justice Report 1999*, Report No 2/2000, Human Rights and Equal Opportunity Commission, Sydney.

Aboriginal and Torres Strait Islander Social Justice Commissioner 2000, *Social Justice Report 2000*, Report No. 2/2001, Human Rights and Equal Opportunity Commission, Sydney.

Agius, P 2001, Challenges of negotiating a state-wide agreement, paper presented to Negotiating Country, Native Title Forum Brisbane, 1–3 August.

Ah Kit, J 2002, *Ministerial Statement on Indigenous Affairs to the Northern Territory Parliament*, 7 March 2002.

Altman, JC 2000, *The Economic Status of Indigenous Australians, Discussion Paper No. 193/2000*, Centre for Aboriginal Economic Policy Research, The Australian National University, Canberra.

Amery, R 2000, *Warrabarna Karuna: Reclaiming an Australian Language*, Swets and Zeitlinger, Netherlands.

Anaya, James 1991, 'Indigenous rights norms in contemporary international law' 8(2) *Arizona journal of comparative and international law* 1.

Anaya, James 2001,"The influence of Indigenous peoples on the development of international law", in *Indigenous Human Rights*, eds S. Garkawe, K. Loretta & F. Warwick, Sydney Institute of Criminology Monograph Series, Sydney.

Anaya, James 2002, "The case of Awas Tinghi v Nicaragua: A new step in the international law of Indigenous peoples", *Arizona Journal of International and Comparative Law*, Spring.

Anderson, I 1997, *I, the 'Hybrid' Aborigine: Film and Representation*. The Australian Aboriginal Studies: Journal of the Australian Institute of Aboriginal Studies, 1: 4–14.

Andrews JA 1978, 'The concept of statehood and the acquisition of territory in the nineteenth century', 94 *Law Quarterly Review* 408.

Arthur, WS 2001, *Indigenous Autonomy in Australia: Some concepts, issues and examples*, Discussion paper No. 220/2001, Centre for Aboriginal Economic Policy Research, The Australian National University.

The Australia Institute 2000. *Resourcing Indigenous Development and Self-Determination, A Scoping Paper*, Prepared for the Aboriginal and Torres Strait Islander Commission, Canberra.

Australian Citizenship Council 2000, *Australian Citizenship for a new Century*, Australian Citizenship Council, Canberra.

Australian Government Solicitor 1998, *Native Title. Legislation with Commentary by the Australian Government Solicitor*, 2nd edn, Australian Government Solicitor, Canberra.

Australian Law Reform Commission 1986, *The Recognition Of Aboriginal Customary Laws*, vol. 2, report no. 31, AGPS, Canberra.

Barsh Russell Lawrence 1994, 'Indigenous peoples in the 1990's: from object to subject of international law?', 7 *Harvard Human Rights Journal* 33.

Bartlett Richard H 1993, 'Inherent Aboriginal sovereignty in Canada and Australia' 11 (1 & 2) *Australian-Canadian Studies*.

Bartlett Richard 1999, 'Native title in Australia: denial, recognition and dispossession' in Paul Havemann (ed), *Indigenous Peoples' Rights in Australia, Canada and New Zealand*, Oxford University Press, Auckland.

Bartlett, Richard 2000, *Native Title in Australia*, Butterworths, Sydney.

Bartlett, Richard 2001, 'Canada: Indigenous land claims and settlements', in B. Keon-Cohen (ed.), *Native Title in the New Millennium: A selection of papers from the Native title Representative Bodies Legal Conference 16–20 April, Melbourne*, Aboriginal Studies Press, Canberra.

Batiste, Marie & Henderson, James (Sa'ke'j) Youngblood 2000, *Protecting Indigenous Knowledge and Heritage,* Purich Publishing, Saskatoon, Canada.

Beckett, J 1988, *Past and Present: the Construction of Aboriginality,* Aboriginal Studies Press, Canberra.

Behrendt Larissa 2000, 'Righting Australia', 45 *Arena Magazine* 24

Behrendt, L 2002, 'Unfinished Journey—Indigenous Self-Determination', *Arena Magazine,* April–May.

Berger, Julian 1988, *Aborigines Today: Land and Justice,* Anti-Slavery Society, London.

Berndt, Ronald & Berndt, Catherine 1992, *The World of the First Australians,* Aboriginal Studies Press, Canberra.

Blakeney, Michael 1997, 'Bioprospecting and the protection of traditional medical knowledge', *European Intellectual Property Reports,* vol 6.

van Boven, Theo 1991, 'The international system of human rights: An overview' in *Manual on Human Rights Reporting under Six Major International Human Rights Instruments,* United Nations, New York.

Brascoupe, Simon & Endemann, Karin 1999, *Intellectual Property and Aboriginal People: A Working Paper,* Research and Analysis Directorate, Department of Indian Affairs and Northern Development & Intellectual Property Policy Directorate, Canada.

Brennan Frank & Crawford James 1990, 'Aboriginality, recognition and Australian law: where to from here?, 1 *Public law review* 53.

Buxton, Jeremy 1998, 'Fair Representation or Racial Privilege?', *Quadrant,* July–August, pp 54–57.

Canby, WC 1998, *American Indian Law in a Nutshell,* 3rd edn, West Group, St. Paul, Minnesota.

Carroll, Lewis 1960, *Alice in Wonderland; Through the Looking Glass,* A. Blond, London.

Case Natasha 1998/1999, ' Tide of history or tsunami?' *Indigenous Law Bulletin,* vol. 4, issue 17.

Cassidy, F 1994, 'British Columbia and the Aboriginal peoples: The prospects for the treaty process', *Options Politiques,* Vol. 15, No. 2, March.

Cassidy Julie 1988, 'The significance of the classification of a colonial acquisition: the conquered/settled distinction', 1 *Australian Aboriginal Studies* 2

Cassidy Julie 1998, 'Sovereignty of Aboriginal people', *Indiana international and comparative law review,* vol. 9.

Chaney, F 2001, 'The National Native Title Tribunal and Reconciliation Australia', paper presented at the Australian Institute of Aboriginal and Torres Strait Islander Studies (AIATSIS) Seminar Series, Limits and Possibilities of a Treaty Process in Australia, Canberra, August 27.

Charlesworth, Hilary 2002, *Writing in Rights: Australia and The Protection of Human Rights,* University of New South Wales Press, Sydney.

Clark, G 2001a, 'Constitutional change: Australian experience and future prospects for a treaty', in G Patmore (ed), *The Big Makeover: A New Australian Constitution: Labor Essays 2002*, Pluto Press Australia, Annandale, NSW.

Clark, G 2001b, ATSIC's role in the treaty process, presented at the Australian Institute of Aboriginal and Torres Strait Islander Studies (AIATSIS) Seminar Series, Limits and Possibilities of a Treaty Process in Australia, Canberra, 2 April 2001.

Collard, Edna 2002, Letter to the Editor, *Koori Mail*, 20 March.

Commonwealth of Australia 2000a, *National Indigenous English Literacy and Numeracy Strategy 2000–2004 Strait Islander Education Policy,*—Supporting Statement package, McMilliam Press.

Commonwealth of Australia 2000b, *Katu Kalpa: Report on the inquiry into the effectiveness of education and training programs for Indigenous Australians*, Senate Employment, Workplace Relations, Small Business and Education References Committee, Canberra.

Commonwealth Grants Commission 2000, *Draft Report on Indigenous Funding*, Commonwealth Grants Commission, Canberra.

Commonwealth Grants Commission 2001. *Report on Indigenous Funding*, Commonwealth Grants Commission, Canberra.

Commonwealth Schools Commission 1987, *Schooling in Rural Australia*, AGPS, Canberra.

Constitutional Centenary Foundation 1994, *Securing a bountiful place for Aborigines and Torres Strait Islanders in a modern, free and tolerant Australia*, Constitutional Centenary Foundation, Carlton, Victoria.

Coombs, HC 1994, *Aboriginal Autonomy, Issues and Strategies*, Cambridge University Press, Melbourne.

Cornell, S 2002a, The importance and power of indigenous self-governance: Evidence from the United States, paper presented at the Indigenous Governance Conference, 3–5 April, Canberra.

Cornell, S 2002b, Governance and economic development, Harvard project on American Indian economic development, paper presented at the Indigenous Governance Conference, 3–5 April, Canberra.

Cornell, S & Kalt, J 1998, 'Sovereignty and nation-building: The development challenge in Indian country today', *American Indian Culture and Research Journal*, 22:3, pp. 197–214.

Cornell, S & Kalt, J P (eds.) 1992, *What Can Tribes Do? Strategies and Institutions in American Indian Economic Development*, American Indian Studies Center, University of California, Los Angeles.

Council for Aboriginal Reconciliation 1993, *'The position of Indigenous peoples in national constitutions'*, conference report, Canberra 4–5 June, Commonwealth Government Printer, Canberra.

Council for Aboriginal Reconciliation 1994a, *Addressing Disadvantage: A Greater Awareness of the Causes of Indigenous Australians' Disadvantage*, Key Issue Paper No. 5, AGPS, Canberra.

Council for Aboriginal Reconciliation 1994b,'*Walking together: the first steps. Report of the CAR to federal parliament, 1991–1994*', Council for Aboriginal Reconciliation, Canberra.

Council for Aboriginal Reconciliation 1994, '*Agreeing on a document*', Key issues paper no. 7, AGPS, Canberra.

Council for Aboriginal Reconciliation 1995. *Going Forward. Social Justice for the First Australians. A submission to the Commonwealth Government*, Commonwealth of Australia, Canberra.

Council for Aboriginal Reconciliation 1998. *Towards a benchmarking framework for service delivery to Indigenous Australians. Proceedings of the Benchmarking Workshop. 18–19 November 1997*, Council for Aboriginal Reconciliation, Canberra.

Council for Aboriginal Reconciliation 2000a. *Reconciliation. Australia's Challenge. The Final Report of the Council for Aboriginal Reconciliation to the Prime Minister and the Commonwealth Parliament*, Council for Aboriginal Reconciliation, Canberra.

Council for Aboriginal Reconciliation 2000b. *Recognising Aboriginal and Torres Strait Islander Rights*, Council for Aboriginal Reconciliation, Canberra.

Crawford James 1989, 'The Aboriginal legal heritage: Aboriginal public law and the treaty proposal', *Australian law journal*, vol. 63.

Creamer, H 1987, 'Aboriginality in NSW: beyond the image of cultureless outcasts', in J. Beckett (ed), *Past and Present: the Construction of Aboriginality*, Aboriginal Studies Press, Canberra.

Crough, G 2001a, A practical critique of practical reconciliation or what is the reality of Indigenous funding, paper presented at the Australian Council Of Social Services (ACOSS) and Australians for Native Title and Reconciliation (ANTAR) Seminar: Practical Reconciliation or Treaty Talks, 25 July, Canberra.

Crough G 2001b, Regional Options for Aboriginal Communities in Central Australia, paper prepared for the Central Land Council.

Cunneen Chris & Libesman Terry 1995, '*Indigenous people and the law in Australia*', Butterworths, Sydney.

Daes, Erica Irene 1995, *Discrimination Against Indigenous Peoples: Protection of the Heritage of Indigenous Peoples, Final Report*, United Nations Economic and Social Council, E/CN.4/Sub.2/1995/26, 21 June.

Davis, Megan 2002, 'The United Nations Draft Declaration', *Inidgenous Law Bulletin*, April, vol. 5, no.16.

De Costa, R 2001, 'Getting treaties right (and wrong) in British Columbia', paper presented to the Rethinking Indigenous Self-Determination conference, University of Queensland, Brisbane, September 25.

Department of Employment, Education and Training (DEET) 1989, *National Aboriginal & Torres Strait Islander Education Policy*, AGPS Press, Canberra.

Department of Employment, Education and Training (DEET) 1994, *National Review of Education for Aboriginal and Torres Strait Islander Peoples—A Discussion Paper*, AGPS, Canberra.

Department of Employment, Education and Training (DEET) 1995, *National Review of Education for Aboriginal and Torres Strait Islander Peoples—Final Report*, AGPS, Canberra.

Department of Indian and Northern Affairs 1995, *Aboriginal Self-Government: The Government of Canada's Approach to Implementation of the Inherent Right and the Negotiation of Aboriginal Self-Government*, Ottawa.

Department of the Parliamentary Library 2001, *Indigenous Affairs Expenditure*, Commonwealth of Australia, Canberra.

Department of Prime Minister and Cabinet 2000, *Final Submission to the Commonwealth Grants Commission Indigenous Funding Inquiry*, Submission No.: IFI/SUB/0068, 22/12/2000.

Department of Sports, Recreation and Tourism 1986, *Aboriginals and Recreation*, Department of Aboriginal Affairs, Canberra.

Dodson, M 1988, 'United nations commission on human rights' *Indigenous law bulletin*, vol. 4, issue 12.

Dodson, M 1994, 'The End in the Beginning: Re(de)fining Aboriginality', *Australian Aboriginal Studies: Journal of the Australian Institute of Aboriginal Studies*, 1:2-13.

Dodson, M & Pritchard S 1998, 'Recent developments in Indigenous policy: The abandonment of self determination?' *Indigenous law bulletin*, vol. 15, issue 4.

Dodson, M 2001, 'An Australian Indigenous Treaty—Issues of Concern', paper presented at the Australian Institute of Aboriginal and Torres Strait Islander Studies Seminar Series, Limits and Possibilities of a Treaty Process in Australia, March 20, Canberra.

Dodson, P L 1991, *Regional Report of Inquiry into Underlying Issues in Western Australia*, Vol 2, Australian Government Publishing Service, Canberra.

Dodson Patrick 2002, 'Reconciliation and the high court's decision on native title', *Aboriginal law bulletin*, vol. 6, issue 61.

Dodson, Patrick 2000a, Beyond the Mourning Gate—Dealing with Unfinished Business, the Wentworth Lecture presented on the 12 May 2000.

Dodson Patrick 2000b, 'Until the chains are broken, Aboriginal unfinished business', *Arena magazine*, issue 45.

Donoghue Louis 1994, 'Australian government and self determination', in Christine Fletcher, '*Aboriginal self determination in Australia*', Aboriginal Studies Press, Canberra.

Dorsett, S & Godden, L 1998, *A Guide to Overseas Precedents of Relevance to Native Title*, Native Title Research Unit, Australian Institute of Aboriginal and Torres Strait Islander Studies (AIATSIS), Canberra.

Dorsett, S & Godden, L 2000, 'The contractual status of Indigenous land use agreements', in *Land, Rights, Laws: Issues in Native Title. Issues Paper*, vol. 2, no.1, Native Title Research Unit, Australian Institute of Aboriginal and Torres Strait Islander Studies (AIATSIS), Canberra.

Dudgeon, P 1999, 'Reflections', in D. Oxenham(ed.) et al, *A Dialogue on Indigenous Identity: Warts 'n' All*, Gunada Press, Perth.

Dudgeon, P 1999, 'Indigenous identity', in P Dudgeon, D Garvey & H Pickett (eds), *Working with Indigenous Australians: A Handbook for Psychologists*, Gunada Press, Perth.

Durie Mason 1998, *Te mana, te kawanatanga the politics of Maori self-determination*, Oxford University Press, Auckland.

Dutfield, Graham 2000, Developing and implementing national systems for protecting traditional knowledge: A review of experiences in selected developing countries, paper delivered at United Nations Conference on Trade And Development (UNCTAD) Expert Meeting on Systems and National Experiences for Protecting Traditional Knowledge, Innovations and Practices, 30 Oct–1 Nov 2000, Geneva.

Edmunds, M. (ed) 1998, *Regional Agreements: Key Issues in Australia*, Native Title Research Unit, Australian Institute of Aboriginal and Torres Strait Islander Studies (AIATSIS), Canberra.

Edwards, H. W. 1993, *An Introduction to Aboriginal Societies*, Social Science Press, Wentworth Falls, NSW.

Elliott, David W. 1997, *Law and Indigenous Peoples in Canada*, Captus University Publications, Ontario.

Falk, Richard 2000, *Human Rights Horizons*, Routledge, New York.

Ferguson, Juanita (ed) 1989, *'Aboriginal People and treaties'* Seminar report, University of New South Wales, Sydney.

Fleiner, Thomas 2001, 'Constitutions & Diverse Communities in the 21st Century', paper presented at Institute for Comparative and International Law and the Centre for Comparative and Constitutional Studies, University of Melbourne, 26 September.

Fletcher, C (ed) 1994, *Aboriginal self-determination in Australia*, Australian Institute of Aboriginal and Torres Strait Islander Studies Report Series, Aboriginal Studies Press, Canberra.

Fletcher Christine, 1999, 'Living together but not neighbors, cultural imperialism in Australia' in Paul Havemann (ed) *Indigenous peoples' rights in Australia, Canada and New Zealand*, Oxford University Press, Auckland.

Flynn Martin and Stanton Sue 1997, 'Another failed sovereignty claim: Thorpe v Commonwealth of Australia' , *Indigenous law bulletin*, vol. 3, issue (7)19

Fforde, Cressida and Ormond-Parker, Lyndon 2001, 'Repatriation developments in the UK', in *Indigenous Law Bulletin*, vol. 5, issue 6.

Fourmile, Henrietta 1996, 'Protecting Indigenous Intellectual Property Rights in Biodiversity', paper presented at Kaltja vs Business Conference, 28 August 1996.

Fourmile, Henrietta 2000, 'Developing a Regime to Protect Indigenous Traditional Biodiversity Related Knowledge' *Balayi: Culture, Law and Colonialism*, vol. 1, no. 1.

Gardiner-Garden, J. (ed) 1992, *Aboriginality and Aboriginal Rights in Australia*, Department of the Parliamentary Library, Canberra.

Gardiner-Garden J. 2000, *From Dispossession to Reconciliation*, Research Paper No. 27 1998–99, Information and Research Services, Department of Parliamentary Library, Canberra.

Gilbert Kevin 1993, *'Aboriginal sovereignty, justice, the law and the land'*, 3rd edn, Treaty '88, Canberra.

Gilbert Kevin 1994, 'Mabo is the turning point for justice', in Irene Moores (ed), *'Voices of Aboriginal Australia'*, Butterfly Books, Springwood, NSW.

Gray Stephen 1993, 'Planting the flag or burying the hatchet: sovereignty and the high court decision in Mabo v Queensland', *Griffith law review*, vol. 2, issue 1.

Griggs, Kim, *Maori Take on hi-tech Lego Toys*, http://news.bbc.co.uk/hi/english/worls/asis-pacific/newsid

Hale, Ken 1992, 'On endangered languages and the safeguarding of diversity', *Language*, vol. 68, pp. 1–42.

Harris Alana 1994 'The big march', in Irene Moores (ed), *'Voices of Aboriginal Australia'*, Butterfly Books, Springwood, NSW.

Harris, S 1978, *'It's Coming Yet…' An Aboriginal Treaty Within Australia Between Australians*, The Aboriginal Treaty Commission, Canberra.

Hooper, Narelle 2002, Aboriginal Remains in England, transcript of ABC AM program broadcast at 0800 3 January, AEST on local radio: http://www.abc.net.au/am/s451332.htm

House of Representatives Standing Committee on Aboriginal Affairs 1979, *Aboriginal Health Report (No.60/1979)*, The Parliament of the Commonwealth of Australia, Canberra.

House of Representatives Standing Committee on Aboriginal Affairs 1990, *Our Future Our Selves*, AGPS, Canberra.

House of Representatives Standing Committee on Aboriginal and Torres Strait Islander Affairs 1997, *Torres Strait Islanders: A New Deal*, AGPS, Canberra.

Huggins, Jackie 2002, 'Unfinished business', paper presented at the Aboriginal and Torres Strait Islander Commission's National Treaty Conference August, 2002.

Human Rights Committee 2000, *Concluding Observations of the Human Rights Committee Australia*, Office of the United Nations High Commissioner for Human Rights, Geneva.

Human Rights and Equal Opportunity Commission 1997, *Bringing Them Home: Report of the National Inquiry into the Separation of Aboriginal and Torres Strait Islander Children from their Families*, Sterling Press for HREOC, Sydney.

Human Rights and Equal Opportunity Commission 2000a, *Social Justice Report*, Human Rights and Equal Opportunity Commission, Sydney.

Human Rights and Equal Opportunity Commission 2000b, *National Inquiry into Rural and Remote Education*, Human Rights and Equal Opportunity Commission, Sydney.

Human Rights and Equal Opportunity Commission 2001, *Social Justice Report 2001*, Aboriginal and Torres Strait Islander Social Justice Commissioner, Sydney.

Hunter, B 1999, *Three nations, not one: Indigenous and other Australian poverty*, The Australian National University, Centre for Aboriginal Economic Policy Research Working Paper No. 1/1999, Canberra.

Hutchinson, J 1994, *Modern Nationalism*, Fontana, London.

Independent Aboriginal Organisations of the Kimberley, October 1994. *Towards Regional Autonomy*, Statement to the Chairman of the Aboriginal Reconciliation Council.

Ivanitz, M 1997, 'The emperor has no clothes: Canadian comprehensive claims and their relevance to Australia', Native Title Research Unit Discussion Papers Regional Agreements No 4, Australian Institute of Aboriginal and Torres Strait Islander Studies (AIATSIS) Canberra.

Ivison, D, Patton, P & Sanders, W (eds.) 2000a. *Political Theory and the Rights of Indigenous Peoples*, Cambridge University Press, New York.

Ivison, D, Patton P & Sanders, W (eds) 2000b, *On the Plurality of Interests: Aboriginal Self-Government and Land Rights*, Cambridge University Press, Melbourne.

Janke, Terri 1999, *Our Culture: Our Future, Report on Australian Indigenous Cultural and Intellectual Property Rights*, Terri Janke and Michael Frankel & Co, Sydney.

Jenkins, G 1979, *Conquest of the Ngarrindjeri*, Raukkan, Port McLeay.

Johns, G 2001, 'The Failure of Aboriginal Separatism', *Quadrant*, May.

Johnson, J, Sweeney, B & Associates 1996. *Unfinished Business, Australians and Reconciliation. An Overview of Community Attitudes, Research Conducted for the Council for Aboriginal Reconciliation*, Council for Aboriginal Reconciliation, Canberra.

Johnson, Vivien 1996, *Copyrites—Aboriginal Art in the Age of Reproductive Technologies*, Touring Exhibition 1996. Catalogue published by National Indigenous Arts Advocacy Association (NIAAA) and Macquarie University, Sydney.

Jonas, W (Bill) 2002, 'Recognising Aboriginal sovereignty: Implications for the Treaty process', paper presented at the Aboriginal and Torres Strait Islander Commission's National Treaty Conference, 27–29 August, Canberra.

Jull P 1989, 'Seeking a framework. Aboriginal identity and political institutions in Central and Northern Australia: some overseas comparisons', paper presented at Conference on the Future of Government for Aborigines in Central and Northern Australia.

Jull Peter 2000, 'Maimed rites', *Arena magazine*, issue 45.

Keating Paul 1994, 'Redfern park speech', in Irene Moores (ed), *'Voices of Aboriginal Australia'*, Butterfly Books, Springwood, NSW.

Kelly Loretta 1993, 'Reconciliation and the implications for a sovereign Aboriginal nation', *Aboriginal law bulletin*, vol. 3, issue 61.

Kee, Sue 2001, 'Indigenous land use agreements: Which, why and where?', in B Keon-Cohen (ed), *Native Title in the New Millennium*, Aboriginal Studies Press, Canberra.

Kickett, T 1998, 'Say where it is', in D. Oxenham (ed.) et al, *A Dialogue on Indigenous Identity: Warts 'n' All*, Gunada Press, Perth.

Kidd, R 1993, *You Can Trust Me—I'm With The Government*, University of Queensland Press, St. Lucia, QLD.

Kidd, R 1997, *The Way We Civilise. Aboriginal Affairs—The Untold Story*, University of Queensland Press, St. Lucia, QLD.

Langton, M 1981, 'Urbanizing Aborigines: the social scientists' great deception', *Social Alternatives*, vol.12(2), pp. 16-22.

Langton, M 1993, *'Well I Heard it on the Radio and I Saw it on the Television': An Essay for the Australian Film Commission on the Politics and Aesthetics of Filmmaking by and about Aboriginal People and Things*, Australian Film Commission, North Sydney, N.S.W.

Langton, M 1994, 'Indigenous self-government and self-determination: overlapping jurisdictions at Cape York', in C Fletcher (ed), *Aboriginal Self-Determination in Australia*, Aboriginal Studies Press, Canberra.

Langton, M 2001a, 'Dominion and dishonour: A treaty between our nations', *Postcolonial Studies*, vol. 4(1), pp. 13–26.

Langton, M 2001b, The Nations of Australia, *Alfred Deakin Lecture*, 20 May.

Langton, M 2002, 'Ancient jurisdictions, Aboriginal polities and sovereignty', paper presented at the Indigenous Governance Conference, 3–5 April 2002, Canberra.

Langton, M & Palmer, L 2002, 'Treaties and agreements as instruments of order in and between civil societies: A rational choice approach', paper presented at the Aboriginal and Torres Strait Islander Commission's National Treaty Conference, August 27–29, Canberra.

Lippmann, L 1994, *Generations of resistance*, Longman Cheshire, Melbourne.

Lui, G 1994, 'Self-government in the Torres Strait Islands', in C Fletcher (ed), *Aboriginal Self-Determination in Australia*, Australian Institute of Aboriginal and Torres Strait Islander Studies Report Series, Canberra.

Mann, Howard 1997, 'Indigenous peoples and the use of intellectual property rights in Canada: Case studies relating to intellectual property rights and the protection of biodiversity', paper submitted to IP Policy Directorate, Industry Canada and Canadian Working Group on Art.8 (j) of the Convention on Biodiversity, 1997.

Mansell Michael 1994, 'The Mabo case, the court gives an inch but takes another mile', in Irene Moores (ed), *'Voices of Aboriginal Australia'*, Butterfly Books, Springwood, NSW.

Mansell, Michael 2002a, paper presented at the Aboriginal and Torres Strait Islander Commission's National Treaty Conference, Canberra.

Mansell, Michael 2002b, *Finding the Foundation for a Treaty with the Indigenous Peoples of Australia in Treaty Framework*, Aboriginal Studies Press, Canberra.

Martin, DF 2001, 'Is welfare dependency 'welfare poison'? An assessment of Noel Pearson's proposals for Aboriginal welfare reform', Discussion paper no. 213/2001, Centre for Aboriginal Economic Policy Research, The Australian National University, Canberra.

Martin, D 2002, Developing strong and effective Aboriginal institutions, paper presented at the Indigenous Governance Conference, 3–5 April, Canberra.

Mathews, R July 1993, *Towards Aboriginal Self-Government*, CEDA Public Information Paper No. 46.

Mattingley, C & Hampton, K 1988, *Survival In Our Own Land, Aboriginal Experiences in South Australia Since 1836*, Wakefield Press, Adelaide.

McCausland, Sally 1997, *Protecting Aboriginal Cultural Heritage in Australia*, Faculty of Graduate Studies, University of British Columbia [unpublished]

McConnochie, K, Hollinsworth, D & Pettman, J 1988, *Race and racism in Australia*, Social Science Press, Wentworth Falls, NSW.

McCorquodale, J 1987, *Aboriginals and the Law: A Digest*, Aboriginal Studies Press, Canberra.

McNeil, K 1989, *Common Law Aboriginal Title*, Claredon Press, Oxford.

McGlade Hannah 2000, 'Not invited to the negotiating table', *Balayi, culture, law and colonialism*, vol. 1, issue 1.

McHugh Paul 1998, 'Aboriginal identity and relations in North America and Australasia', in Ken Coates, *Living relationships Kokiri Ngatahi*, Victoria University Press, Wellington

McHugh Paul 1999, 'From sovereignty talk to settlement time' in Paul Havemann (ed), *Indigenous peoples' rights in Australia, Canada and New Zealand*, Oxford University Press, Auckland.

McRae H, Nettheim G & Beacroft L 1997, *Indigenous legal issues, commentary and materials*, LBC Information Service, North Ryde, NSW.

Meyers, G, Nettheim, G & Craig, D 1999, Australian Research Council Collaborative Research Project: Governance Structures for Indigenous Australians on and off Native Title Lands, Discussion Papers 1–9, Sydney.

Miller, James 1985, *Koori: A Will To Win, The Heroic Resistance Survival and Triumph of Black Australia*, Angus & Robertson, Australia.

Ministerial Committee on Mabo 1993, *Mabo: The High Court Decision on Native Title*, AGPS, Canberra.

Ministerial Council on Education, Employment, Training and Youth Affairs 1995, *A National Strategy for the Education of Aboriginal and Torres Strait Peoples*, Department of Employment, Education, Training and Youth Affairs, Canberra.

Moisiadis Valentia, 'A treaty between Aborigines and the white Australian community. achieving a settlement; on whose terms?', Unpublished Honors Thesis, University of Melbourne.

Moreton-Robinson, A 2000, *Talkin Up to the White Woman: Indigenous Women and Feminism*, University of Queensland Press, St. Lucia, QLD.

Moreton-Robinson, A 2001, *Treaty Talk: Past, Present and Future*, The Ngunnawal Lecture Series, Aboriginal and Torres Strait Islander (ATSIC) News, Autumn.

Morgan, S 1987, *My Place*, Fremantle Arts Centre Press, Perth.

Mulgan, Richard 1998, 'Citizenship and legitimacy in post colonial Australia', in N Peterson & W Sanders (eds), *Citizenship and Indigenous Australians*, Cambridge University Press, New York.

National Native Title Tribunal 1999, *Native Title: A Five Year Retrospective 1994-1998*, National Native Title Tribunal, Perth.

Neate, G 2001, 'President's overview', in the *National Native Title Tribunal Annual Report 2000-2001*, National Native Title Tribunal, Perth.

Nettheim Garth 1993, "'The consent of the natives': Mabo and Indigenous political rights", *Sydney Law Review*, vol. 15.

Nettheim Garth 1998a, 'The international law context' in Nicholas Peterson & Will Sanders (eds.), *Citizenship and Indigenous Australians, changing conceptions and possibilities*, Cambridge University Press, Melbourne.

Nettheim, Garth 1998b, "'Native Title, Fictions and 'Convenient Falsehoods'" in C Perrin (ed) in *The Wake of Terra Nullius*, Prospect Media, St. Leonards, NSW.

Nettheim Garth 1999, 'Reconciliation and the constitution', *University of New South Wales Law Journal*, vol. 22, issue 2.

Nicholls, Christine 1998, 'Secondary education for the Northern Territory's Indigenous students: "The Missing Link" in the so called life long education process', in Roz Walker (ed.) et al, *Indigenous Education and The Social Capital*, Black Swan Press, WA.

Nicholls, Christine 2001, Speaking out for an Australian Languages Act: the case for legislative activism for the maintenance of Australia's Indigenous languages, the Paulo Freire Memorial Lecture, December 13th 2001.

O'Brien, S 1989, *American Indian Tribal Governments*, University of Oklahoma Press, Norman, USA.

O'Shane Pat 1991, 'A treaty for Australians?' in William Renwick (ed.), *Sovereignty and indigenous rights, the treaty of Waitangi in an international context*, Victoria University Press, Wellington.

Otto Dianne 1995, 'A question of law or politics? Indigenous claims to sovereignty in Australia', *Syracuse journal of international law and commerce*, vol. 21, issue 65.

Patton, P 2001, 'Constitutional paradoxes: Native title, treaties and the nation', paper presented at the Australian Institute of Aboriginal and Torres Strait Islander Studies (AIATSIS) Seminar Series, Limits & Possibilities of a Treaty Process in Australia, 28 May.

Pearson Noel 1994, '204 years of invisible title: from the most vehement denial of a people's right to land to a most cautious and belated recognition', Irene Moores (ed), *Voices of Aboriginal Australia*, Butterfly Books, Springwood NSW.

Pearson, N 2000a, 'Passive welfare and the destruction of Indigenous society in Australia', in P Saunders (ed.), *Reforming the Australian Welfare State*, Australian Institute of Family Studies, Melbourne.

Pearson, N 2000b, 'The light on the hill', Ben Chifley memorial lecture presented at the Bathurst Panthers League Club on Saturday 12 August 2000.

Pearson, N October 2001, 'On the human right to misery, mass incarceration and early death', Dr. Charles Perkins Memorial Oration presented at McLaurin Hall, the University of Sydney, 25 October 2001.

Pearson, N March 2002, 'Working at the sharp end', lecture presented at The Australian and New Zealand Social Entrepreneurs Network Conference, Carlton Crest Hotel, Melbourne, 4 March.

Plumtree, T & Graham, J 1999, *Governance and Good Governance: International and Aboriginal Perspectives*, Institute of Governance, Ottawa.

Pritchard, S 1994, 'Self Determination under International Law', in *Controlling destinies*, key issues paper No.8 for the Council for Aboriginal Reconciliation, AGPS, Canberra.

Pritchard, S (ed.) 1998, *Indigenous Peoples, the United Nations and Human Rights*, Federation Press, Sydney.

Pritchard S 2000, 'From welfare to rights', *Arena magazine*, issue 45.

Pritchard, S 2001, *Setting International Standards. An Analysis of the United Nations Declaration on the Rights of Indigenous people and the First Six Sessions of the Commission on Human Rights Working Group*, 3rd edn, Aboriginal and Torres Strait Islander Commission, Canberra.

Pybus, C 2002, 'Shades of black', *The Age Saturday Extra*, Saturday March 2.

Quiggin, Robynne 2001, 'Boobera Lagoon', *Indigenous Law Bulletin*, February-March, vol. 5, issue 6.

Read, P 1998, 'Whose citizens? Whose country?' in N Peterson and W Sanders (eds), *Citizenship and Indigenous Australian*, Cambridge University Press, New York.

Reynolds, Henry 1987a, *Frontier*, Allen and Unwin, NSW.

Reynolds, Henry 1987b, *The Law of the Land*, Ringwood Penguin, Australia.

Reynolds Henry 1993, 'Terra Nullius, Never, Never', *The Weekend Australian Newspaper*, July 3–4.

Reynolds Henry 1998, 'Sovereignty', in Nicolas Peterson & Will Sanders (eds.), *Citizenship and Indigenous Australian. changing conceptions and possibilities*, Cambridge University Press, Melbourne.

Reynolds Henry 1999, 'New frontiers: Australia', in Paul Havemann (ed), *Indigenous peoples' rights in Australia, Canada and New Zealand*, Oxford University Press, Auckland.

Rintoul, S 2002, 'The third wave', *The Weekend Australian*, March 2–3.

Ritter David 1996, 'The rejection of terrra nullius in Mabo: a critical analysis', *Sydney Law Review*, vol. 18, issue 5.

Royal Commission into Aboriginal Deaths in Custody 1991, *National Report of the Royal Commission into Aboriginal Deaths in Custody*, AGPS, Canberra.

Rowse, T 2001, 'The treaty debate 1979-1983 and the continuing problem of federalism', paper presented at the Australian Institute of Aboriginal and Torres Strait Islander Studies (AIATSIS) Seminar Series, Limits and Possibilities of a Treaty Process in Australia, 30 April, Canberra.

Ruddock, Philip 2002, 'Changing Direction', speech delivered at the Aboriginal and Torres Strait Islander Commission's National Policy Conference, 26th March.

Sanders, W 1999, 'Torres Strait Governance Structures and the Centenary of Australian Federation: A Missed Opportunity?', Australian National University Centre for Aboriginal Economic Policy Research, Canberra.

Sanders, WG & Arthur, WS 2001, 'Autonomy rights in Torres Strait: From whom, for whom, for or over what?', discussion paper no.215/2001, Centre for Aboriginal Economic Policy Research, the Australian National University, Canberra.

Schmidt, Annette 1990, *The Loss of Australia's Aboriginal Heritage*, Aboriginal Studies Press, Canberra.

Scholz, C 2001, 'Land claims: A negotiated option', paper presented at Australian Institute of Aboriginal and Torres Strait Islander Studies (AIATSIS) Seminar Series, Limits and Possibilities of a Treaty Process in Australia, 27 August, Canberra.

Schwab, RG & Sutherland, D 2001, 'Building Indigenous Learning Communities', Discussion Paper, no. 225/2001, Centre for Aboriginal Economic Policy Research, The Australian National University, Canberra.

Senate Standing Committee on Constitutional and Legal Affairs 1983, *Two Hundred Years Later*, AGPS, Canberra.

Senior Secondary Assessment Board of South Australia (SSABSA) 1996, *Australia's Indigenous Languages*, Senior Secondary Assessment Board of South Australia, Adelaide, Australia.

Shaw, G 2002 'Native Title, sovereignty and treaty—do they mix?', paper prepared for the National Treaty Think Tank.

Shuter, Angie 2002, 'Scoping paper: Sui generis protection of traditional knowledge', presented at the Te Puni Kōkiri, New Zealand, February.

Skari, A 1992, 'The tribal judiciary: A primer for policy development' in S Cornell & JP Kalt (eds.), *What Can Tribes Do?*, American Indian Studies Centre, University of California, Los Angeles.

Smith, D 2002, 'Towards a fiscal framework for resourcing Indigenous community governance in Australia', paper presented at Indigenous Governance Conference, Canberra, 3–5 April.

Solomon, Maui 2000, 'Intellectual property rights and Indigenous peoples rights and obligations', paper presented at Global Biodiversity Forum 15, UNEP Headquarters, Gigiri, Nairobi, Kenya, May 2000.

Stavenhagen, Rudolpho 1996, 'Self-determination: right or demon?', in D Clark & R Williamson (eds.), *Self-Determination: International Perspectives*, St Martin's Press, New York.

Steiner, H & Alston P (ed) 1996, *International human rights in context, law politics morals*, Oxford University Press, Oxford.

Stephenson, M 1997, 'Negotiating Resource Development Agreements with Indigenous People: Comparative International Lessons', in B Horrigan & S Young (eds.) *Commercial Implications of Native Title*, Federation Press, Sydney.

Sterritt, N 2002, 'Defining Indigenous governance', paper presented at Indigenous Governance Conference, Canberra, 3–5 April.

Strelein, L 2000, 'The courts of the conqueror: The judicial system and the assertion of Indigenous peoples' rights', *Australian Indigenous Law Reporter*, vol. 5, no. 3.

Strelein, L 2001a, 'Conceptualising native title', *The Sydney Law Review*, Vol. 23 No. 1.

Strelein, L 2001b, 'Missed meanings: The language of sovereignty in the treaty debate', paper presented at Australian Institute of Aboriginal and Torres Strait Islander Studies (AIATSIS) Seminar Series, Limits and Possibilities of a Treaty Process in Australia, 20 August, Canberra.

Sutton, P 2001, 'The politics of suffering: Indigenous policy failure in Australia since the seventies', a revised version of the Inaugural Berndt Foundation Biennial Lecture given at the annual conference of the Australian Anthropological Society, University of Western Australia on 23 September 2000.

Taylor, R 2001, 'About Aboriginality: questions for the uninitiated', in I Keen & T Yamada, Identity and Gender in Hunter and Gathering Societies, *Senri Ethnological Studies*, 56.

Thornbery Patrick 1989, 'Self determination, minorities, human rights: a review of international Instruments', *International and comparative law quarterly*, vol. 38.

Tickner Robert 2001, *Taking a stand, land rights to reconciliation*, Allen & Unwin, Crows Nest NSW.

Tonkinson, M 1989, 'Is it in the blood? Australian Aboriginal identity', in J Linnekin & L Poyer (eds), *Cultural Identity and Ethnicity in the Pacific*, University of Hawaii Press, Honolulu.

Toyne, Peter 1993, *Report on the Education Placement of Aboriginal Secondary-Aged Students in the Southern and Barkly Regions*, Northern Territory Department of Education, Alice Springs.

Triggs, Gillian 1999, 'Australia's Indigenous peoples and international law: Validity of the Native Title Amendment Act 1998 (Cth)', *Melbourne University Law Review*, vol. 23, no. 2.

United Nations Human Rights Committee, *Concluding Observations of the Human Rights Committee Australia*, United Nations Doc. 24.7.2000, A/55/40

Unrepresented Nations and Peoples Organisation 1997, *UNPO Monitor of the United Nations Working Group on Indigenous Populations*, Unrepresented Nations and Peoples Organisation, The Hague.

Van den Berg, R 1998, 'Intellectual property rights for Aboriginal people in Australia', in *Mots pluriels*, No 8, October 1998.

Wade, R 2001, 'Indigenous land use agreements: their role and scope', paper presented at Negotiating Country, Native Title Forum, Brisbane, 1–3 August.

Waia, Terry 2002, 'Greater autonomy and improved governance in the Torres Strait region', paper presented at National Treaty Conference, August 27–29, Canberra.

Wallace-Bruce Nii Lante 1989, 'Two hundred years on: a reexamination of the acquisition of Australia', *GA Journal of international and comparative law*, vol. 19.

Walsh, M & Yallop, C 1993, *Language and Culture in Aboriginal Australia*, Aboriginal Studies Press, Canberra.

Walter, Robert Mayne 2000, 'Crossing the divide', *Panorama*, Ansett Australia, pp26–32.

Wanganeen, E 1987, *Point Pearce Past and Present*, Narrunga Community College, South Australian College of Advanced Education, South Australia.

Watson Irene 1997, 'Indigenous peoples law ways: survival against the colonial state', *The Australian feminist law journal*, vol. 8.

Webber, J 2000, 'Beyond regret: Mabo's implications for Australian Constitutionalism', in D Ivison, P Patton & S Sanders (eds.), *Political Theory and the Rights of Indigenous Peoples*, Cambridge University Press, Melbourne.

Webber, J 2001, 'Foundations of the modern treaty process in Canada: The relationship to native title', paper presented at the Australian Institute of Aboriginal and Torres Strait Islander Studies (AIATSIS) Seminar Series, Limits and Possibilities of a Treaty Process in Australia, 21 May.

Westbury, N & Sanders, W 2000, 'Governance and Service Delivery for Remote Aboriginal Communities in the Northern Territory: Challenges and Opportunities', Centre for Aboriginal Economic Policy Research, discussion paper No. 6/2000, Australian National University, Canberra.

Williams, David 2001, *Matauranga Maori and Taonga: The Nature and Extent of Treaty Rights Held by Iwi and Hapu in Indigenous Flora and Fauna, Cultural Heritage Objects and Valued Traditional Knowledge*, Waitangi Tribunal Publications, Wellington.

Williams, G 2002, 'Bills of Rights, The Republic and a Treaty: Strategies and Lessons for Reform', paper presented at Australian Institute of Aboriginal and Torres Strait Islander Studies (AIATSIS) Seminar Series, Limits and Possibilities of a Treaty Process in Australia, 3 September.

Williams Robert A Jnr 1990, 'Frontiers of legal thought III: encounters on the frontiers of international human rights law: redefining the terms of Indigenous peoples survival in the world', *Duke law journal*, vol. 60.

Williams Robert A Jnr 1991, 'Columbus's legacy: law as an instrument of racial discrimination against Indigenous peoples right to self determination', *Arizona journal of international and comparative law*, vol. 8, issue 2.

Wimmer, A 1998, 'Australia's history of hoaxes', in A Wimmer and D Callhan (eds.), *European Association for the Study of Australia Newsletter*, No.19.

Wrend, J & Smith, C (eds.) 1998, *American Indian Law Deskbook*, Conference of Western Attorneys Generals, University Press of Colorado.

Yencken, D & Porter, L September 2001, *A Just and Sustainable Australia*, published on behalf of The Australian Collaboration by the Australian Council of Social Service, Melbourne.

Yu, P April 1994, 'Kimberley: The need for self-government and a call for radical change', in C Fletcher (ed.) *Aboriginal Self-Determination in Australia*, Australian Institute of Aboriginal and Torres Strait Islander Studies, Report series, Aboriginal Studies Press, Canberra.

Yu, P 1997, 'Multilateral Agreements—a new accountability in Aboriginal affairs', in G Yunupingu (ed), *Our Land is Our Life, Land Rights—Past, Present and Future*, University of Queensland Press, St. Lucia, QLD.

Yu, P 2002, 'Aboriginal rights and governance, a Kimberley perspective', paper presented at Indigenous Governance Conference, 3–5 April, Canberra.

List of Statutes

Native Title Act 1993 (Cth)

Constitution Act 1982 (Canada)

Case Law

Calder v Attorney-General of British Columbia (1973) SCR 313

Cherokee Nation v Georgia 30 US 5, Pet. 1 (1831)

Coe v C/W (1979) 24ALR 118 ; *Coe v C/W* (The Wiradjeri claim case) 118 ALR 193

Cooper v Stuart (1889) 14 App. Cas, 286

Delgamuukw v British Columbia (1997) 3 SCR. 1010

Johnson v McIntosh 21 US 543, 5 L.Ed. 681 (1823)

Mabo and other v State of Queensland [No. 2] (1992) 107 ALR 1

Mayagna (Sumo) Awas Tingni Community v. Nicaragua (2001) (Inter American Court of Human Rights—Eng. translation) 31 August

Worcestor v Georgia 31 US 515, 6 Pet. 515 (1832)

Notes

[1] Inherent Right to Self Government Policy. At p. 23. The role of the Provinces as perceived by the Federal Government is set out in the policy document in 'Part III: Process Issues' under the heading of 'Establishment of Negotiation Process.' The policy notes that: 'Accordingly, the Government is prepared to enter into negotiations with duly mandated representatives of Aboriginal groups and the Provinces concerned, in order to establish mutually acceptable processes at the local, regional, treaty or provincial level.'

[2] The Constitution Act 1930 entrenched the Natural Resource Transfer Agreements between the Federal Government of Canada and the Provinces of Manitoba, British Columbia, Alberta and Saskatchewan.

[3] I use the term Kauwawa (Uncle) Ngarpadla (Aunty) in this paper in a Narungga cultural sense of respect and recognition. These terms are not used here in a genealogical/biological western sense.

[4] Dr Alitja (Alice) Wallara Rigney is a Narungga, Kaurna and Adnyamathanha woman. She was the First Aboriginal female principal in Australia. Dr Rigney was also instrumental in establishing the first urban Aboriginal school in Adelaide, the Kaurna Plains School. In 1998 she was awarded an honorary doctorate from the University of South Australia.

[5] The Kaurna people are the custodians of the Adelaide plains area in and around the Adelaide area in South Australia.

[6] This single was released in 1991 from the album 'Tribal Voice' – —among other awards 'Treaty' won the ARIA for Best Single in 1992. Mandawuy Yunupingu (lead singer of the band) collaborated with Paul Kelly and Peter Garrett to create the song—the lyrics were sparked by comments from former Prime Minister Bob Hawke regarding the negotiation of a treaty between Indigenous and non-Indigenous Australians.

[7] *The Australian* newspaper, Tuesday 1/6/2001, pg 11.

[8] McCorquodale (1987) recorded 67 definitions of Aboriginality used by both State and Commonwealth Governments in the past 200 years.

[9] See for instance: Aborigines Protection Act 1886, Aboriginals Ordinance Act 1913 (NT), Aborigines Amendment Act 1936, Native Administration Ordinance (1940), Aborigines Act 1957.

[10] For example, we were not counted "in reckoning the numbers of the people of the Commonwealth, or of a State or other part of the Commonwealth, aboriginal natives shall not be counted" unamended section 127 Commonwealth Constitution.

[11] Creamer (1988:48) uses the phrase "defined to confine' spatially, legally and culturally".

[12] For example when prominent NSW Magistrate Pat O'Shane was admitted to the bar a number of members of the Women's Electoral Lobby in NSW refused to support a resolution congratulating her because she didn't look Indigenous enough.

[13] Here I mean to refer to Aboriginal people who fall outside the category of what is considered 'tradtional' or 'authentic' by non-Aboriginal people.

[14] The level of misinformation surrounding the 'benefits' that an Aboriginal person is entitled to continues to astound me. Any talkback radio station on any given day provides proof of this. As an example I once replied to a 'letter to the editor' in the Sydney news paper *'The Telegraph Mirror'* stating that Aboriginal NSW Higher School Certificate students were given extra marks purely because they were Aboriginal.

[15] The notion of 'pan-Aboriginality' itself is subject to debate. I use it here to encompass the idea that regardless of the urban/rural (traditional) dichotomy there remains a common 'Aboriginality' amongst us all—a shared experience of living Aboriginal, a common feeling of cultural belonging. The idea that urban Aboriginal people share in the experience of, or are as 'Aboriginal' as, their rural/remote brothers and sisters, remains a difficult concept for many non-Aboriginal people to comprehend.

[16] It seems to my that this term 'elite' black or Aboriginal is used to refer to Aboriginal people who are perceived as educated, articulate, successful, urbanised. At a conference I attended on Treaty recently this term was used frequently by a non–Aboriginal academic in reference to the 'damage' caused to Aboriginal remote communities by well-meaning elite blacks. I dislike the term 'elite' black intensely although it appears to be increasing in use. I would argue that it is often utilised as a tool for undermining 'elite' views on 'community' issues, as if somehow our participation in mainstream, non-Indigenous society, precludes us from living or experiencing the problems our communities face daily.

[17] By this I mean a move away from living community life, a move away from poverty, substance abuse and violence—a move toward education and career opportunities.

[18] I see the 'elite'(with all that the term implies) and others dichotomy as very similar to the urban/rural dichotomy. Langton (1981:) in her seminal paper on urban Aborigines two decades ago contends that "the integrity of urban Aboriginal culture " must be recognised. With the emergence of this new distinction I would argue that to a degree we urban Aborigines (including those considered part of the 'elite') are still awaiting that recognition of our unique position in the Indigenous community by non-Indigenous people.

[19] See *The Commonwealth v Tasmania; The Tasmanian Dams Case* (1983) 158 CLR, *Gibbs v Capewell* (1995) 128 ALR 577. See also *As a Matter of Fact: Answering the myths and misconceptions about Indigenous Australians*, Commonwealth Government 1998, ATSIC Office of Public Affairs, Canberra.

[20] I readily acknowledge that this is a very simplified version of how a treaty might be formulated and implemented. Regional Agreements and Native Title Representative Bodies are themselves the subject of criticism and debate. I do not intend to explore this aspect more completely given the scope of the paper, I simply use them as a reference point for the process that might be developed in response to a treaty.

[21] Dudgeon concurs: "There needs to be some sort of evidence that people are indeed of Indigenous Australian descent; I find it hard to accept that 'just a feeling' qualifies as Indigenaity."

[22] To my knowledge there is little contention within the Aboriginal community regarding the requirement of this criteria.

[23] The book went on to win the Dobbie Award for Women's Writing, the award carries a prize of $5000. The award was accepted on 'Wanda's' behalf by her agent because 'Wanda' was overseas. To date Carmen has not returned the $5000 prize—awarded to him, a non-Aboriginal man, as an Aboriginal woman.

[24] Matthews comments: "I had experienced first hand what it felt like to grow up Aboriginal in mainstream Australia. I knew about discrimination towards Indigenous Australians. I had suffered that. Like any fundamental experience, you don't unlearn that."

[25] The story of Roberta Sykes also provides a poignant example of how children of mixed heritage were almost automatically attributed Aboriginality. See *Snake Cradle, Snake Dancing, Snake Circle.*

[26] Sally Morgan for example Aboriginal author of *My Place* was told that she was of Indian descent.

[27] Wimmer 1998:10 comments: "Mudrooroo may have given us an incorrect line about his heritage (and it is not even certain that he did so knowingly), but it seems a real tragedy that the man who has done most for the acceptance of Aboriginal literature, who served as a role model for many aspiring young authors and has given much help to start their careers is now unfairly treated like an outcast by the Aboriginal community."

[28] [1998] 389 FCA, 20 April 1998.

[29] Personal Communication.

[30] This is curious given that in most situations, ie: applying for an Indigenous Identified employment position, applying for Absutdy, qualifying for University alternative entry schemes, the onus is on the person asserting a claim to Aboriginality to establish authenticity— usually by way of a stamped certificate from a local land council or other representative body.

[31] (1938) 60 CLR 336. The principal is as follows per Dixon J at 362: "The seriousness of an allegation made, the inherent unlikelihood of an occurrence of a given description, or the gravity of the consequences flowing from a particular finding are considerations which must affect the answer to the question whether the issue has been proved."

[32] Merkel J noted: "The present case offers a good example of the difficulties thrown up by issues of Aboriginal identification. That some descent may be an essential legal criterion required by the definition in the Act is to be accepted. However, in truth, the notion of 'some' descent is a technical rather than a real criterion for identity, which after all in this day and age, is accepted as a social, rather than a genetic, construct. The solution to such problems is a matter for the legislature rather than the courts."

[33] These include issues raised in papers at the three Treaty conferences in 2002: 'Unfinished Business Conference' 3-5 June Melbourne; 'Treaty—Advancing Reconciliation' 26-28 June Perth; 'National Treaty Conference' 27-29 August Canberra.

[34] See M. Dodson's chapter, *Unfinished Business: A Shadow across our relationships* in this book.

[35] Some historical instances of recognition of Islanders distinct identity and position: Islanders were kept out of the *Aborigines Protection and Prevention of the Sale of Opium Act 1897* and the 1901 Amendment until 1904 by the influence of the Government Resident of the time John Douglas. In 1936, following the Marine Strike, Islanders negotiated concessions to the Act which were accommodated via separate legislation enacted through The Torres Strait Islanders Act 1939. In the mid-1990's Islanders negotiated the separation of funding from ATSIC and the establishment of the Torres Strait Regional Authority.

[36] House of Representatives Standing Committee on Aboriginal and Torres Strait Islander Affairs. (1997). Torres Strait Islanders: A new deal. Canberra: The Parliament of the Commonwealth of Australia.

[37] The Committee found Islanders to be so dispersed geographically on the Australian mainland that they did not have the collective numbers to gain representative seats on the ATSIC board. With no representative voice and only moral support from the TSRA, Islanders on the mainland stated that they felt abandoned without support. The Torres Strait Islander Advisory Board and the Office of Torres Strait Islander Affairs were set up to monitor the delivery of government programs and services to Islanders on the Australian mainland but its advisory and monitoring role did not equate to being part of the decision-making process in ATSIC. The Committee considered it economically not viable to separate governance structure or an extension of TSRA on the mainland, as it would duplicate the number of ATSIC agencies and services. The federal government remains firm on this position. However, the Committee did find that Islanders on the mainland "do require special considerations by ATSIC" (p. 100) and recommended that: ATSIC continues to represent the interests of Islanders on the mainland; the Chair of the Torres Strait Islander Advisory Board (TSIAB) replaces the Torres Strait Zone Commissioner on the ATSIC board; a Torres Strait Contact Officer be appointed to each regional office of ATSIC; each regional office of ATSIC be required in its Annual Report to report on measures taken to identify and respond to Islander concerns within their region; and, or ATSIC to develop a program to encourage Commonwealth, State, Local and non-Government agencies into partnerships and joint ventures with Islanders and the mainland. In the light of the federal government's slow response to these issues, the current regional autonomy forum in the Torres Strait is working to incorporate a voice for mainland Islanders into any model of regional governance.

[38] House of Representatives Standing Committee on Aboriginal and Torres Strait Islander Affairs, 1997, p. 43.

[39] Ibid, p. 41.

[40] Ibid, p. 41.

[41] Royal Commission into Aboriginal Deaths in Custody, National Report, Vol 2, pp.501–02; & Vol.4, p. 2.

[42] House of Representatives Standing Committee on Aboriginal and Torres Strait Islander Affairs, 1997, p. 42.

[43] Ibid, p. 43.

[44] Ibid, p. 77.

[45] Ibid, p. 78.

[46] Ibid, p. ix.

[47] Public speech by John Howard on 8 July 1997 on Thursday Island reported in House of Representatives Standing Committee (1997), p. 26.

[48] See for example, McFarlane, S. (1888). Among the cannibals of New Guinea. Philadelphia: Presbyterian Board of Publication and Sabbath School Work; Haddon, A.C. (1908). *Reports of the Cambridge Anthropological expedition to Torres Straits: Vol. VI. Sociology, magic and religion of the Eastern Islanders*. Cambridge: Cambridge University Press; Sharp, N. (1993). *Stars of Tagai: The Torres Strait Islanders*. Canberra: Aboriginal Studies Press; and Ganter, R. (1994). *The pearl-shellers of Torres Strait: Resource use, development and decline 1860s–1960s*. Melbourne: Melbourne University Press.

[49] See Moore, D. (1979). Islanders and Aborigines at Cape York: An ethnographic reconstruction based on the 1848-1850 'Rattlesnake' Journals of O.W. Brierly and information he obtained from Barbara Thompson. Canberra: Australian Institute of Aboriginal Studies. New Jersey: Humanities Press Inc.

[50] See Ganter, R. (1994). *The pearl-shellers of Torres Strait: Resource use, development and decline 1860s-1960s*. Melbourne: Melbourne University Press.

[51] For further readings see Beckett, J. (1987). *Torres Strait Islanders: custom and colonialism*. New York: Cambridge University Press; and, Sharp, N. (1993). *Stars of Tagai: The Torres Strait Islanders*. Canberra: Aboriginal Studies Press.

[52] See Sharp, N. (1993).

[53] See Douglas, J. (1899–1900). The islands and inhabitants of Torres Strait. *Queensland Geographical Society*, 15, 25–40.

[54] See Raven-Hart, R. (1949). *The happy isles*. Melbourne: Georgian House.

[55] For a history of the maritime strike see Sharp, N. (1993).

[56] See page 2 of Government response to Torres Strait Islanders: A new deal. (June 1998). Online document located at http://www.aph.gov.au/house/committee/atsia/tsi.pdf

[57] Figures from Standing Committee's Report, p. 11 and based on the 1996 census figures.

[58] See Sanders, W. (1999). Torres Strait governance structures and the centenary of Australian Federation: A missed opportunity. Online paper at http://www.anu.edu.au/caepr/1999/1999_DP184.pdf.

[59] For an explanation on the use of the term 'polity' instead of the more contentious term 'nation' see Langton-Marcia & Palmer, L. (2002). *Treaties and agreements as instruments of order in and between civil societies: A rational choice approach*. National Treaty Conference, Canberra. Online paper at http://www.treatynow.org/conference.asp

[60] Sanders, W. (1999).

[61] See also Government response to the Standing Committee recommendations (June 1998).

[62] See Waia, T. 2002. Greater autonomy and improved governance in the Torres Strait region. Paper delivered at Indigenous Governance Conference, Canberra, 3–5 April 2002. Online paper at: http://www.reconciliationaustralia.org/docs/speeches/governance2002/07_terry_waia.doc.

[63] The Torres Strait Treaty is worthy of reference. Islanders were not signatories but played a critical part in the eventual outcome. In what was a clear coincidence of interest between the Australian government and Islanders, Islanders' continuing traditional rights of occupation, movement and customary practices in relation to sea resources and relations with their Papua New Guinea neighbours were upheld. The Treaty affects Islanders north of 10 degrees and supports the customary movement and subsistence practices of Islanders and Papuan New Guineans in those waters.

[64] See Standing Committee Report (1997), p. 73.

[65] See for example, The Queen versus Benjamin Ali Nona & George Agnes Gisu in Haigh, D. (1999). Fishing war in the Torres Strait. Indigenous Law Bulletin, 4(22), 20–21.

[66] Since the final Report of the Standing Committee in 1997 an autonomy task force was established by TSRA to disseminate information and to coordinate discussions across the islands on the Standing Committee's proposed New Deal for Islanders. Membership of the task force has been reconstituted three times since its establishment. See TSRA News No. 24, January 1999; No. 35, October 2000; & No. 45, June 2002.

[67] See details in TSRA News, No. 40, October 2001.

[68] See House of Representatives Standing Committee (1997) recommendation No. 3.

[69] Ibid, recommendation No. 13.

[70] See Langton-Marcia & Palmer, L. (2002).

[71] Waia-Terry. (2002). *Greater autonomy and improved governance in the Torres Strait region*. National Treaty Conference, Canberra. Online paper at http://www.treatynow.org/conference.asp

[72] See Jonas-Bill. (2002). *Recognising Aboriginal sovereignty: Implications for the treaty process*. National Treaty Conference, Canberra. Online paper at: http://www.treatynow.org/conference.asp

[73] See Michael Mansell's discussion on the moral compromise in this book, and the lingering moral illegitimacy acknowledged by Bill Jonas (2002).

[74] For an articulation of this important concept, 'coincidence of interest', to agreement making between nation states and Indigenous peoples see Langton & Palmer (2002).

[75] Ibid.

indigenous people have argued that they won't negotiate on the original text and some states have expressed an unwillingness to accept the text in its original form while others can accept it in its current form. In recent sittings of the working group, some states have commenced the drafting of an entirely alternative text that reflects the political objections of some of the more powerful states like the US, UK, Canada and Australia to articles such as land rights, rights to natural resources, self-determination and cultural protection. These alternative texts are being annexed to the official working group reports.

One major controversy about this is that the drafting of the alternative text is conducted by states during the two allocated weeks of meeting time, in 'informal consultations' outside of the meeting room in the absence of indigenous people. This creates resentment, as it is extremely expensive for Indigenous people to attend these meetings for two weeks in Geneva. They attend to participate in the work on the original text of the Draft Declaration as adopted by the Sub-Commission and not the drafting of an alternative text. States argue that the drafting of this alternative Declaration is aimed at reaching a states consensus. Yet the cumulative effect of the official annexes will result in a considerably modified and effectively watered down version of the text from the original.

Permanent Forum on Indigenous Issues

On 28 July 2000, the United Nations ECOSOC approved the establishment of a Permanent Forum in which indigenous experts and nation state experts will have equal representation and deal exclusively with indigenous issues (E/RES/2000/22). The resolution established the Permanent Forum as an advisory body to the Council, with a mandate to discuss indigenous issues relating to economic and social development, culture, the environment, education, health and human rights. According to the United Nations, the Forum is specifically expected to: (a) provide advice and recommendations on indigenous issues to the Council, as well as to programmes, funds and agencies of the UN through the Council, (b) raise awareness and promote the integration and coordination of activities relating to the indigenous issues within the UN system; and (c) to prepare and disseminate information on indigenous issues.

The Forum is a 16 member panel. The Australian region is called the Pacific and the first representative is Mililani Trask from Hawaii. The distribution of governmental seats is based on the five United Nations regional groups, with three additional seats rotating among the regions. For the first Permanent Forum panel, the three regional groups are Latin America and the Caribbean, Western Europe and Asia who each have two seats. The Permanent Forum is seen as a major development in indigenous international issues, however it has also met with some suspicion based upon a view that it is an example of the states attempting to institutionalise or assimilate indigenous issues within the limitations of a restrictive agenda and formal mandate. It has been argued that the establishment of the Permanent Forum will lead to the closure of the WGIP, which many believe will limit indigenous peoples access because the PF unlike the WGIP, has restrictive attendance requirements and at the moment is based in New York as opposed to Geneva. It is not inconceivable to consider that the PF may be an example of states attempting to domesticate indigenous peoples within rigid Western political structures and agenda methods to control the dissemination of information about human rights violations to the UN and the international media. On the other hand, it may become another effective vehicle in highlighting indigenous peoples grievances and uncovering major human rights violations committed by states. For example the United Nations envisages that it may provide an entry point for implementation of the principles of ethical globalization. According to Mary Robinson, the current High Commissioner for Human Rights, 'The guidance and recommendations emanating from the permanent forum can and should make a significant contribution to improvements in the well-being of indigenous people' (Mary Robinson, U.N. High Commissioner for Human Rights). It is to early to predict but the fact that indigenous people have a permanent presence within the UN system is of itself a significant development.

Conclusion

It is clearly important that international human rights law including the international human rights covenants and treaties, the Draft Declaration and the growing body of international customary law will play an important role in the Australian domestic treaty process. It can provide a valuable framework for negotiations between indigenous peoples and the state of Australia. International law, unlike many domestic legal systems, has and continues to develop a level of recognition of indigenous peoples' rights. Many of the issues raised by ATSIC in its treaty literature are addressed in the Draft Declaration such as the recognition of distinct indigenous identities, the protection of indigenous laws, cultures and languages, law and justice issues, reparation and compensation and economic and social development. The Draft Declaration also reflects existing human rights standards relating to CERD and racial discrimination, CROC and the rights of children, ICESCR and cultural, economic and social rights, ICCPR and civil and political rights and CAT and rights relating to the prevention of torture. Comparative case law such as *Awas Tingni* and the jurisprudence of the Human Rights Committee will also be of great significance and guidance. While it is important to keep in mind Mick Dodson's qualification that 'international law is not a panacea to all our problems' (Pritchard 1998, p. 20), the important thing for the domestic treaty process is that there is an available and discernable body of law pertaining to the human rights of indigenous peoples at international law. While a treaty between Australia and its indigenous peoples will be tailored to the unique circumstances and traditions of Australia's first peoples, there does exist a body of international norms and standards that can assist if necessary in the development of a modern and dynamic document of rights and standards. All indigenous Australians should have the right to enjoy these rights and standards that in an ideal democracy, the Australian parliament is obliged to respect and apply.

Megan Davis specialises in international law.

Indigenous Disadvantage, Indigenous Governance and the Notion of a Treaty in Australia: An Indigenous Perspective

Darryl Cronin

Introduction

Overcoming disadvantage, strengthening or rebuilding governance and recognising Indigenous rights through negotiated agreements or treaties are all fundamental issues in Indigenous affairs. These issues are part of a broad Indigenous strategy to address the issues of social and economic disadvantage, acquire more autonomy and control and achieve the recognition of Indigenous rights. This paper looks at the common thread between these issues and discusses and examines the characteristics and causes of Indigenous disadvantage in two contexts:

1. the issue of Indigenous governance; and,

2. the issue of a treaty or treaties between Australian Governments and Indigenous peoples.

Indigenous disadvantage has been the focus of much public debate, however past and present solutions and efforts have been ineffective or insufficient. Most Indigenous people feel that Australian governments have failed them and they have called for more autonomy and control for their communities. Indigenous governance is seen as a way of dealing with social and economic disadvantage as well as giving effect to the principles of self-determination. However Indigenous governance appears to be confined to delivering government programs and services rather than a framework for recognising Indigenous autonomy and authority. The issue of treaty or treaties is seen as the means of developing new relationships between Indigenous peoples and the Australian nation. A treaty or treaties will provide a framework for justice and protection of rights, however the treaty issue is in danger of being perceived as another process that will not deliver any tangible benefits to Indigenous communities. In the treaty strategy there is an inevitable tension between the pursuit of Indigenous rights and redress of Indigenous social and economic problems. To be meaningful the treaty strategy must realise tangible outcomes and benefits for Indigenous people.

Indigenous Disadvantage

Indigenous disadvantage is the product of inequality. Inequality exists in many forms, including discrimination, unequal access to basic human services, inequalities of power and inequality of wealth, income and employment (Yencken and Porter 2001,

p. 38). Indigenous people are the most politically and economically disadvantaged group in Australian society and make up 2.1% of the total Australian population. Examination of material well-being is one method of determining the social and economic inequalities of Indigenous people in comparison to the dominant population. Social indicators such as employment, education, health, occupation, income and housing are the measuring sticks of economic status (Altman 2000, pp. 1–4). When these factors are analysed it can be shown that high unemployment, lack of job prospects, lack of economic or business opportunity; low incomes, dependence on government pensions and allowances, low home ownership, inability to accumulate capital, greater school drop out rates, lower post school qualifications, and lower life expectancy are characteristics of Indigenous communities. Comparative disadvantage is greater for Indigenous people who live in rural areas (Altman 2000).

But Indigenous disadvantage is not confined to material or economic disadvantage. Disadvantage has many forms and dimensions and can include matters arising from the history of dispossession, including loss of self-determination, dignity, self-confidence, sense of identity and spiritual heritage (Council for Aboriginal Reconciliation 1994, p. 11). Other factors such as overcrowded housing, poor health outcomes, lack of access to land, the high levels of arrest and victimisation of Indigenous people (Hunter 1999) and the alienation and exclusion of Indigenous people from education and training by systemic and institutional bias (Schwab & Sutherland 2001, p. 5) are also relevant when analysing Indigenous disadvantage.

The Royal Commission into Aboriginal Deaths in Custody looked in detail at issues of Indigenous poverty, inequality and disadvantage in health, housing, education, employment and income and it made recommendations about reducing and eliminating disadvantage (Johnston 1991, Volumes 2 & 4). The Royal Commission saw the "extraordinary domination" of Indigenous people by non-Indigenous people as the underlying cause of disadvantage and that disadvantage could only be eliminated by ending domination and empowering Indigenous people to control their lives and their communities (Johnston 1991 Overview and Recommendations, pp. 15–20).

Historical and continuing factors have largely influenced the social and economic position of Indigenous peoples in Australian society. Dispossession is regarded as the core of Indigenous disadvantage because it has denied Indigenous rights to natural and cultural resources replacing them with 'handouts' and dependence on non-Indigenous society. It has also supplanted Indigenous control over natural and cultural resources with non-Indigenous legal and administrative control which has had a devastating spiritual and psychological impact on people (Council for Aboriginal Reconciliation 1994, p. 13).

- The continuing causes of disadvantage include such matters as:
- Exclusion from citizenship entitlements up until the 1960's and 1970's;
- Social security payments can be more attractive than the wage economy in providing monetary support for dependents;
- Many communities are in remote locations, far from urban centres, formal labour markets and commercial opportunities;

- There is a high economic burden in raising a large young population (Altman 2000, pp. 8–11);

- Continuing inter-generational impact created by the long periods of formal exclusion and control;

- Exclusion from social and economic opportunities through discrimination and through systemic factors;

- The special programs aimed at overcoming disadvantage have not been successful;

- The history of control and exclusion strongly influences the way Indigenous people and communities relate to the mainstream society and economy (Council for Aboriginal Reconciliation 1994, p. 19).

Some commentators have argued that contemporary problems or issues including Indigenous culture contribute to continuing disadvantage, rather than the underlying causes as outlined by the Royal Commission into Aboriginal Deaths in Custody. For example such problems or issues are:

- the corruptive effect of "passive welfare" and the destructive effects of substance abuse epidemic on individuals families and on Indigenous society (Pearson 2000a, pp. 136–154; Pearson 2001);

- Aboriginal self-determination is a form of separatism and an impediment to economic and social integration into the modern world (Johns 2001, pp. 9–18);

- the separation of service delivery to Indigenous people, the denial of the need for cultural change, and the misplaced emphasis on rights (Sutton 2001);

- Cultural factors such as family formations, ceremonial obligations, low labour migration and use of languages (Altman 2000, pp. 10–11).

Pearson's (2000a, 2001) discussion about welfare dependency is not new in the Indigenous domain because such discussions have been happening for some time. The perpetuation of substance abuse and violence in Indigenous communities needs to be tackled immediately through societal change because they are major barriers to improving the social and economic position of Indigenous people. However most Indigenous people recognise there is more to Indigenous disadvantage than welfare dependency. Welfare dependency is only one factor in a range of factors, which cause community dysfunction. Pearson's arguments ignore the impact of other factors (Martin 2001, p. 20). The arguments of Johns (2001) and Sutton (2001) focus on dealing with disadvantage in the context of assimilating or mainstreaming Indigenous people into the dominant culture and appear to argue against the right of Indigenous people to pursue their own political, social, economic and cultural development. Altman's (2000) view is that cultural and language factors are constraints on Indigenous people to economically incorporate into mainstream society. But cultural and language factors are merely cultural considerations that need to be taken into account in adapting to a modern economy especially in regards to Indigenous labour market strategies.

Noel Pearson has articulated a strategy to deal with the problems in Indigenous communities in the Cape York region. He has used the idea of 'mutual obligation' to explain how Indigenous people can strengthen their society and move away from a relationship of dependency on a "passive welfare" system created by Government (Pearson 2000a, 2000b). Pearson argues about changing the individual's relationship with Government and in doing so focuses on what individuals are expected to do for society not what society can do for the individual. However he is also advocating for Indigenous governance and the role of government in facilitating greater Indigenous autonomy and control. His underlying argument is for the development of real economies for Indigenous communities and greater Indigenous autonomy and control in the Cape York region (Pearson 2000a).

Again the issue of Indigenous autonomy and control is not new. In the late 1980s the Land Councils in the Northern Territory were examining options for new Indigenous political structures (Jull 1989). In the early 1990s the Kimberley Land Council and a Coalition of Kimberley Indigenous Organisations were calling for a comprehensive regional autonomy agreement (Yu 1994; Independent Aboriginal Organisations of the Kimberley 1994) and the Cape York Land Council were considering the future possibility of self-government in Cape York (Langton 1994). The Torres Strait Islanders were already developing a framework for regional government (Lui 1994) and the Aboriginal Provisional Government was calling for an Aboriginal Government (Aboriginal Provisional Government 1992).

Indigenous groups and organisations are calling for more autonomy and control, for change to the Indigenous affairs structure and for greater equality. However Indigenous equality and participation in the Australian nation will not be achieved without positive reciprocation from non-Indigenous society (Dodson 1991, p. 778). Indigenous people are frustrated with the failure of Australian Governments to redress their disadvantage. Equally they are frustrated with the policy and practical approaches of Australian governments whereby Indigenous peoples are categorised as disadvantaged Australian rather than as distinct political communities with rights and responsibilities. Indigenous peoples are seeking new arrangements and relationships with Government. But Indigenous peoples do not want further piece meal solutions but a major overhaul and restructure of the relationship with governments (Dodson 1991, p. 781). These new arrangements and relationships extend to establishing Indigenous governance and formalising new constitutional relationships with the Australian nation.

Indigenous Governance

Governance is defined as the formal and informal structures and processes through which a group, community or society conducts and regulates both its internal affairs and its relations with others (Martin 2002). Governance involves the interactions among structures, processes and traditions that determine how power is exercised, how decisions are taken, and how citizens or other stakeholders have their say (Plumtree & Graham 1999, p. 3). It is the means (process and structure) by which communities exercise jurisdiction or control (Sterritt 2002). But governance is more than structures, processes, people and power; it is also about having authority over financial, social, cultural and natural resources (Smith 2002).

Australia has never recognised Indigenous sovereign rights through treaties or agreements. The response of Australian Governments to Indigenous demands is through administrative or statutory arrangements by the various Federal, State or Territory Governments. These arrangements have been piecemeal and often bureaucratically driven (Martin 2002) and have not adequately addressed Indigenous self-governance or matters of "unfinished business". Different forms and levels of Indigenous organisational and administrative structures already exist and these are often referred to as forms of self-government or Indigenous government. Under Australian incorporation laws Indigenous groups or communities are able to establish corporations to represent their interests and provide services. Governments have also created statutory corporations by legislation, to undertake specific functions.

In the Northern Territory, there are community organisations, Community Government Councils, Aboriginal and Torres Strait Islander (ATSIC) Regional Councils, Land Councils, Native Title Corporations, Indigenous Housing Authority and Indigenous Health Boards. The Community Organisations are generally incorporated Associations that provide a range of services. Community Government Councils provide services under the Local Government Act. ATSIC Regional Councils have authority under the ATSIC Act to make decisions about allocating ATSIC funding. Land Councils have authority under the Aboriginal Land Rights (NT) Act to manage and control Indigenous lands. Native Title Corporations have certain responsibilities under the Native Title Act including holding title on trust for native title holders and undertaking functions relating to or affecting native title. The Indigenous Housing Authority makes decisions on expenditure of pooled housing funds from the Northern Territory and the Commonwealth Governments. Similarly Indigenous Health Boards make decisions on pooled health funds to either purchase or provide health services to Indigenous and non-Indigenous communities.

The major problem with this statutory and administrative structure of Indigenous governance is that the vast majority of Indigenous organisations have no jurisdictional authority and are dependent upon annual grant funding. Where there is jurisdictional authority through some statutory mechanism, that authority is either a limited delegation of authority or it is exercised on behalf of Indigenous groups by a centralised authority. Federal and Northern Territory jurisdictional authority primarily apply over Indigenous lands and peoples, although under the Land Rights (NT) Act, Traditional Aboriginal Owners have some authority in relation to control and management of land. Further, the existing forms of Indigenous governance are based on administrative arrangements whereby Indigenous organisations administer Government programs and services or they exercise delegated jurisdiction by undertaking the statutory responsibilities of other governments.

Governance structures in Indigenous communities in the Northern Territory are limited to having local government or local government type functions. The powers and responsibilities of local government are delegated from the Northern Territory Parliament. This is a limited form of governance, which does not protect Indigenous rights or meet the unique social, cultural, political and economic needs of Indigenous peoples. Indigenous communities are seeking greater levels of authority and power and better funding arrangements to protect their social, cultural, political and economic rights. The current trend is for more regionalised forms of governance. Models of Indigenous regional autonomy are currently being articulated, developed or implemented in the Kimberley region of Western Australia (Yu 1997 2001), the Torres Strait, Tiwi Islands, Miwatj region in East Arnhem Land, and Murdi Paaki region of western New South Wales (Arthur 2001). In recent times there have been initiatives in housing and health in the Northern Territory allowing greater Indigenous participation and control over service delivery. Service delivery is being undertaken by regional organisations through regional service delivery agreements to deliver services to regional Indigenous populations (Westbury & Sanders 2000). A number of reports have also referred to the development of governance and greater regional autonomy to facilitate greater Indigenous participation and cooperation in service delivery and decision-making.

Control over Service Delivery

Much of the focus of Indigenous governance relates to controlling service delivery. Indigenous people can rightly feel aggrieved about the intractable nature of their social and economic problems because it is apparent that past and present government policies and programs have failed. Australian governments have failed on a range of matters including service delivery, recognition and respect for Indigenous rights, the creation of employment and economic opportunities and to facilitate a greater level of autonomy and control to Indigenous communities. Many Indigenous communities want to control service delivery priorities, and the design and delivery of citizenship type services. But government is considered the main barrier because it is bureaucratic, authoritarian and paternalistic (Mathews 1993, p. 8) and such bureaucracy is considered wasteful, unaccountable and unable to meet Indigenous needs (Yu 1994 p. 119). Government is unable to think outside the existing government program and service delivery paradigm and so they do not understand that current service delivery methods contribute to passive welfare dependency (Pearson March 2002 p. 4). There is very little indication that reducing inequality between Indigenous and non-Indigenous people is a priority of government (Aboriginal and Torres Strait Islander Social Justice Commissioner 2000 pp. 88–89). Indeed welfare is viewed as a method by which government can manage marginalised groups at minimal cost (Pearson 2000a p. 142). Failure of government policy is a failure of institutional imagination because policy, programs and structures are usually replicated and imposed on Indigenous people (Behrendt 2002, p. 26).

The failure of Australian governments is attributable to state and territory agencies, which appear to be under no legal obligation to take responsibility for provision of services or to address long standing inequities (ATSIC 2000 pp. 11–12). There are no adequate performance targets, benchmarks and mechanisms to ensure government accountability and transparency in funding and service delivery arrangements (Aboriginal and Torres Strait Islander Social Justice Commissioner 2000 pp. 89–91). In a draft report released in October 2000 the Commonwealth Grants Commission (CGC) noted that the intergovernmental arrangements to address Indigenous disadvantage are inadequate because they do not address long term disadvantage, build Indigenous community capacity, encourage Indigenous participation, priority setting or decision making, and deal effectively with coordination, fragmentation and cross-functional issues (Commonwealth Grants Commission 2000, p. 53).

Much of the work of the CGC on intergovernmental arrangements was taken out of their final report because the federal government said the CGC had diverted from its terms of reference (Department of Prime Minister and Cabinet 2000). However in its final report the CGC identified some key areas for action aimed at reducing Indigenous disadvantage, including the establishment of funding arrangements that reflect the long term and wide ranging nature of Indigenous need; establishing a defined role for Indigenous people in making decisions on allocation of funds and service delivery; and building the capacity of local Indigenous organisations to manage service delivery (Commonwealth Grants Commission 2001, p.90).

The public has not supported Indigenous views and arguments in relation to addressing Indigenous disadvantage. Research by the Council for Aboriginal Reconciliation found that Indigenous people are not perceived as victims of social injustice and inequity because the public believes that large amounts of public money are put into programs and services directed at Indigenous people. The general public response is to blame these problems on Indigenous behaviour or lifestyle and to perceive special funding measures as discriminatory. There is little understanding of the need for proactive funding of Indigenous programs (Johnson & Sweeney 1996, p. 8). The Australian public has very little understanding of the lack of accountability and transparency in relation to State and Territory expenditure of federal grants for the provision of services to Indigenous communities. Further it also appears there is very little understanding of human rights and Indigenous rights.

There are other factors or motivations, which explain why Indigenous peoples are pursuing greater levels of autonomy and control over their affairs. These other factors are:

- the right to self-determination;
- economic development;
- direct funding arrangements;
- greater autonomy and control;
- asserting Indigenous authority and power.

The right to self-determination

The right to self-determination is a right held by Indigenous peoples in Australia.
Although it is not a right to secession it is a right to some form of autonomy within
the Australian nation (Aboriginal and Torres Strait Islander Social Justice
Commissioner 2000, pp. 28–31). It is the right of Indigenous peoples to organise
themselves politically, socially, economically and culturally to meet their needs and to
freely determine ways in which they can use their land, resources and people to
achieve a common good (Skari 1992, pp. 93–94).

Self-determination is a mechanism to re-empower Indigenous peoples within
society. It is the right of Indigenous peoples to negotiate freely their status and
representation in the state in which they live on mutually agreed and just terms. This
does not mean assimilation of Indigenous individuals but it does mean the
recognition and incorporation of Indigenous people as distinct peoples into the fabric
of the state through constitutional reforms designed to share power democratically
(Aboriginal and Torres Strait Islander Social Justice Commissioner 2000, pp. 31–32).
Self-determination requires that Indigenous peoples have a right and ability to
determine their own priorities and strategies and be recognised as political
communities with their own governance arrangements (The Australia Institute 2000,
p. 5).

In the Northern Territory, Indigenous people have been attempting to move their
relationship with Government to one that is underpinned by recognition and
protection of rights. However 25 years of one party rule, which has largely been
hostile to Indigenous interests has been the main barrier to any progress. Indigenous
Territorians have called for greater recognition of rights, self-determination and
change to the Indigenous affairs structure. This is apparent from the Barunga
Statement 1988, and other statements such as Eva Valley Statement 1993, Kalkaringi
Statement 1998 and Standards for Constitutional Development, Batchelor 1998 (See
ATSIC News, February 2001 & Indigenous Constitutional Strategy, Northern
Territory).

A number of fundamental issues are put forward in each statement. Some of the
main issues are control over and enjoyment of land, recognition of Aboriginal law,
protection of culture and tradition, control over the delivery of social services, direct
funding of communities, the right to self-determination, the right to be self-governing
and the need for a lasting settlement or treaty. Each of those statements reflects the
ongoing process of Indigenous people in the Northern Territory in developing their
own agenda to deal with existing issues. Indigenous people are calling for change and
have been doing so for some time. However the growing assertiveness of Indigenous
people in seeking recognition and protection of rights is viewed as a threat to the
fabric of white Australian nationhood. Various attempts have been made to
undermine or extinguish Indigenous social and political aspirations. The ATSIC
Report to the United Nations Committee on the Elimination of Racial Discrimination
reported on federal government policy and strategy, which undermined Indigenous
rights and aspirations (ATSIC 1999, pp. 115–127).

Economic Development

Economic development and the creation of employment opportunities are important issues in the Indigenous domain. However the economic development focus is detached from human development and there is an assumption that economic development created for "passive" community recipients will lead to sustainable human development and elimination of disadvantage. The economic development focus derives largely from within the dominant institutional economic framework and is more about imposing the dominant institutional and economic system over indigenous people. Indigenous culture is usually regarded as an obstacle to economic development and the practical aspects of creating economic opportunities in Indigenous communities is largely a "jobs and income" approach. But economic development is only a means to improving the well-being of Indigenous communities. It is not the only solution but should be part of a broader developmental approach, which enhances economic activity and human and social development through Indigenous nation building.

Research on Indian country in the United States has found that although there is a persuasive logic to the "jobs and income" approach to economic development, it does not work because it is short term and non-strategic. Here the solutions are focused on getting grants, creating a business, finding a joint venture partner or other solutions for generating jobs and income. The result is usually failed enterprises because outsiders, primarily government, set the development agenda. The alternative is a more sustainable approach to economic development. In the "nation-building" approach the problem is the lack of jobs and income, however the solution is to build a nation in which both businesses and humans can flourish and the creation of an environment which encourages investment. Nation-building focuses on laying sound institutional foundations, strategic thinking and informed action (Cornell 2002b; Cornell & Kalt 1998, pp. 5-9).

In this model economic development is a political problem, not just an economic problem, because it is about decision-making power, the capability of effectively asserting that power and matching it to Indigenous ideas about how authority should be organised and exercised. Nation-building is about equipping Indigenous nations with the institutional foundations that will increase their capacity to effectively assert self-governing powers in relation to their own economic, social and cultural objectives. Research by the Harvard Project on American Indian Economic Development points to key factors to successful economic development, these are: sovereignty (self-rule and control over decision making); effective governing institutions, institutions culturally matched with Indigenous culture; strategic thinking and leadership that serves the interests of the Indigenous nation (Cornell 2002a, 2002b).

Direct Funding Arrangements

The broader issue of direct funding of Indigenous communities and organisations entails the recognition of Indigenous governance as another order of governance within the Australian governmental framework. Unlike Canada and the United States, Australia is not prepared to accept an Indigenous order of governance. The approach in Australia is confined to finding ways of improving the prevailing directed community services model of funding Indigenous organisations. This arrangement for funding Indigenous organisations aims to provide services to Indigenous peoples as a category of disadvantaged Australians and such funding is at the discretion and direction of the Commonwealth, States and Territory government agencies. Indigenous organisations are conceived as non-government community service organisations (The Australia Institute 2000, pp. 1–5).

The funding arrangements for Indigenous organisations are political relationships devoid of any recognition of Indigenous rights; Indigenous people and organisations are heavily dependent on grant funding from government and the legal framework does not adequately provide for the establishment of Indigenous models of governance (The Australia Institute 2000, p. 22). This funding framework is no longer applicable to the contemporary rights agenda and contemporary development issues of Indigenous communities. Self-determination is linked with a political community or people having a right and ability to determine their own priorities and design their own systems of governance (The Australia Institute 2000, p. 5). Ideas and discussion about Indigenous governance must move beyond the situation, where Indigenous organisations are non-government community service organisations or another tier of local government or where service delivery is at the direction and discretion of government funding agencies.

Indigenous governance organisations should be part of the Australian fiscal and governmental framework. They would receive more flexible and varied funding arrangements and be provided with a share of the national tax revenue. They would provide services to agreed standards, exercise jurisdictional authority, levy taxes and raise own revenue. Indigenous groups would develop their own models of governance and their own internal governance mechanisms to ensure adequate community representation, deliberation, decision-making and accountability (The Australia Institute 2000, pp. 6–10). A strong legislative base and constitutional protection should also underpin such right to self-governance.

Greater Autonomy and Control

The level of governance within Indigenous communities is reflected in their ability to control the important matters and is also reflected in the scope of their decision-making powers. Indigenous governance is a means to achieving a greater level of control because governance involves the exercise of jurisdictional authority with secure funding arrangements. Governance will enable Indigenous groups and communities to develop a stronger institutional and political base for their society to undertake a range of governance functions, including having the ability to:

- Take responsibility for dealing with social and economic problems;
- Develop Indigenous systems and institutions of law and authority;

- Re-assert authority to manage and control land, seas and communities;
- Assert rights to the natural and cultural resources;
- Re-assert identity and culture and sustain or revitalise cultural practices and beliefs;
- Develop institutional mechanisms to participate in the public government of the Commonwealth, State or Territory;
- Develop and manage new relationships with Governments based on rights and equity.

In order to define their status and the extent of their authority and power, Indigenous groups must look to their cultural values, the traditions, customs, and institutions that constitute the basis of their society. They must also develop practical ways to exercise that authority and power. Indigenous governance must be based on the exercise of authority and power whether it is inherent flowing from culture and tradition or delegated by other levels of Governance. This is the essence of Indigenous governance. Adequate jurisdictional authority is a requirement of effective governance because governance without jurisdiction is governance without strength and power. Indigenous governance strategies must also focus on rebuilding or strengthening Indigenous authority and power in a modern form, which reflects Indigenous culture and tradition, is legitimate in the Indigenous community and is able to effectively engage with the dominant society.

Asserting Indigenous Authority and Power

Indigenous or Aboriginal authority is described as the legitimate authority of distinct peoples to make their laws, design their governing institutions and govern themselves as they see fit (Cassidy 1994, p. 13). Indigenous rights to land and native title and the authority that flows from these rights are manifestations of Indigenous authority. Indigenous authority derives from culture and tradition, which in turns derives from prior occupation and cultural rights and responsibilities to land, seas, and natural resources. The recognition of native title and rights to land has provided the basis for recognising an "autonomous source of legal and political authority" within Australia whose source lies outside the common law (Webber 2000, p. 77) and which predates the authority of Australian governments.

In Australia the relationship between governments and Indigenous peoples proceeded on the assumption that Indigenous peoples had neither laws nor a worthwhile culture, therefore they had no system of law and government. But the recognition of native title has changed that assumption. Native title and rights to land are not just property rights, although governments have defined them as such. Native title "is inherent to the occupation of land and identical to the kind of dominion that people of different societies assert over land" (Pearson 1997, p. 122). Native title is a right or title in a group to order their own affairs in relation to land and to exercise a level of authority and autonomy within the group and externally against all others (Strelein 2001a, pp. 123–124). It is recognition of an inherent sovereignty (Strelein 2001b, p. 1) and accordingly it manifests as jurisdictional authority. The issue of

Indigenous rights to land is inseparable from the issue of sovereignty because the key issues for Indigenous cultural survival are a separate political jurisdiction and the establishment of a land base. The first step in regaining lost sovereignty is claiming traditional lands (Scholtz 2001).

The notion of a Treaty or Treaties

In North America, Indian tribes have a government to government relationship with the United States. A tribe is a group of Indians recognised as constituting a distinct and historical political entity for at least some governmental purposes (Canby 1998, p. 4). The basic element of this relationship is that it is based on the inherent sovereignty of each party and it acknowledges the right of the tribes to self-determination, including the right to operate their own governments, control their own resources, and protect their culture. It also includes federal protection of tribal resources and sovereignty, it bars state interference with tribal affairs without federal or tribal approval, and it involves a weaker sovereign taking the protection of a stronger sovereign without extinguishing its own sovereignty (O'Brien 1989, p. 293). Sovereignty is described as the inherent right or power to govern (Canby 1998, p. 68). Indian sovereignty is another level of sovereignty within the American federal system of government and the manifestation of this sovereignty is tribal government. An Indian tribe is a distinct political community, with its own territory and its own exclusive authority (Cherokee Nation v Georgia 1831). The source of tribal sovereignty is Aboriginal or Indian title that predates European colonisation but which is now recognised by treaties, statutes, executive orders and actions (Wrend & Smith 1998, pp. 44–45). Therefore a tribe is its own source of power and its authority and power to act are not delegated by the federal government, but are inherent (O'Brien 1989, p. 292).

The position of Indigenous peoples in Australia is different because Indigenous authority is not recognised by Australian law. The colonial occupiers of Australia refused to acknowledge the prior existence and authority of Indigenous law and custom. The English took possession of the Australian continent on the assumption that Indigenous people did not own the land, were not 'civilised' and did not have an established system of law. Therefore the Australian continent was regarded as *terra nullius* and open to settlement or occupation. Colonial governments did not make agreements with Indigenous peoples because they adhered to English law, which asserted that Australia, was unoccupied without settled inhabitants or settled law (McNeil 1989, p. 121; Cooper v Stuart 1889). This fiction was further entrenched into the Australian system of government, when in 1901 the States excluded Indigenous peoples and created a federation. It was not until 1993 that the High Court of Australia declared that Australia was not *terra nullius* at the time of European settlement (Mabo and others v State of Queensland [No. 2] 1992).

But *terra nullius* still lives on. Australian law still denies the existence of Indigenous sovereignty (Clark 2001a, p. 161). The recognition of native title and rights to land has not translated into recognition of the underlying Indigenous authority which emanates from those titles. Native title and rights to land have been confined to mere property titles, another form of land tenure. But native title is more than recognition of a particular land tenure. It "is intrinsically bound up with issues of political organisation and self-government" because the title is determined by Indigenous societies, which have their own legal orders and their own political capacity. Also the recognition of native title requires the development of institutions and political organisation (Webber 2000, p. 68).

The recognition of Indigenous title involves the recognition of Indigenous self-governance but it also raises broader considerations of relations between non-indigenous and Indigenous societies (Webber 2000, pp. 86–87). The issue of Indigenous title or authority is related to the question of the status and place of Indigenous people in the Australian nation. The recognition of Indigenous title should ultimately lead to the recognition and accommodation of an Indigenous legal order within the Australian federation. Such recognition and accommodation must involve political negotiations between Indigenous peoples and Australian governments leading to negotiated agreements or treaties. A treaty or treaties could provide protection for Indigenous rights and establish the framework of new constitutional and political relationships between Indigenous groups and the governments of Australia (Clark 2001a).

The issues of Indigenous rights and overcoming disadvantage have been portrayed by the federal government as distinct and separate. Indigenous rights are seen as a distraction (Aboriginal and Torres Strait Islander Social Justice Commissioner 2000, p. 22). The Federal Government sees the past treatment of Indigenous people and the issues of rights and justice as irrelevant to the achievement of practical outcomes in Indigenous health, housing, education and employment. There is no disagreement that social and economic reform is a priority, and indeed Indigenous people agree that governments need to be held accountable for their lack of action. However rights to land, culture and self-determination are also important in redressing disadvantage.

The federal government proposes a "practical" approach, which emphasises limited and specific arrangements around particular services, programs and processes. However the policy of practical reconciliation excludes debate about addressing disadvantage on the basis of rights and it maintains a situation where Indigenous people are subject to the beneficence and good intentions of government (Aboriginal and Torres Strait Islander Commissioner 2000, pp. 22–23). Practical reconciliation represents little more than the continuation of the official government policy towards Indigenous people that has been in place for three decades. That policy, which is spending by the federal government on programs and services for Indigenous people for the delivery of mainstream citizenship-type services and programs, has rarely been underpinned by a rights agenda (Crough 2001a, p. 3). Further practical reconciliation has not resulted in any significant expenditure to address the backlog of infrastructure deficiencies in Indigenous communities or address the widening gap in terms of living conditions and access to basic services (Crough 2001a, pp. 4–8).

Past experience with Australian governments has engendered frustration, distrust and cynicism because Indigenous people perceive that nothing is going to change. Indigenous people have witnessed or have participated in a number of public policy processes, such as commissions, inquiries, reports or reconciliation processes and believe that the outcomes of these processes have been very limited or of little benefit to them. Indeed some Indigenous people believe government foist these processes on Indigenous people to make it look as though something is being done about their problems or claims for recognition of rights. There may indeed be concerns that the ATSIC treaty strategy is another process with little outcome for Indigenous people.

While there may be a diversity of opinion in the Indigenous community about the desirability of a treaty, most Indigenous people acknowledge that there must be recognition of Indigenous rights and some form of settlement between Indigenous peoples and the Australian nation. However treaty discussions have highlighted the tensions between the Indigenous rights agenda and the need to deal with Indigenous social and economic problems. Some Indigenous people are asking how a treaty might improve housing, health, education and provide employment. This response lacks understanding of the interrelationship between Indigenous needs and rights. Further it "simplifies the problems, as well as the solutions to socio-economic disparity" and may entail a lack of understanding of the need for a rights framework to protect existing rights and create and protect rights to economic self-sufficiency so that people are not dependent on welfare or the benevolence of government (Behrendt 2002, pp. 25–27). Some Indigenous people also perceive treaty as being a top down or national approach to an issue that should be developed and controlled at a regional or local level.

To be meaningful the treaty strategy must have tangible outcomes and benefits for Indigenous communities. It must deal with the substantive issues that currently affect Indigenous communities. These substantive issues are not only confined to service delivery matters such as health, housing, education, employment, and other social programs to reduce violence and abuse, but also extend to such issues as reparation and compensation, land and water rights, cultural heritage and intellectual property rights, rights to the natural resources, law and justice, direct funding, the right to self-governance and recognition of Indigenous authority and power. Indigenous governance is the mechanism for dealing with the substantive issues. It will also build or strengthen Indigenous capacity to take on the broader issue of a constitutional settlement. In that regard one of the cornerstones of any treaty process must be the pursuit of the right to self-governance through the development of Indigenous governing structures, and this includes determining the authority and financial aspects of Indigenous governance.

Indigenous governance processes are happening now. Some Indigenous communities are discussing how they might acquire more control over their affairs and are putting in place strategies to do so. The treaty strategy needs to be linked more closely with the processes of Indigenous governance because it is an area in which Indigenous groups are beginning to assert their authority. Indigenous authority should underlie the basis of any treaty strategy and form the basis of any negotiations or agreements. In the long run, though, a governance arrangement or agreement will not amount to a treaty because the basis of the treaty is in developing new constitutional relationships. But Indigenous governance will lay the foundations for a treaty process because it will strengthen or rebuild governance structures, rebuild

Indigenous economies and foster healthy communities. Governance will also deal with some of the immediate issues that confront Indigenous communities.

Conclusion

Australian governments will not genuinely and successfully redress Indigenous disadvantage through their normal policy and program approaches because they are either incapable or in some cases unwilling to deal with such issues. Indeed there is very little indication that Australian Governments are committed to addressing the needs of Indigenous peoples or their relative disadvantage compared to the non-Indigenous population.

Indigenous governance is the means for Indigenous communities and groups to take responsibility for their own decisions, manage their own affairs and exercise authority to deal with a range of political, social and economic matters. Indigenous organisations currently undertake a range of functions to address Indigenous needs and protect rights and interests. New service delivery and decision making models of governance are being implemented, however Indigenous governance must go further than just providing Indigenous organisations with the status of non-government community service organisations or recognising them as another tier of local government. Indigenous governance must extend to recognising Indigenous authority and accommodating such autonomous authority within the Australian federal system of governance.

The authority and power to negotiate treaties or agreements derives from within a peoples or a community. The idea of treaty or treaties between Indigenous peoples and Australian governments is an issue that must emanate from the culture and tradition of a peoples or a community. Therefore a treaty strategy must be grounded in these ideals otherwise it will be seen as being detached from the problems and issues that confront Indigenous communities on a daily basis. It will also be seen as a top down approach. The treaty strategy must be linked more closely with the processes of Indigenous governance that are currently developing as a way of dealing with the current issues and problems and as a means of providing tangible outcomes and benefits to Indigenous communities. Dealing with and resolving the substantive issues at a local or regional level will build a much firmer foundation for a future treaty process.

Daryl Cronin is a research fellow for the Centre for Indigenous Natural & Cultural Resource Management at the Northern Territory University.

Treaty and the Self-determination Agendas of Torres Strait Islanders: A Common Struggle

Dr Martin Nakata

Introduction

This chapter, like others in this book, contributes to the conversations underway within the Treaty Think Tank. It draws from experiences in the Torres Strait with the aim of speaking to some of the issues raised by members of the Think Tank and other contributors to Treaty conversations.[33] Whilst the Torres Strait context provides no clear way through any of the issues it does perhaps provide substance to the issues involved in negotiating and developing models for political autonomy or governance in a regional context. The Torres Strait example illustrates how the issues, as discussed and understood by both parties (Islanders and governments), are anchored both in principles (for example rights) and practicalities (for example how to achieve better representation and determination of Islander interests, better control over local resources and better delivery of externally funded services into the region). But it is *the task of developing processes and mechanisms to deliver both and satisfy all interests that is the real difficulty in the Torres Strait and with the current Treaty process.*

A consideration of the difficulties that have arisen in Torres Strait negotiations may point up the areas that will need to be clarified for sceptic members of Indigenous communities elsewhere if they are to be encouraged to see the value in any proposals being discussed by the Treaty Think Tank. The difficulties in the Torres Strait example also point up the amount of work to be done in developing clearer understanding of the components of regional autonomy or self-government (an untried concept in this context). Clear understanding is critical in contexts where historical colonial legacies and more recent administrative practices cloud, even obstruct, the creation of more effective and workable systems of governance, and where the intersections of traditional customary practices, colonial practices and Western democratic practices and their various interests also complicate matters. A consideration of these difficulties may assist the arguments for the creation of a national standards framework for local and regional agreement making, as well as the details of any such framework.

At the very least, the Torres Strait example illustrates the extent of work to be done to connect the rhetoric of top down (the national, universal perspective) and bottom up (on the ground, practical and locally appropriate) approaches being pursued to address the 'unfinished business'[34] in Australia. It may also be useful in gaining a realistic sense of timelines in a treaty process.

Autonomy in the Torres Strait context

Torres Strait Islanders in the Torres Strait are arguably further along the road to self-government than any other Indigenous group in Australia, and have got to this position without exciting too much controversy. Indeed there has been little public discussion of our progress outside of the Torres Strait community and very little reference to our position in any broader national discussions of Indigenous sovereignty, rights, treaty, or even practical issues. This is perhaps due to the fact that we have historically pursued our struggle by emphasising our cultural distinctiveness, and have on that basis and also the basis of geographical isolation, and minority numbers chosen the path of political independence [35] when pursuing self-determination agendas. This stance of independence reflects our distance from the centralised bureaucracies that have determined policy and made decisions on our behalf. It is also perhaps distance and small numbers that limits contributions to national discussions, as well as respect protocols on the part of both the Islander and Aboriginal leadership. However, in the current context of local and regional agreement-making on the Australian mainland, it is perhaps timely for Islanders to share their experiences and to look around at the strategies others are pursuing and the progress being made in Aboriginal Australia.

The Torres Strait Islander strategy of always appealing to local, regional, historical and cultural specificities has enabled a long slow process of negotiating by increment towards the goal of self-determination. Cutting deals has often depended on leveraging between governments and taking advantage of, or at least benefiting from, particular historical moments.

One of the distinctive features of Islander negotiating is a lack of preciousness about the language used. Islander politics is and always has been a struggle to reassert political independence as a response to external control of our affairs and this has never been disguised. How others define and use the concepts and principles on which that aspiration may be curtailed or progressed matters not to Islanders. The goal remains the same viz., an effective role in decision-making and policy-making in regard to the issues that affect Islander lives and futures in the Torres Strait.

Islander negotiating has also been characterised by a notable absence of loyalty or allegiance to any particular ideology, party political persuasion or government, nor to any particular personalities, although appeals to these are readily deployed to gain leverage in cutting deals and in reaching short-term goals. This has sometimes been hard for non-Islanders to understand, particularly left-liberals who worry we do not understand conservative agendas.

Islanders thus are sometimes seen as 'unprincipled' enough to 'get into bed with the enemy'. Our own reading of this practice is one of maintaining the Torres Strait standpoint regardless of who holds the reigns of power and remaining steadfast in the pursuit of self-determination agendas whatever the changing determinations of others are.

In August 1997, and ninety-three years after Torres Strait Islanders came under the all encompassing terms and regulations of *The Aborigines Protection and Prevention of the Sale of Opium Act 1897 (1901)* in 1904, the final Report[36] of the House of Representatives Standing Committee on Aboriginal and Torres Strait Islander Affairs (1997) inquiry into greater autonomy for Torres Strait Islanders was delivered to parliament. The Standing Committee consulted institutions, communities and individuals across the nation and finalised 25 recommendations in support of regional autonomy in the Torres Strait region, and improved processes within ATSIC for Islanders on the mainland[37]. From these consultations they were convinced that "Torres Strait Islanders could take responsibility for their own affairs".[38]

Although the Committee accepted that a greater degree of autonomy means different things to different people, they identified three dimensions of autonomy that Islanders sought. These were: representative structures to influence public sector expenditure and delivery of services to Islanders (greater political/structural roles); control over the natural resources and government expenditure in the Torres Strait region (greater economic independence); and a higher degree of emphasis on Torres Strait heritage, languages and traditions (greater cultural interpretations).

In outlining the benefits of regional autonomy for the Torres Strait, the Committee synthesised from submissions and accepted what essentially constitutes the set of premises on which Islanders base their arguments for regional autonomy. The first was expressed as 'returning a right'. Islanders were recognised as the original inhabitants of the region: "These people had total control over their lives, their culture and the local economy, before that autonomy was taken away after European contact and formal annexation to Queensland in 1879. By giving Torres Strait Islanders a greater degree of autonomy, the Commonwealth and Queensland governments will be returning a right that was taken from them".[39] Islanders consider this principle a basic and necessary element of Reconciliation agendas.

The second premise was the important role of Torres Strait culture. The Committee accepted arguments about the link between formal decision-making processes and respect for local customs, and recognised "that by having greater autonomy, Torres Strait Islanders will be able to integrate program design and delivery with their cultural values. The result should be the preservation of Ailan Kastom through its continuing relevance and application in daily life".[40] A Council of Elders to advise elected representatives was supported and recommended by the Standing Committee.

The third premise centred on the link between effective change and greater Torres Strait Islander responsibility for their own affairs. In upholding submissions from Islanders, the Committee cited the Royal Commission into Aboriginal Deaths in Custody[41] arguing that "substantial change for Aboriginal people in Australia will not occur unless governments and non-Indigenous people accept the necessity for allowing Aboriginals to identify, effect and direct the changes which are required".[42] The Committee accepted that "if Torres Strait Islanders are given a greater degree of responsibility for making the decisions that affect them, they will then seek their own solutions to problems and establish their own economic initiatives".[43]

The final premise centred on service-delivery issues. It was accepted that greater regional involvement in decision-making processes was also likely to lead to better program co-ordination and more effective use of resources and funding. But the Committee felt this premise also had the potential to blur distinctions between greater autonomy and greater self-management. It cautioned that self-management (via input and administration of government policy and programs) was complementary to political autonomy but a poor substitute for it. It therefore encouraged specific-agreement making between Islanders and agencies that involved Islanders in "an integral role in high level policy development".[44] It cited as a best practice example the, *Agreement on Aboriginal and Torres Strait Islander Health between the Queensland Minister for Health, the Commonwealth Minister of State for Health and Family Services and the Chairperson of the Aboriginal and Torres Strait Islander Commission, July 1996*. The Committee recommended that Islanders develop "generic guidelines for negotiation by people of the Torres Strait region, that can be used by Commonwealth and State agencies which are developing policies that particularly affect the region".[45]

In accepting the arguments for autonomy in the Strait, the Committee made a number of recommendations for greater autonomy in the Torres Strait region. The first and principal recommendation was the establishment of a joint Commonwealth-State government statutory body, conceived as an elected *Regional Assembly*, to carry out the coordinating functions for all people in the Torres Strait region.

The model proposed included a representative structure for all people in the region, not just Islanders. This was argued to be democratic and in the interests of the region and ensured effective representation of Islander interests because Islanders constituted the majority. Islanders accepted this qualifier on democratic and inclusive principles of justness and fairness, and as part of the modern reality of living within the bounds of the Australian State.

The Committee acknowledged that the three tiers of government—local, state and federal—did not deliver services to such an isolated and small population in a satisfactory way but was characterised by "inefficiency, duplication, a lack of services and dilution of real autonomy".[46] The proposed model essentially called for the conflation of bureaucratic control over what is effectively the funding for local government infrastructure that comes to the Torres Strait from Commonwealth and State sources. This is currently dispersed via three institutions: Torres Strait Regional Authority, Torres Shire Council and the Island Coordinating Council. The Island Coordinating Council operates on behalf of 17 discrete Island community councils. A large proportion of funding to ICC and TSRA comes by way of the Federal Government's work for the dole scheme, or CDEP (Community Development Employment Program).

Amongst a list of recommended roles and functions for the proposed Assembly was included an advisory role to advise Commonwealth and State Ministers on policy for the region. Whilst Islanders are already involved in a number of advisory and consultative processes in relation to separate government policies that affect them, the proposal provides a space perhaps for more effective cross-portfolio coordination of policy and a mechanism under which frameworks for regional agreements and negotiation can be developed. It also broadens the regional role beyond local government concerns into what many regard as the real business of Islander self-determination—social and economic policy determinations to improve Islander well-being along the range of social and economic indicators. The details of how Islanders might discharge this function were not outlined. This point will be returned to later in this chapter.

It was also proposed that the model of a Regional Assembly be incorporated with processes and structures that could lead to *self-government under Territory status* when the region was more economically self-reliant. The report called for the positive support and action from the State and Commonwealth authorities to develop legislation to facilitate processes towards this end. In the final months when the Committee was drafting its report, the Prime Minister, John Howard, lent his support to the process. On a visit to the Torres Strait, he announced a promise to Islanders that the Torres Strait Regional Authority (TSRA) would have separate enabling legislation by the end of 2000[47] as a move towards this end. This is yet to be enacted.

However, Islanders had concerns with the proposed Regional Assembly despite it having the potential if not the detail to move the region towards a greater degree of autonomy, and self-government via territory status at a later date. Five and a half years on, Islanders are yet to reach agreement on the proposed governance structures for the Torres Strait. If the Torres Strait is cited as one of the contexts where regional self-government is most likely to be achievable then why has the negotiation been so fraught and protracted so close to the end goal?

Torres Strait Islander participation in external systems of local and regional governance—past and present

In pre-colonial times, Islanders lived in politically autonomous but inter-connected communities on Islands across the Strait and had extensive trade and kin networks within the Strait and extending north into Papua New Guinea and south along coastal communities of Cape York.[48] They also traded with other voyagers who passed through the Strait.[49] In the colonial period, legislation aimed at regulating the frontier marine industry and gaining some control over missionary activity became, in the space of two decades, legislation that severely restricted the freedom of Islanders and limited their participation in and negotiation of the emerging new order.[50] Whilst the entire history of colonial administration is relevant in some way to the current context, the need for brevity does not permit its explication.[51] In relation to systems of governance all aspects of Islander lives from 1904 were controlled by the Queensland government via the *Aborigines Protection and Prevention of the Sale of Opium Act, 1897* and the subsequent *Torres Strait Islanders Act 1939* until the entry of the Commonwealth government into Islander affairs following the 1967 Referendum. Moreover, to Islanders, the locus of power of the Queensland government resided entirely in the hands of the singular Local Protector acting on behalf of the Chief

Protector who was the arbiter of all fate, and seemingly as powerful as any autocrat.[52] The principles of liberal democracy were certainly not on view in the Torres Strait.

However, in a quirk of history perhaps, Islanders were given a means of limited participation in the new order of government and this aspect of colonial experience has significance in terms of current models for political autonomy. A simple system of 'local' Island Councils was instituted in 1899 by a liberal-minded Government Resident, John Douglas, who viewed Islanders as people of intelligence and capacity, capable of exercising the rights of British citizens.[53] The Council system operated through elected councils of village 'headmen' with magisterial powers and village constables. In practice, as controls over Islanders tightened during the colonial period, this limited form of participation in government made a mockery of the democratic process[54] and co-opted Islanders into a process of self-regulation to uphold external agendas. With white teacher/supervisors in effective day to day control of communities, the power of veto located in the Local Protector, and no such thing as a secret ballot, the Island Councils were a structural reflection of the paternal relationship. We were little more than agents of the new order, actively policing its terms and participating in our own humiliation.

However, on the positive side, this mechanism achieved a number of things. It established a degree of recognition of Islanders as occupiers with a continuing presence and visibility. Diminished and powerless though we were at the bottom of the new order, most communities remained Islander communities even as many customary practices were transformed to incorporate new realities. This system also allowed a degree of participation in and exposure to external systems of governance, providing a space where Islanders could measure what these systems meant to and for them and where customary practice could be accommodated to a degree. It entrenched an Islander ambivalence towards external authority whilst developing an active, often resistant local politic with a recognised leadership that positioned itself between external authority and the community. It provided a channel and protocols through which leaders could communicate grievances and through which government officials could coerce and persuade Islander leaders to cooperate with government policy.

This history has provided the structure for political negotiation and representation of Islanders living in the outer Islands today. This history has also helped preserve the discrete identities of many pre-contact communities as new circumstances forged the Torres Strait collective identity. Since the maritime strike of 1936,[55] the Council system has been a legitimate means for Islanders to assert themselves as a collective. Designated inter-Island meetings of Island Chairmen since this time have facilitated pan-island unity on issues of concern to Islanders.

The continuity of the Island Council system means it is now an integral part of political organisation in the Torres Strait and instrumental for maintaining unity and equitable distribution of resources and services across the collective. The concept further developed over the reform period, post 1970s. Now legislated under the Queensland Government's Community Services Act 1984 (descendent of previous

Aboriginal and Torres Strait Islander Acts), the Councils currently discharge the functions of local government, employ Islander police officers, administer Island courts and control entry onto land (whether it be land granted under Native Title or Deed of Grants in Trust). Only Islanders or Aborigines can run for office. The Island Coordinating Council (ICC) established under the same Act is now the peak Queensland body representing all Island Councils. It has an advisory role but can also contract, implement and administer programs and projects. 17 Island Councils are represented in this Council, including the suburb of Tamwoy on Thursday Island (previously a Reserve) and the Cape York communities of Bamaga and Seisia, which are relocated Torres Strait communities.

With regard to the Commonwealth presence in the region, Island Councils are also represented on the Torres Strait Regional Authority by their Chairpersons. The Torres Strait Regional Authority (TSRA) carries out all the roles and functions of the former ATSIC Torres Strait Regional Council which it replaced. Both the Torres Strait Regional Council and the Torres Strait Regional Authority were legislated under the ATSIC Act. TSRA, under new legislation[56], now receives its budget from the Federal Department of Finance and Administration and is considered a milestone on the path to self-determination in the Torres Strait, and legislation has been promised by the current Government to reconstitute TSRA outside of the ATSIC Act 1989. The Island Councils, ICC, and the TSRA have elected and administrative arms.

Islanders and the Torres Shire Council

Not all Islanders in the Torres Strait are represented at the local government level through Island Councils. Also a product of the colonial period but with a different evolution is the Torres Shire Council (TSC) based on Thursday Island. Thursday Island was the colonial administrative centre and off limits to Islanders until the post-war period. Once the enclave of the Europeans, Asians and the 'mixed-races', Thursday Island and the nearby islands of Horn Island and Prince of Wales Island (Ngurapai and Muralug) now have significant numbers of Islanders. Many of the Islanders of mixed descent identify strongly and are accepted as Torres Strait Islanders and have roots in traditional communities. Many outer-Islanders come to Thursday Island to reside for education and employment opportunities. A significant proportion of the population of these three inner Islands are non-Indigenous (in the vicinity of 40%).[57]

The Torres Shire Council from the 1950s, and for almost forty years, was run by an administrator appointed by the State. Now, incorporated under the Queensland *Local Government Act 1993,* all people who meet the normal Queensland local government eligibility criteria may stand and vote at elections. Since 1991, Islander representation on the Torres Shire Council has grown to closely reflect the population proportion. Since 1994, an Islander has held the office of Mayor.

Torres Strait Islanders who live within this local government jurisdiction also have representation on the Torres Strait Regional Authority through two directly elected positions. Non-Indigenous people, of course, have no representation on TSRA.

Integrating two previously politically separate local government domains into one regional structure

In short, the local governance structure consists of seventeen (17) Island Community Councils operating under one set of legislation and derivative of old traditional communities that were gazetted Aboriginal Reserves under former Queensland Acts. It also includes one (1) Torres Shire Council that whilst nominally responsible for the entire Torres Strait effectively deals with local government jurisdictions in the areas formerly not gazetted as Reserves. This shire operates under different legislation that represents the interests of all residents whether they are Islanders or not. It effectively operates in the administrative centre of Thursday and nearby Islands.

All eighteen (18) Councils have representation in the current regional governance structures. The seventeen (17) outer-Island communities are represented in the ICC and TSRA. The Torres Shire Council does not have representation on the ICC but two directly elected positions representing its Islander residents are preserved on the TSRA. This arrangement reflects historical developments, which have maintained a divide across local and regional governance structures between the more traditional/homogenous Island communities and the much more mixed population in the administrative area who were historically not subjected to the restriction of the Queensland Acts that controlled Islander people on Reserves.

Perhaps not understanding the strength of feeling of Islanders[58] living within the boundaries of the Torres Shire Council, the Standing Committee recommended that the TSC be abolished and its functions be incorporated directly into the business of the Regional Assembly largely because of the close physical proximity. The Committee proposed that the local government area of the TSC would be replaced by five (5) elected positions within the Regional Assembly. At the same time, the seventeen Island (17) Councils were to remain intact and independent because they were distant and isolated and because it was considered important to retain the integrity of these more traditional Island polities.[59] This was rejected by the Torres Shire Mayor, an Islander, who felt it was discriminatory.[60] He (and others) argued that it was undemocratic that local government services in the former Torres Shire region would be reduced to a structure where only 5 of the 22 member Regional Assembly represented 63 per cent of the population and where the role of Mayor would be abolished, and where the remaining 17 members represented other much smaller local councils (23 per cent) and who would stay in control of their local government business. He was particularly upset that the TSC was being dismantled as an entity so soon after Islanders under its jurisdiction had been given the opportunity to participate in local government. Current alternate proposals being put forth by Islanders therefore argue to retain the Torres Shire Council as the 18th local government structure in the region and there is understandably general agreement on this by both the Queensland and National governments.[61]

In relation to overseeing local government functions, the Standing Committee's proposal for a Regional Assembly is essentially about establishing a joint Commonwealth-State coordinating mechanism rather than continuing with two separate bodies—the ICC (State) and the TSRA (Commonwealth). It is also about integrating two historically different political domains at the regional level and including non-Indigenous residents under the same structure, although accounting for budget streams would still have to reflect the Indigenous/non-Indigenous basis of funding allocations. If the Torres Shire Council were to be retained in its current form then the proposal for a Regional Assembly would seem to be a small change from the current situation, or a streamlining of the current regional mechanisms across the two previously politically separate local government domains. Aspirations for regional autonomy, however, extend beyond the functions of local government.

Other tiers of governance in the Torres Strait

The regionalising—bringing together of the discrete local councils under a broad regional structure—of what are essentially local government systems is an important part of self-determination. Much improvement has occurred in the Torres Strait by improved regional coordination of local government service planning, implementation and resource use.[62] The role and contributions of Torres Strait Islanders in developing and implementing new processes has made enormous differences that support the basic premises for regional autonomy. However, Indigenous communities are also overlaid by an array of Commonwealth and State government interests that extend far beyond local government jurisdiction, and the Torres Strait is an excellent example of the complex web of government policy and practice that conditions many aspects of daily life.

The Torres Strait may be remote but it lies across an international seaway and an international border subject to an international Treaty and all that entails.[63] It lies in a sensitive environmental region at the most northern end of the Great Barrier Reef. This reality means that Islander lives are overlaid in the portfolio sense by a foreign affairs presence, an immigration presence, quarantine presence, a customs presence, a Federal police presence, a Queensland police presence, a water police presence, a fisheries presence, and aerial surveillance among other things. These are not just jurisdictional referents but involve a material physical presence of all these interests in the region. And this is before we get to service provision in the basic areas of health, education, employment, housing, welfare, communications, utilities, transport and justice all of which are represented by various agencies at various tiers of government. Thursday Island is therefore a veritable outpost of Federal and State bureaucracies but still distant from the policy and decision-making centres of Brisbane and Canberra.

Some of these government interests (eg. quarantine and fisheries concerns) are weighted toward regulatory regimes and some (eg. health and education) are weighted towards service provision for Islanders. But all impact in some way. Regulatory regimes associated with the Border and with marine resource and environmental issues require the co-operation of Islanders. Whilst Islanders are generally co-operative there are absurdities and ironies that do not escape them in what is a culture of regulation and policing.

For example, one of the demands of the 1936 strike was for a lifting of restrictions on inter-Island travel. Islanders had been denied freedom of movement by the Protector and had to have permission and a pass to travel on the seas for any purpose. Failure to comply resulted in penalty. In 2003, Islanders have free passage across their seas and beyond but their activities are regulated to an extraordinary degree. Boat licensing, fishing licensing, the regulation of 'subsistence' and traditional marine activity, safety regulations, quarantine regulations, the limits of protected zones associated with the Border Treaty, seasonal and catch limits to name some. These are actively policed and carry a penalty if breached. Most of these regulations are for good reason—and well understood—some for our protection, some for resource protection, some for territorial reasons. These regulations may be accepted by Islanders for their 'good' but the inequities, for example, between the regulation of Islanders and outside commercial fishermen (in effect as well as in intent) lay the grounds for grievance and serve to reinforce the ongoing quest for self-determination in the islands. As in Aboriginal coastal communities, there is evidence in the Torres Strait experience that suggests that protection of traditional rights and pursuit of local interests has led to over-regulation of Islanders rather than the external players. What constitutes a legitimate 'subsistence' catch of a particular marine species can be enshrined in regulation down to a particular number and also regulate who may be in the boat and who may not. Trawlers that annually remove around $20 million of prawns, lobsters and mackerel[64] (the profits of which leave the Strait) and damage the sea floor in the process are exercising legitimate rights and do not have to account to Islanders or the region but to licensing boards far away in southern cities. Application of penalties in this web of legislation adds to the growing 'criminalisation' of Islanders who for customary subsistence or commercial reasons breach any regulations. This bears resemblance with colonial times where Islanders were harshly regulated by government to 'protect' them from the external interests that intruded into their lives and region. The struggle to 'self-determine' therefore continues to be concerned with the regulation of external interests in local resources. This issue is closely associated with regional economic development and aspirations for self-reliance, is becoming increasingly contentious[65] and provides impetus to the pursuit of sea rights as an extension of Native Title.

Service provision beyond local government jurisdiction in the three key areas of health, education and employment but also in other areas such as communication is also a major issue of regional governance. Whilst consultative and advisory mechanisms have been in operation for a couple of decades, and the influence of Islanders is increasing through participation in key positions, especially in health, real improvement in outcomes is slow and continues to frustrate Islanders. Policies which are developed on a state-wide or nation-wide basis often contain funding criteria or program guidelines that do not always fit local needs. A regional approach, especially sanctioned by an elected polity, can facilitate much in traversing the State-Commonwealth funding and policy domains to service local needs more effectively.

But there is also an aspiration on the part of Islanders to make government departments more directly accountable to Islanders. The Standing Committee did not in any measurable way satisfy Islander aspirations in this context. Whilst it left a space in the functions and roles it suggested, which Islanders could have taken up within the Assembly, it did not outline details. The current autonomy forum[66] is developing ideas in these areas but as yet has no elaborated strategy through which to work towards any policy goals beyond the formation of a portfolio executive elected on a sub-regional basis. The legacy of the two separate political domains that was evident in discussion about electoral representation issues is of less import in bringing these portfolio concerns under a regional focus. These concerns are seen to be central to issues of economic development and capacity building over the long-term. In a sense they are seen to precede local government concerns. For instance how can there be effective and autonomous governance at the local level across the region if the outcomes in the key areas of education, employment, self-reliance (economic development) and health are not improved.

These areas are critical to improved futures and the real guts of self-determination aspirations. Regional governance has to be conceived as a mechanism for better joint coordination between Commonwealth-State agencies, which operate in the region. But this mechanism can not just be limited to facilitating local government responsibilities. It must commit equally to facilitating an upward mechanism to the more centralised policies and programs associated with State and Commonwealth responsibilities. In this regional context, the concept of 'local' or 'regional' cannot be equated to 'local' government responsibilities but as critically must be about 'localising' State and Commonwealth responsibilities in key areas under regional frameworks. Mechanisms for making these interests more directly accountable for outcomes are considered central to any conceived regional governance structure. Policy input is no longer considered sufficient. The failure of the Standing Committee to clearly distinguish proposed changes in terms of the tiers of government being dealt with considerably weakened the chance of acceptance from Islanders concerned about improving opportunities for influencing decision-making across the entire spectrum of government on a regional basis.

Issues in moving forward

The Standing Committee's report was arguably a remarkable, generous, indeed historic document in terms of recognising Torres Strait Islanders' call for greater autonomy. However, in response to some concerns about the Standing Committees recommendations for a Regional Assembly, the Islander leadership embarked on a program of community consultation and established processes to develop their own model, which are still ongoing in 2003. Instead of negotiating through points of issues, Islanders have given themselves the considerable task of generating another proposal and selling it to their own constituents and to the governments—a much harder task. Reaching consensus on all matters a priori is much more difficult than negotiating key points in a set of recommendations and using a process to review, and adjust over time. Perhaps it is beneficial in the long-term but, as proven by the current process, it lengthens the process considerably, and can be problematical in areas not foreseen by the people.

Could Islanders in the region have gained a degree of autonomy more quickly if they had worked from the recommendations? Undoubtedly there were many points of issue to be negotiated by Islanders. The Torres Shire Council issue is one case in point. Spaces were provided in the original proposal to revisit electoral constituent issues, and to consider ways to develop better policy input and consideration of mainland Islanders relationship to the Regional Assembly. The potentially most contentious issue of developing a regional governance structure that is not Torres Strait Islander specific has not been a sticking point. And yet there are questions that perhaps Islanders should be raising in terms of protecting rights to self-govern that derive from their status as original inhabitants rather than just relying on rights to autonomy being derived form their current status as residents of the region.

Taking on the additional agenda of mainland Islanders following their dissatisfaction with the Standing Committee's deliberations on issues faced on the Australian mainland has introduced a complication that may take much longer to resolve and for which it will be much harder to gain government support. It is my view that the current attempts at the eleventh hour to include formal representative mechanisms for mainland Islanders in an expanded or overarching governance structure, envisioned initially and argued consistently for decades to overcome problems in the lives of Islanders in the remote Torres Strait region, is misguided and counter-productive at this stage. The issues surrounding this are indeed legitimate but need to be negotiated separately by mainland Islanders and are unnecessarily complicating issues that need resolution in the Torres Strait region. Further, they undermine the strong position that Islanders in the Torres Strait have reached and risk the chances of a satisfactory resolution of the regional issues in the Torres Strait. However, the Standing Committee did acknowledge the significance of links between mainland Islanders and their homelands and attended to this by recommending observer status and membership on the Council of Elders.

The Torres Strait Islanders' response illustrates the difficulties of connecting broad aspirations and rhetoric to the development of processes for implementation. The following points attempt to tease out some of the key obstacles in moving forward.

In both the Standing Committee report and in the *Bamaga Accord* [67] proposal developed by Islanders four years on, the staging of the implementation from Assembly to self-government was considered necessary to move forward by increment as capacity developed. Islanders chose to defer the advantage that the historical moment of 1997 offered. Instead of negotiating on the issue of the Torres Shire Council and pursuing the necessary legislative changes to constitute a Regional Assembly that would begin the process, Islanders opted for building their own governance model from the ground up. In doing this they envisioned the final goal of self-government and concentrated on representational and structural issues of a governance model that would serve that eventual goal. Though reference was made to staging the process no great detail was provided and community-wide agreement on a 'self-government' model was pursued rather than community agreement on *the simpler principle of a regionally elected Assembly to begin an incremental journey toward eventual self-government.* In contrast, the Standing Committee had clearly envisioned the Regional Assembly as the first step in the process.

By beginning with representational and structural details for eventual self-government, the governance structure put forward in the Bamaga Accord has begun to look rather complicated. The Standing Committee's proposal recommended 22 elected members representing the local government regions, the Bamaga Accord opted for 21 members. The Bamaga Accord also added another layer—an Executive consisting of 6 representatives elected from its members on a sub-regional basis with as yet unspecified 'portfolio' and specified higher level responsibilities in the Assembly. This formulation of an 'inner circle' in essence establishes a hierarchical structure within the Assembly that concentrates decision-making processes on a 'formalised basis'. Thus the model looks more concerned with the details of 'allocating' and 'distributing' responsibilities ahead of determining what the details of the different aspects of roles and functions within the Assembly's brief are to be. Apart from the difficulties associated with gaining agreement across the community on a more detailed proposal, this approach is less about 'what' to determine and more about 'who' is to determine it within a regional governance structure.

Determining what the roles and functions of the Assembly are to be in moving forward incrementally as capacity develops is the real guts of 'self-determination' agendas. Incremental capacity-building in this sense is the most important part of moving forward towards eventual self-government. The middle ground between the rhetoric of aspirations for self-determination and the detail of regional governance structures revolves around clarifying what the roles and functions of the proposed structure should be. That is, what is the business and what form should it take within a regional structure that would progress towards more effective regional policy and practice across the Commonwealth-State domains? What processes will move things forward?

In determining roles and functions it would seem most important to be clear about which functions of the regional governance structure in the Bamaga Accord will articulate to which Islander aspirations for autonomy—which articulate to the 'regionalising' of local government and which articulate to the 'regionalising' of State and Federal government department policies and practices in the Torres Strait region. This is recognition of the three tiers of government which operate across the region, and recognition that Islander aspirations articulate to more effective control over the three tiers. It is also recognition of the differences between how local government functions in communities and how the State and Commonwealth government departmental activities function in relation to communities. From an observer's perspective, there is a lack of clarity in both the Standing Committee's proposal and the discussion in the Torres Strait community on how to sort out the quagmire produced by different historical political domains, different levels of government, different agencies, programs, policies and how these relate to the content of broad Islander aspirations and community functioning.

The concept of the Regional Assembly as a joint Commonwealth-State statutory body to replace the ICC and TSRA functions as they presently stand meets Islander aspirations for a more effective mechanism to coordinate and make use of funding from these sources. But this only relates to the regionalisation of local government functions. It restructures what is (in)effectively already operating, and does not in itself address other Islander aspirations to greater autonomy. If the Torres Shire Council is maintained as a separate entity on the same basis as the Island Community Councils but with representation proportional to its greater population, the Standing Committee's proposal would seem to satisfy Islander concepts of regionalised local governance. This aspect of regionalisation could have begun the longer journey towards greater autonomy and eventual self-government. Whilst only an incremental gain in real terms it would have nonetheless been an historic and important symbolic one.

In relation to State and Commonwealth government departments who oversee the key areas of economic and social policy determination and implementation such as education, employment, health, fisheries, justice etc., the Standing Committee suggested a policy development role for the Regional Assembly.[68] The Committee clearly saw a role for the Assembly in negotiating regional agreements in different areas and recommended that the proposed Assembly develop a set of guidelines[69] to be used by government departments in negotiating with Islanders to support this practice. Building guidelines as part of building a regional framework for agreement-making would contribute greatly to the process of extending influence and control over policy determination and strategies to achieve policy goals for Islanders in key areas. This approach is currently being used widely in Indigenous communities across Australia[70] including the Torres Strait and represents the basic blocks of any future regional framework.

Islanders are working toward but have a lot more work to do in relation to this issue. As part of this aspect of greater autonomy, a regional economic development plan is figured as central to progressing regional policy across all government activity in key areas. Underneath this there is policy development work being done in the key areas. However, in terms of roles and functions of the proposed regional governance structure, attention has been diverted from the task of developing processes to incrementally stage progress in this area. It is important that a focus be developed for achieving this as this aspect of greater autonomy differs considerably to that of simply regionalising local government functions. It therefore should not be conflated under the same process but needs to be developed differently. It is important that the differences be clearly understood.

The regionalising of local governance is about coordination and streamlining of processes to make the most effective use of funds coming into the region to develop local government infrastructure and implement projects in this jurisdiction. In terms of self-determination it is about Islanders making their own decisions according to self-determined interests and priorities. Direct funding lines are already established for this purpose.

But this is not the case with Commonwealth and State government activity in key portfolio areas. In moving towards regional frameworks for these it is important to remember that the eventual devolution of control will not occur as a local government function and therefore cannot occur through them. Regional frameworks will devolve no further than the Regional Assembly because agreements will be between the Assembly and the organisations responsible for delivering services such as schools, TAFE, hospitals, health organisations etc and the relevant Commonwealth and State government departments. Yes, agreements and frameworks serve the needs of communities at a local level but they will never be within the jurisdiction or function of local governance as it is presently structured. Elected members will be responsible for ensuring that regional agreements and/or frameworks meet the needs of their constituents and that parties to the agreement can be made accountable to the Regional Assembly at the end of the day, and thus to communities via that process. Islanders have expressed a desire for eventual regional control of budgets in these areas but this will only occur in step with economic development and governance and professional capacity-building, and therefore continues to be a long way off.

This aspect of greater autonomy therefore requires a different approach from that which has already developed in relation to the regionalising of local government and will produce a different outcome no doubt. The Bamaga Accord dealt with this by recommending an Executive to manage this aspect. However, this is perhaps jumping the gun and placing structural issues ahead of functional ones. Less formal structures may provide more flexibility in the shorter-term as the whole Regional Assembly begins the work of developing processes to manage the incremental implementation of staged goals. It would seem important that the entire Assembly feel ownership with respect to this aspect of the Assembly's work, and that all members develop greater expertise, experience and capacity in respect of the issues where possible. This is complicated and long-term work and progress will not be uniform across the key areas. It may be that the first step is a budget line for this aspect of the Regional Assembly's work and a Committee program to move the issues forward systematically and incrementally. This seems difficult to organise a priori in any regional structure and it could quite legitimately fall within the brief of any proposed Regional Assembly. In the meantime, there is a general climate for agreement-making across the whole country which allows Islanders to keep developing this strategy in the Torres Strait context in the interim. Parties currently involved in these processes need to be involved in the transition process to incorporate the processes under a more formal regional framework system within the Assembly's realm.

By distinguishing more clearly between the regional aspects of local and other tiers of government, a way forward can be more easily negotiated. Accepting the basic principles recommended by the Standing Committee for a Regional Assembly, whilst it still requires some negotiation, would allow for the continuance of the already commenced process to improve local governance on a regional basis. From there, as well, can begin the hard work of building a staged process for gaining a greater degree of autonomy in relation to other spheres of government influence. This process can be included as a distinct aspect of the work of the Regional Assembly on the basis that it forms a legitimate part of the move towards greater autonomy and eventual self-government.

At the same time, distinguishing clearly between issues of political representation within the governance structure and the roles and functions of the Assembly as it relates to progressing self-determination agendas across the key areas of Commonwealth and State government policy is a necessary first step in staging progress towards longer-term goals. Efforts to formalise structures a priori should be resisted in the interest of flexibility as the issues are worked through. It is easier to gain agreement on the broad principles than it is on fine detail if the process is seen to be open-ended rather than pre-determined.

These discussions in no way cover all the recommendations made by the Standing Committee or all the events and discussions that have taken place in the Torres Strait community since then. It has attempted to highlight the main difficulties in *translating the space between aspirations and implementation to illustrate how complex governance issues are at the intersections of traditional, colonial and contemporary experience, different tiers of government and the underdevelopment of Islander capacity.*

How Torres Strait experience fits with Treaty discussions

What does all this have to do with current treaty discussions? It speaks to pressures on Indigenous leadership at the grass-roots level as they attempt to find ways to exercise more control over their affairs and make practical improvements in the lives of people. It also speaks to the connections between their pursuit of practical improvements on the ground and the desire of the current national Indigenous leadership to anchor the broader concepts of acknowledgement, sovereignty, self-determination and inherent rights in the terms of a nationally orchestrated agreement or treaty.

In speaking to this connection, the Chairman of the Torres Strait Regional Authority expressed a widely held community sentiment when he said:

> The people... will continue to face real problems such as border security, health service access issues, loss of language, welfare dependency regardless of whether the Torres Strait becomes independent, autonomous or not. Those issues will continue to be there regardless of the existence of a Treaty between the Australian government and Indigenous Australians.... If an agreement such as a Treaty can deal with these real problems then yes let's go for it....[but] a Treaty for Indigenous people, or autonomy for Torres Strait Islanders for that matter, is not going to make these problems go away.[71]

In this address to the National Treaty Conference, Waia argued that concepts such as sovereignty and independence do not begin with 'governments systems and flags' but with individuals taking control of their lives and that the bigger movements such as Treaty and autonomy should begin from this vision. The most important aspect of the pursuit of autonomy in the Torres Strait therefore had to be the agreement of the members of the community at each step of the way and for this reason he conceded that the aspiration of self-government in the Torres Strait might take decades. Many of these sentiments are common on the ground across Indigenous Australia.[72]

A further theme developed in this same address spoke to the issue of co-existence. Islanders in their thinking (if not entirely in their hearts) have subordinated the alternative reality of independent and autonomous sovereign status via secession from Australia because that holds no more guarantee of a better future, and quite possibly less, than remaining with Australia. In this, the great moral compromise[73] has been made and accepted by Islanders between the import of the original colonial injustice and the practicalities of living with the modern global reality. Waia conceptualises Islander sovereignty in limited terms viz., a 'relative' sovereignty, a 'realistic' sovereignty, a 'level' of sovereignty. This concept of coexistence and relative sovereignty expressed by Waia depends on recognition of Islanders as the original inhabitants, the traditional owners, the bearers of a different culture.

In making this compromise and proceeding with ways to improve the intersections between Islanders and governments' jurisdictions, Islanders have clearly developed what Bill Jonas has called "the 'recognition space' for the ongoing exercising of [their] sovereignty" (2002, p. 6). However hard Islanders have argued, and whatever the gains they have made towards exercising any ongoing or residual or inter-related sovereignty, they have had to proceed on the terms of others and at the largesse of governments, with the exception of the Mabo judgement. The traditional and customary rights recognised in the Torres Strait Treaty were an 'unusual' example of a co-incidence of interest[74] between Islanders who wished to remain within Australian waters, and the Australian government of the time who were interested to retain as much jurisdiction over these waters and their economic and strategic resources as they could.

The task for any Treaty process might be given clearer form if Islanders were to ask 'What will the treaty proposal do for us?' There is much that can be done for them. Islanders are in a vulnerable position. In focusing on the practical issues, the exercise of 'rights' is assumed by them. Islanders are clearly exercising citizen rights and in some of their arguments make consistent claim to inherent rights. But when do Islanders know when they undermine their own claims to inherent rights or traditional rights by the agreements and compromises they make. I would argue that they do not know with any certainty. Islanders require as much protection for traditional and customary rights as is possible in what is a shared space, which positions them as the less powerful actors. But how much protection is possible and what is being conceded that doesn't have to be, or shouldn't be? When the distinctions between traditional, customary, colonial and Western practices are so blurred and overlaid how do Islanders remain clear about particular domains? How do they know when the protection of traditional rights is not going to lead to over-regulation of them as citizens or discriminate against them in relation to, for example, commercial rights? With each concession and compromise of each agreement what is being signed away. For example, in accepting their place within the Australian polity they have accepted the notion of co-existence and included non-Indigenous

Australians within the concept of regional autonomy with only the assurances of majority status to see their interests through the long-term. What must be clearly included in the constitution of any regional governance structure to protect Islanders from future changes in population distribution?

Viewed from the Torres Strait context, the growing consensus emerging in the Think Tank meetings, general debates and discussions, and papers for the encouragement of local and regional agreement-making that meets the needs and particularities of different communities and contexts would seem to be an essential part of a move towards a national, overarching position as articulated by Marcia Langton and Lisa Palmer.[75] It is abundantly clear that any position that does not begin in the local is unlikely to resonate at the local level.

The legal protection of these agreements through some sort of national framework that can set standards and benchmarks holds promise for connecting this practice at the local level to a broader understanding of both protection and exercise of rights in the legal and constitutional sense. But this would have to be presented as a facilitative, research, assessment, supportive process rather than an administrative hoop for communities and agreement-makers to jump through. Islanders would be greatly assisted by expert opinion and research assistance in assisting them to reach policy determinations and agreed positions that uphold their inherent rights as much as possible in the deeper legal sense. But they would not accept interference or cumbersome administrative red tape so complicated that it hindered rather than aided the process. If that were the case they would prefer to operate independently. That is, a national framework approach would need to work from the ground up, responding to local and regional issues. Islanders, like other communities need support on the ground, rather than another accountability regime imposed from above.

But building a national framework does not necessarily make the connection with the concept of a treaty or the need for constitutional change. The Torres Strait example suggests that struggles on the ground occupy the time and efforts of peoples in communities, including the leadership of communities who are critical in disseminating and encouraging any acceptance of concepts of Treaty. The concept of Treaty needs to be articulated clearly for people on the ground in terms of what it will deliver them as they work towards the practical improvements necessary to improve life in communities. If there is no great connection bar the entrenchment of rights and the acknowledgement of status and injustice then that should be clearly argued on its own merits and not through a false argument that change on the ground ultimately depends on it. Protection of rights and examples that clearly outline the vulnerability of hard fought for positions should connect practical agendas with the stronger symbolic ones. Anything that involves more work or expense for overworked communities is unlikely to gain support and further alienate the national leadership from people on the ground. Approaches to selling the concept for treaty would be well advised to present it as complementary or protective of what is being done on the ground. The language of this will need to become a common discourse if the necessary support is to build motive for a common direction.

Concluding remarks

The preoccupation of people on the ground with practical issues suggests that the simpler the final proposition for the case for constitutional change the easier it will be to make the case viz., that Constitutional change would protect the rights being fought for on the ground and provide further leverage where rights were being limited by any particular government. Communities have consistently expressed the sentiment that the real work is on the ground. The building of a national framework that is helpful would perhaps be the more welcomed proposition in the interim. Certainly a useful reference point and guidelines for negotiation of agreements on social policy determinations, service delivery and accountability procedures would cut the work for Torres Strait Islanders.

Dr Martin Nakata is the first Torres Strait Islander to receive a PhD from an Australian university. He is currently working as the Director of the Aboriginal Research Institute at the University of South Australia in Adelaide. His current work is in the Research and Curriculum Development areas with a particular focus on Indigenous education and English language teaching in Indigenous communities.

Mabo Ten Years On—Small Step or Giant Leap?

Aden Ridgeway

This year was the tenth anniversary of the High Court's Mabo decision. It has created a valuable opportunity to reflect on what has been achieved in Indigenous Affairs over the last decade, and whether or not Indigenous Australians have really reaped the rewards the High Court opened up to us in this landmark case.

It also provides an opportunity to ask some challenging questions about how we can remove the obstacles that stand in the way of a better and more equal relationship between black and white Australians.

As part of this chapter I want to focus on the current political leadership in Canberra, which I think is a serial underachiever when it comes to reducing Indigenous disadvantage. This is because it is driven by the conviction that better economic opportunities and individual initiative alone will deliver real equality between all Australians.

I also want to highlight some of the obstacles to progress that exist within Indigenous communities and why these need to be confronted and addressed if we are to see a new generation of Indigenous leaders coming forward.

The *Mabo* decision and the *Native Title Act*—best outcome or political back-peddle?

The *Mabo* decision must be seen within the broader context of public policy making in Indigenous Affairs over the last 100 years and more particularly the period since the 1967 referendum.

This latter date marks a real turning point in the history of Indigenous Affairs in Australia. It was an era when, for the first time, the emergence of a truly national social conscience in relation to Indigenous peoples in Australia can be recognised. Without this shift in the national psyche, I do not think the States and Territories would have passed land rights legislation and we certainly wouldn't have had the Royal Commission into Aboriginal Deaths in Custody or a ten year dialogue about reconciliation.

But has Australia really maximised the opportunities these achievements opened up to us, or have they been squandered by half-hearted political responses?

Just as many people thought the 1967 referendum and the citizenship rights it conferred on Aboriginal people and Torres Strait Islanders would transform our life experience and deliver equality, so too many people placed great hope in the ability of the *Mabo* decision to right the wrongs of the past and belatedly deliver social justice to the original owners of the land.

After all, the High Court affirmed in law what Indigenous people had always known in their hearts:—

> **that we have a basic right to our traditional country** (where native title has not been extinguished—which occurred without the consent of Indigenous peoples); and

> **this right exists because of our cultural identity**, our laws, traditions and customs.

The Mabo decision achieved legal recognition of our status as the First Nation Peoples of Australia and gave us the ability to move towards a better position in the social, economic and political life of this country. It presented us with both the imperative and the tools to negotiate our relationship with the rest of the Nation. Despite the rhetoric of new forms of political correctness and popularism, it was never about being 'separate and equal' but creating an 'equal and inclusive' agenda.

Many Indigenous people were also heartened by prospect of native title legislation being able to deliver better legal protection of our cultures, especially in relation to significant sites and objects. Taking the High Court's finding that native title has its origins in the culture and traditions of Indigenous people, it was logical to assume that heritage protection and other cultural rights would need to be included in the concept of native title.

In addition to the development of a *Native Title Act,* it was also proposed that there would be:

> *a social justice compact between the Commonwealth Government and Indigenous Australians that would set out how Indigenous people could exercise and protect their inherent rights*, ranging from cultural integrity and heritage protection, to regional self-governance and a treaty, to economic development; and

> *a National Indigenous Land Fund* that would provide a long-term financial base for the acquisition of land by Indigenous communities who had been dispossessed and would be unlikely to be able to claim native title.

But a social compact never eventuated.

The Indigenous leadership only gave their consent and support to the enactment of native title legislation on the basis that this package of measures would follow. In this respect, the original agreement that was brokered was not honoured.

The proposal for a treaty or national framework agreement to overcome the destructive cultural, social and economic consequences of dispossession is yet to be pursued by any national government. Even now, ten years on, the concept of a treaty to settle the 'unfinished business' of the last two hundred years, remains acutely controversial—amongst the broader population and our own mob.

The *Native Title Act* that resulted in 1993 is one of the most ambitious, complex and far-reaching pieces of legislation ever embarked upon. It is comparable only in scope to the Australian Constitution—with implications for all federal and state property laws.